GURU DEV

Paul Mason learned the practice of transcendental meditation in 1970 when he visited the Maharishi's ashram at Rishikesh after having hitchhiked to India. This experience spurred him to dig deeper into the history of the teaching of meditation, which in turn led to his being commissioned by Element Books to write the biography of Maharishi Mahesh Yogi - published in 1994 as *'The Maharishi: the Biography of the Man Who Gave Transcendental Meditation to the World'*.

Maharishi's *guru,* referred to simply as Guru Dev, was Swami Brahmananda Saraswati, Shankaracharya of Jyotirmath (the most prominent religious position in Northern India). Paul Mason hopes that by offering Guru Dev's lifestory and teachings, readers will be able to obtain a clearer perspective on traditional Indian teachings.

Titles by Paul Mason:

Via Rishikesh: A Hitch-Hiker's Tale

The Maharishi:
The Biography of the Man Who Gave Transcendental Meditation to
the World
Element Books – First English edition 1994
Evolution Books – Revised English edition 2005
Maharishi Mahesh Yogi - Aquamarin – German edition 1995
O Maharishi - Nova Era – Portuguese editon 1997

Mala: A String of Unexpected Meetings

108 Discourses of Guru Dev:
The Life and Teachings of Swami Brahmananda Saraswati,
Shankaracharya of Jyotirmath (1941-53) Volume I

The Biography of Guru Dev:
The Life and Teachings of Swami Brahmananda Saraswati,
Shankaracharya of Jyotirmath (1941-53) - Volume II

Guru Dev as Presented by Maharishi Mahesh Yogi:
The Life and Teachings of Swami Brahmananda Saraswati,
Shankaracharya of Jyotirmath (1941-53) - Volume III

Kathy's Story

The Knack of Meditation: The No-Nonsense Guide to
Successful Meditation

Dandi Swami: The Story of the Guru's Will,
Maharishi Mahesh Yogi, the Shankaracharyas of
Jyotir Math & Meetings With Dandi Swami
Narayananand Saraswati

108 Discourses of Swami Brahmananda Saraswati
Shankaracharya of Jyotirmath (1941-1953)
* Specially Revised Translations *
Indica Press - ISBN 978-93-81120-04-0

Roots of TM: The Transcendental Meditation of Guru Dev &
Maharishi Mahesh Yogi

GURU DEV

AS PRESENTED BY
MAHARISHI MAHESH YOGI

The Life and Teachings of
Swami Brahmananda Saraswati,
Shankaracharya of Jyotirmath (1941-53)

Volume III

by
Paul Mason

PREMANAND
www.paulmason.info
premanandpaul@yahoo.co.uk

First published by Premanand, 2009
© Paul Mason 2009, 2016
ISBN 978-0-9562228-2-4

Cover design by Premanand

Foreword

Having hitch-hiked from England to India in 1970, I wondered whereabouts to visit. When I remembered hearing of The Beatles' involvement with Maharishi Mahesh Yogi and also of their connection with Ravi Shankar, it seemed like a good opportunity to go and meet them both. First I decided to go to see Maharishi, at his *ashram* at Shankaracharya Nagar near Rishikesh. There I learnt transcendental meditation, a practice that I continued even after returning to the west – I found the process settled me down and simulaneously pepped me up. Several years later, in 1978, I returned to India, this time by jet plane. On this second trip I brought with me a resolve to search out the monastery of Jyotirmath, formerly run by 'Guru Dev' the master of Maharishi, and to visit Uttarkashi, a place where both Guru Dev and Maharishi had spent periods of time in *sadhana*. I visited both, and even ended up staying for a period in the very room that Maharishi is supposed to have lived in after his master passed on. Indeed, underneath the old wooden bedstead was the cave in which he spent long periods in meditation.

Over the ensuing years I collected as much information as I could about Maharishi Mahesh Yogi and meditation. Element Books commissioned me to write a book intended for inclusion in a series on twentieth century teachers. My biography of Maharishi was published in 1994 as *'The Maharishi: the Biography of the Man who Gave Transcendental Meditation to the World'*. Since writing that book I continued collecting data about Maharishi and Guru Dev, particularly information relating to the early formative years of Maharishi's mission to spread the philosophy of meditation, prior to the adoption of the practice globally.

I returned to India, again and again, and on one such trip I felt spurred to return Jyotirmath so I found myself arranging to retrace my journey there via Rishikesh, and to visit the holy towns of Badrinath, Kedarnath and Gangotri. I was rewarded in so many ways, not least in being provided with a book by Swami SuryaSatyanand, allegedly himself a direct disciple of Gurudeva. The book turned out to be **another** book of quotations of Guru Dev, one collected by a young monk named Bal Brahmachari Mahesh. This being the very same Mahesh who after his master's passing assumed the mantle of master himself, as Maharishi Mahesh Yogi.

'Amrit Kana' contains a selection of quotations on a wide selection of subjects and was published in 1952, several months before Guru Dev's death. Indeed, since the book was published whilst Guru Dev was still alive it is also likely the selection of quotations contained in it met with his approval. One can assume it also contains many of Maharishi's own favourite quotations. Surprisingly, the existence of this compilation by Maharishi was kept secret, even from his confidantes. Jerry Jarvis, one of his closest aides had never heard of it. However, on at least one occasion Maharishi alluded to a Hindi book on Guru Dev. In a tape recording made on the 1968 course The Beatles attended in India, Maharishi remarked:-

'I have written long ago, maybe twenty or thirty years ago, I wrote a book, a small cover, about two hundred pages, and that was in Hindi, account of Guru Dev. But in that description, hear what I said! Not the instances were cited, but the inferences drawn from the instances. Not the instances make history!'

'Nothing pleases me more than speaking about him all the time.... A very great blessing to the world.' [1]

Within the covers of this volume are also other published quotations of Guru Dev, and examples of Maharishi's representation of Guru Dev's life and his teaching. Initially I placed the rough translations on my website (www.paulmason.info), but reading these quotations on a computer screen is less pleasant than having them in a printed form, so I am pleased to present my translations in book form and make them available through the website.

The translation would really have been much more difficult had it not been for the use of a piece of computer programming devised by Richard Mason called the *Handi Hindi Gizmo Innit*. Generation of the Hindi text would have been so painful but for the existence of *Itranslator99* for which I am eternally grateful to Omkarananda Ashram, and especially to Swami Satchidanand who has also helped me through some glitches in the work.

Jerry Jarvis has been very supportive to this project, offering material, feedback and, most importantly, becoming a friend. Sita Agarawal (Mata Ji of *'Hermit in the House'* fame) gave permission for her copy of *'Amrit Kana'* to be photographed. Thanks to Suradeva in England, Ulrich and Hans in Germany, Dana Sawyer and his connections in Benares, Michael Speight, Lynn Napper, Amrit, and everyone else who has assisted in the hunt for suitable material.

Last but not least, I would like to thank those who have encouraged me to see this project through, Tony who expressed a strong desire to see the finished product even before I had properly started. To Kathy, who would try the subtle approach, saying things like; "Would you like to see the translation in a book one day?" and "Oh, it would be nice if it had pictures - people like to see pictures."

Well, here it is, far too much for just one book, best to spread the material over three volumes. Happy reading!

जय गुरु देव

Jai Guru Dev

Premanand Paul Mason

Contents

—★—

अमृत कणा

श्री निर्भूषित जगद्गुरु भगवान श्री शंकराचार्य
श्री ज्ञानज्योतिर्मठीठपीठ पर
स्वामी श्री ज्ञानानन्द सरस्वती जी महाराज
ज्योतिर्मठ-बदरिकाश्रम
के आर्ष वचनों का संग्रह

बालब्रह्मचारी श्री मुदेशजी

Amrit Kana
(Nectar Droplets)

**A Collection of Authorative Discourses
from
Ananta Shri Vibushit Jagadguru
Bhagwan Shri Shankaracharya Shri
Majjyotishpiithaadhishwar**

Swami Shri Brahmanand
Saraswati Ji Maharaj

Jyotirmath – Badarikashram

Balbrahmachari Shri Maheshji

अमृत-कण

Amrit-Kana

[Introduction]

भगवान् का भक्त होकर कोई कभी दुखी नहीं रह सक्ता, यह हमारा अनुभव है ।

Being Bhagwan's devotee nobody can be unhappy, this is our experience.

ईश्वर प्राप्ति की वासना जब तक दृढ़ न होगी तब तक अनेकों वासनाओं के चक्कर में पतंग की भाँति न जाने कहाँ हाँ उड़ते फिरोगे ।

Whilst the longing to gain Ishwar (God) is not resolutely strong, and for so long as you are in the spin of many habitual tendencies, then in the manner of a kite you will fly - turned about, twisted around not knowing indeed where.

अनेक वासना-सूत्रों को इकट्ठा करके भगवद्-वासनारूपी मोटी रस्सी तैयार करो और उसी के सहारे भवकूप से बाहर निकल जाओ ।

Many threads of desire are gathered. Possessed of desire for Bhagavad (God), make ready a thick rope and enable escape beyond the *bhavakupa* (birth-well).

यदि कोई पाप कर्म हो जाय तो परमत्मा से यही प्रार्थना करनी चाहिये कि - भगवान्! हमारा इन्द्रियों पर अधिकार नहीं है क्षमा दिया जाय, भविष्य में फिर ऐसा नही होगा । परन्तु ऐसा नहीं कि पाप भी करते जाओ और भगवान का भजन भी । भगवान की कृपा

के बल पर पाप करने का विधान नहीं है ।

If you have gone and done any sinful action then right here you
should pray - "Bhagwan!" Our own faculties do not have the
ability to give pardon. In future do not the like again. But do not
do this wrong action again and also worship Bhagwan too. The
benevolence of Bhagwan is strong but it is not a transaction to sin.

पाप और पुण्य में शास्त्र ही प्रमाण है । शास्त्र-दृष्टि से अपने
अधिकार के अनुसार चेष्टा करना पुण्य और शास्त्र-दृष्टि से अनधिकार
चेष्टा पाप है ।

In determining sin and meritous action, the *Shastra* is indeed the
measure. We have the ability to act in accordance with *Shastra,* to
perform right action, but sin is done by not observing the
restrictions of *Shastra.*

वेद शास्त्र का सहारा लेकर चलोगे तो पतन से बचे रहोगे ।

If you move with the support of *Veda Shastra* you will avoid ruin.

लोग इसीलिये दुःखी हैं कि उनका कोई इष्ट नहीं । बिना इष्ट के
सब लोग अनाथ हो रहे हैं ।

People who do not have an *ishta* (beloved) are therefore unhappy.
Without having an *ishta* all people are being orphaned.

शक्तिशाली बनना चाहते हो तो सर्वशक्तिमान भगवान की शरण
में आओ ।

You who desire to be made become strong come into the shelter
of Omnipotent Bhagwan.

कुसंग से सदा बचते रहो ।

Always refrain from bad company.

परमात्मा को अन्धा मत बनाओ। चारित्रवान् बनो और पाप करने से डरो।

Have blind faith in Paramatma. Perform traditional rites and fear doing sin.

यदि शान्ति चाहते हो तो व्यवहार में मन को अधिक मत फँसओ।

If you desire peace, do not get the mind excessively involved in your daily business.

मन को संसार में कोई नहीं चाहता। तन और धन ही सब चाहते हैं।

In worldly existence nobody desires the mind. Health and wealth are all that are needed.

वर्तमान में सुख मिले और भविष्य भी उज्ज्वल रहे, ऐसे ही कार्य करो।

अपने योग्य, शास्त्रानुसार कर्म ही ऐसे कार्य हैं।

In the present meet with happiness and in the future also be radiant. Do the work precisely in this way, by only doing work that accords to the *Shastras*.

शास्त्र-मर्यादाओं को लिये रहोगे तो लोक में ऐसे ही कार्य होगे जो परलोक को भी उज्ज्वल बनायेंगे।

The rules of the *Shastra* are for deciding what we do in the world, so that we will make both this and the other world bright.

भवसागर से पार होने के लिये मनुष्य शरीर रूपी सुन्दर नौका मिल गई है।

सतर्क रहो कहीं ऐसा न हो कि वासना की भँवर में पड़कर नौका
डूब जाय ।

The human being has got the beautiful form of body as a boat to
get across to the other shore of the *bhava sagar* (ocean of birth).
Be careful not to sink anywhere or to drop into a whirlpool of
desire.

धन-संग्रह से अधिक प्रयत्न बुद्धि शुद्ध करने के लिए करो ।

Whilst working for a living utmost care should be taken to work
with a clear mind.

भगवान दीन दयालु हैं, दुखी दयालु नहीं, दीन होकर उनकी शरण
में आने से उनकी दयालुता काम करेगी ।

Bhagwan is "Dinadayalu" – 'generous to the humble', not
"Dukhidayalu" – 'generous to the miserable'. Those who are
humble come take refuge in Bhagwan have their desires fulfilled.

दीन वह हैं जो सर्वथा निराधार हो गया हो, संसार में कहीं भी
जिसको कोई भी आधार न रह गया हो, संसार सर्वथा जिसको निरस
लगने लगा हो, किसी भी वस्तु में - जिसका मन न लगता हो -
शब्द, स्पर्श रूप, रस, गन्ध आदि विषयों से जो सर्वथा उपराम हो
गया हो और जिसकी वृत्ति के लिए कोई भी सांसारिक आधार न रह
गया हो ऐसा निराधार जीव ही वास्तव में दीन कहा जा सकता है

Humble are you who are altogether without a basis, who
anywhere in the material world are not being supported, who are
attached to the worldly existence, whose mind is not connected to
anything [spiritual], who has through sound, touch, appearance,
smell etc become altogether attached to worldly pleasures and
whose existence is not supported by anyone else. That life can be
said to be genuinely poor and baseless.

जब पुत्र बीमार होता है तो वह पिता से - प्रार्थना करे, तभी पिता उसकी चिकित्सा कराये - ऐसी बात नहीं है । पिता स्वयं ही अपने पुत्र को रोगी नहीं देख सकता, बिना कहे ही वह रोग को हटाने का प्रयत्न करता है । इसी प्रकार जो भगवान को अपना कर उनके हो जाते हैं । जो एक बार भगवान कि कृपा खींच लेते हैं, उनके लिये भगवान बिना प्रार्थना किये ही सब कुछ करते रहते हैं ।

यह अनुभूति सत्य है कि भगवान का भक्त कभी दुखी नहीं रह सकता ।

At whatever time the son becomes unwell then there is a request made to the father for healing to be done? Such is not the method. Actually the father cannot bear to see our son ill, so of his own accord, indeed without anything being said, effort is made to remove the ailment. It is this very method which applies to those that go to Bhagwan. Whoever is one time pulling a favour of Bhagwan, indeed for them everything is done without prayer. This perception is true, that on no occasion can there be suffering for Bhagwan's devotee.

फूटे घड़े से जैसे बुंद बुंद गिर कर जल कम होता जाता है वैसे ही क्षण-क्षण करके आयु समाप्त हो रही है । अभी से सावधान हो जाओ ।

Like the little drops of water that drip from a cracked earthenware pitcher, the moments of the life are passing. From right now become careful.

सावधानी यही है कि मन को संसार में मत फंसने दो । उस परमात्मा की ओर झुकाओ ।

Right here, heed that it is the mind's belief in worldly existence that gives the difficulty. Bow to the direction of That Paramatma.

यदि एकान्त में न रह सको तो अच्छे लोगों के संग में रहो ।

If you cannot be alone then be in the company of good people.

पेट के धर्म मत छोड़ो ।

Don't give up the stomach for righteousness.

पेट तो चिता तक ही रहेगा परन्तु धर्म उससे भी आगे साथ जायेगा ।

Be reminded about the stomach (capacity for good action) but also be aware that righteousness will go with you beyond.

तुम तो स्वयं सच्चिदानन्दमय परमेश्वर के आंश हो परन्तु अपने को भूल कर अज्ञान के कारण इधर उधर लावारिस कुत्तों की तरह पूंछ हिलाते, विषयों में धक्का खाते फिरते हो ।

You are yourself a part of the Sat Chit Anand – the Absolute Bliss Consciousness - of the Almighty, but out of ignorance don't make the mistake of going here and there in the manner of stray dogs wagging the tails, as taking pleasure in worldliness pushes a return experience.

अमृत-कण
Amrit-Kana

1

मर्यादा की रक्षा से ही व्यवहार और परमार्थ दोनों उज्ज्वल रहते हैं ।

Really, by the protection of *maryada* (principled code of conduct) business and salvation remain bright.

मर्यादा की अवहेलना हुई और व्यवहार में मद्यापन आया तो परमार्थ भी बिगड़ जाता है ।

If you neglect those restrictions and come to intemperance in your behaviour, then salvation is spoiled as well.

वास्तव में मर्यादानुकूल व्यवहार हो परमार्थ का पथ है ।

In truth the way to salvation is by behaving within suitable limitations.

सत्संग की कमी से ही भगवान में प्रवृत्ति नहीं होती ।

For want of *satsang* (company of the pious and hearing of the Truth) the mind is not inclined towards Bhagwan.

सत्संग में भगवान के स्वरूप का बोध होता है ।

In *satsang* the true nature of Bhagwan is sensed.

जितने दिन जीना है शान्ति से जियो । अधिक हाय-हाय करना व्यर्थ है: क्योंकि जो प्रारब्ध में है, उससे अधिक नहीं मिल सकता ।

और उतना तो मिलेगा ही ।

सन्तोषपुर्वक जीवन बिताओ, अधिक परेशान होकर मारे-मारे मत फिरो ।

However many days there are to live, cause them to be lived in peace. It is to no purpose to be self-pitying since this is destiny, more than that cannot be got. That much only will be got. Satisfactorily pass this life, return for the sake of being more troubled.

साकार-निराकार के झगड़े में मत पड़ो, जो निराकार है, वही साकार होता है ।

Drop the dispute about whether God has a form or is incorporeal, That which is formless, the very same exists having a form.

स्थिर प्रशान्त महासमुद्र ही तरङ्ग के रूप में ऊपर उठकर दिखलाई पड़ता है । जो निराकार है वही साकार होता है - तत्वतः दोनों में कोई अन्तर नहीं है । भगवान निराकार भी हैं और साकार भी । जिसकी जिसमें निष्ठा हो उसकी उपासना करके संसार समुद्र को पार कर जाओ ।

Upon a completely still calm ocean appears the shape of a wave. That shapeless is taking a form - actually in neither of them is there a difference. Bhagwan is shapeless and also has form. Worship that in which you believe in order to go beyond the ocean of worldly existence. Happiness is not to found in the superficial, happiness comes from faith. The time in this worldly existence is very precious thing.

वेष कल्याणकारी नहीं, निष्ठा से कल्याण होता है ।

Happiness does not come from appearance, from faith is *kalyana* (happiness) to be.

समय ही संसार में सबसे अधिक मूल्यवान वस्तु है ।

Time is more precious than any other thing in material life.

राष्ट्र के चरित्रबल की बुद्धि और हर प्रकार से राष्ट्र की उन्नति के लिए देश में धार्मिक शिक्षा की आवश्यकता है ।

Instruction in religious teaching is indispensable for improvement and for making a place in the region of the mind relating to force of habit.

वस्तु में राग न रखो तो वियोग का अवसर ही न आयेगा ।

Don't set desire on anything then the chance of loss will not come.

देर अपनी ओर से है परमात्मा तो कल्याण करने के लिए तैयार ही है ।

Delay is from one's own side, Paramatma is very ready for to do *kalyana* (to give happiness).

मन में नित्य अविनाशी आनन्दस्वरूप परमात्मा को स्थान दो ।

Give a place in the mind for Paramatma's eternal everlasting form of bliss.

मन में सदा भगवान का स्मरण करना रहे और मर्यादा का उल्लंघन न हो यही महात्मापन है ।

In the mind always remember Bhagwan and also, don't transgress the restrictions, then in this very place you are a *mahatma* (great soul).

सत्संग के द्वारा जब तक भगवान के स्वरूप, उनकी भक्तवत्सलता और सर्वशक्तिमत्ता का बोध नहीं होता तब तक उनमें इष्ट बुद्धि ठीक से नहीं होती ।

इसलिए प्रयत्न करके समय निकालकर सत्संग करो ।

The *swaroop* (true nature) of Bhagwan is gained by means of *satsang*. He is kind to devotees and the feeling of Bhagwan's Omnipotence is not felt if the mind has not become fit for the *ishta* (beloved). Therefore make an effort to find time and do *satsang*.

परमात्मा को चाहते हो तो आस्तिक बनो ।

If you want Paramatma then make yourself religious.

वेदोक्त धर्माधर्म में विश्वास करना ही आस्तिकता है ।

Belief in God is indeed to trust in what is enjoined by Holy Scriptures regarding virtue and vice.

जब तक वेद-शास्त्र में विश्वास नहीं करोगे तब तक परमात्मा के स्वरूप का कुछ निश्चय नहीं हो सकता और स्वरूप का निश्चय हुये बिना विश्वास किस पर करोगे?

Whilst you don't trust in the *Veda Shastra* then you can't have faith in the *swaroop* of Paramatma and if you don't have trust then what will you base your decision about the *swaroop* upon?

जब तक विश्वास दृढ़ न होगा तब तक परमात्मा का यथार्थ-दर्शन सम्भव नहीं ।

Until that time you have belief then you won't be able to have a true *darshan* (sight) of Paramatma.

वेदोक्त धर्माधर्म में विश्वास करो ।

Trust in that which is taught by the *Vedic* Scriptures about virtue and vice.

धर्म करो और अधर्म को छोड़ ।

Do *dharma* (righteousness) and let go of
adharma(unrighteousness).

स्वधर्मानुष्ठान ही भगवान के निकट पहुँचने की सीढ़ी है।

One's own religion and one's religious work is really a staircase
to reach close to Bhagwan.

स्वधर्मानुष्ठान करो और संसार से राग कम करते हुए परमात्मा में
राग बढ़ाओ।

Do your religious undertaking and having little attachment for
worldliness, grow in attachment to Paramatma.

जिसको मनुष्य सुख का साधन मानता है उसी में इष्टबुद्धि होती
है। धन, स्त्री पुत्रादि से सुख मिलेगा ऐसा निश्चय होने पर ही उसकी
प्राप्ति के लिए मनुष्य प्रयत्न करता है।

इसी प्रकार इष्टबुद्धि जब परमात्मा में हो जाती है तब परमात्मा
की प्राप्ति के लिए भी मनुष्य अभ्यास करता है। परन्तु अभ्यास में
दृढ़ता तभी आती है जब शास्त्र और गुरुओं से यह निश्चय हो जाता
है कि परमात्मा की प्राप्ति में सुख होगा और शान्ति मिलेगी।

In the man who by *sadhana* surrenders the life of pleasure, then
understanding of the *ishta* occurs. In order to gain the pleasures of
wealth, a wife and a son etc a man has to decide to make an effort.
This is the method to get the knowledge of Paramatma's *swaroop*
(true nature), that personal exercise is done to gain Paramatma.
But for this reason become strong in practice and when from
Shastra and *gurus* you become certain of more pleasure of
benefitting from Paramatma, you will meet with peace.

आगे की यात्रा के लिए अभी से कुछ तैयारी कर चलो।

Before going on a journey, go and prepare.

काम, क्रोध, मद, लोभ और मोह यही अपने वास्तविक शत्रु हैं। अन्दर के यही शत्रु बाहर निकल कर व्यवहार में अनेकों शत्रु बना लेते हैं।

इन पर विजय प्राप्त करो यही वास्तविक विजय होगी।

Desire, anger, arrogance, greed and ignorance, right here are our true enemies. In practice many enemies are made, turn out those enemies from within. Gain mastery over them and in this very place will be real victory.

अपने आन्तरिक शत्रुओं का यदि दमन कर लिया तो बाहर व्यवहार में कोई शत्रु उत्पन्न ही नहीं होगा।

Suppress our internal enemies and then in our outer dealings no enemy will be born.

जो राष्ट्र शत्रुओं से मुक्त होकर विश्व सदा सुख-शान्ति का अनुभव करना चाहता है। उसके लिए यह आवश्यक है कि उसके राष्ट्र निर्माता अथवा कर्णधार अपने आन्तरिक शत्रुओं पर विजय प्राप्त करें।

The kingdom has to be set free of enemies if the world wants to experience pleasure and peace always. Therefore the one that builds or directs must gain victory over the kingdom's internal enemies.

जिसने एक बार सतर्क होकर अच्छी तरह मनन करके विचारपूर्वक संसार की क्षणभंगुरता अपने हृदय में पुष्ट कर ली, वही आन्तरिक शत्रु वर्ग पर विजय प्राप्त करता है।

He who with a strong heart carefully reflects on the transitory worldly existence, he gains mastery over the very same internal enemy [which desires worldly existence].

जिस मनुष्य को समस्त लौकिक प्रपञ्च की क्षणभंगुरता पुष्ट हो गई है उसे किसी वस्तु से लोभ और मोह नहीं हो सकता; क्योंकि वह जानता है कि जिसका लोभ और मोह आज करेंगे कल उसका स्वयं ही नाश हो जाना है; इसलिए व्यर्थ लोभ-मोह करके उसके परिणाम में पश्चाताप और अशान्ति ही हाथ लगेगी। इसलिए उसके अन्तःकरण में लोभ और मोह अंकुरित ही नहीं होते। उनका बीज ही नष्ट हो जाता है।

That man to whom worldly affairs have come to be very transitory does not act out of greed and ignorance; because he knows that those who act out of greed and ignorance today automatically fade/decay tomorrow; therefore the consequence of greed and ignorance are useless remorse and disquiet. Therefore, for this reason greed and ignorance of the inner self do not begin to sprout. Truly he goes to destroy their seed.

जैसे चारपाई का एक पाया खींचने से बाकी तीनों पाये अपने आप खिंच जाते है उसी प्रकार आन्तरिक शत्रुओं में से किसी भी एक का दमन कर देने से बाकी तभी शिथिल हो जाते हैं।

In the manner that if one pulls one leg of a bedstead leaving the other three [then all four move] if in a similar way one subjugates one's internal enemies the remainder then become loosened.

विचार पूर्वक संसार की क्षणभंगुरता पुष्ट करो, उसी से कामनायें संकुचित होंगी।

Together, strongly consider the transitoriness of mundane existence. Actually, from doing just that, desires will then be [just] limited desires.

लौकिक वासनाओं को कम करते हुए भगवत् परायण वनो।

Having little earthly desires become attached to the Lord.

जगत् के व्यवहार में केवल कर्त्तव्य बुद्धि रहे उसमें इष्टबुद्धि मत करो ।

Do not mind the business of the world without mindfulness of the *ishta* in you.

संसार में ऐसे रहो जैसे कमल का पत्ता जल में रहता हुआ उससे अलग रहता है ।

In worldly existence be like the leaf of the lotus, which stays upon the water whilst remaining separate from it.

आन्तरिक शत्रु निग्रह ही स्थायी रूप से वाह्य शत्रु-दमन का एक मात्र उपाय है ।

Really, the inner enemy is the impediment, the subjugation of the outer enemy of the person is just one mere project.

जो वस्तु जैसी है वैसा ही देखना समदर्शिता है ।

With equanimity look at all things as being very similar.

समदर्शी वही है जो मिथ्या संसार को मिथ्या समझता है । और सत्य परमात्मा को सत्य समझता है ।

Very impartially understand that the delusory worldly existence is an illusion. Also understand that the truth of Paramatma is real.

मिथ्या संसार में सत्य की भावना करने वाला, व्यवहार में इष्ट बुद्धि रखने वाला कभी भी समदर्शी नहीं हो सकता ।

सर्वत्र आत्मदर्शी ही वास्तव में समदर्शी हो सकता है ।

In the illusion of mundane existence be a person who has a feeling for truth. In the business of being someone with knowledge of the *ishta,* sometimes you cannot be impartial.

You can be dispassionate if you are determined always to behold the soul.

मोक्ष या परमांत्मा की प्राप्ति की लिये जो पुरुषार्थ किये जाते हैं उन्हें ही परमार्थ कहा जाता है ।

Who has laboured for *moksha* or for the gaining of Paramatma (the Supersoul), he is said to go to salvation.

समस्त संसार को अपना कुटुम्ब मानकर "आत्मवत्सर्वभूतेषु" की भावन से प्रभावित होकर; यह समस्त जगत् परमात्मा का ही स्थूल शरीर है; इस प्रकार समझकर ईर्ष्या, द्वेष आदि से रहित होकर भगवद् ।भाव में रहता हुआ सौभाग्वान पुरुष जो भी पुरुषार्थ करता हैं वह वह सब परमार्थ ही है ।

Appreciate all the world as one's own family; be influenced by the pleasing [phrase]:-

"आत्मवत्सर्वभूतेषु"

"atmavatsarvabhuteshu"
'Treat everyone as if they were yourself'
[Shri Shankaracharya's *Sarva Vedanta Siddhanta Sarasangraha* 366]

This whole world is really the gross body of Paramatma; understand that if you remain free from envy, malice etc then everyone can be a fortunate soul and work for complete spiritual knowledge.

अपने क्षुद्र लौकिक स्वार्थों में निमग्न रहोगे तो यह उन्नत अवस्था प्राप्त नहीं हो सकती ।

If you will become drowned in your appetite for earthly pleasures
then you cannot gain the higher state.

जिससे सुख प्राप्त हो वही अर्थ है । अपने को या दूसरों को क्षणिक
लौकिक सुखों की प्राप्ति हो वह "स्वार्थ" और अपने को तथा दूसरों
को नित्यानन्द स्वरूप स्थायी सुख रूप परमात्मा की प्राप्ति हो वह
परम अर्थ (परमार्थ) कहा जाता है ।

From the pleasure gained, that really is the *"artha"* wealth. The
gain to one another of transient earthly pleasures is self-interested,
but for those who wish to attain a permanent form of happiness
the *"param"* (best) *"artha"* (wealth) is said to be *"parmartha"*
(salvation).

इष्ट ही अनिष्टों से बचाता है ।

Actually the *ishta* defends one from *anishton* (calamities).

इसी से लोग दुःखी हैं कि उनका कोई इष्ट नहीं ।

People are unhappy because they do not have any *ishta*.

समय का सदुपयोग करो ।

Make proper use of the time.

संसार सागर से पार होने के लिए मनुष्य शरीर रूपी सुन्दर नौका
मिलीं है । यह नौका सदा अपने अधिकार में रहनेवाली नहीं है ।

जब तक यह अपने अधिकार में है तब तक ऐसा प्रयत्न करो कि
इसके सहारे भवसागर से पार हो जाओ ।

जब तक यह अपने अधिकार है इसका सदुपयोग करो ।

यदि समय रहते इसका सदुपयोग न किया तो जब इसे छोड़ने का परवाना आयेगा तो निराधार होकर चारों तरफ रोते फिरोगे। उस समय कोई सहायक न होगा, और यह भी निश्चय हैं कि उस समय एक मिनट की भी मोहलत नहीं मिलेगी; नौका हाथ से छुट जायगी और फिर न जाने कब तक संसार सागर में निराधार होकर डूबते उतराते, जन्म-मरण की घोरातिघोर यातनायें सहनी पड़ें।

The human being has the beautiful form of body as a boat to get to the other side of the ocean of *samsara* (wordliness and transmigration). This boat is not always in our control. Until control is gained then go and make an effort to get assistance to cross the ocean of experiences.

Make good use of our power until then.

If the proper use is not made of the time here, then, when the warrant order will come to relinquish (the life), then you will be turned to weep without support from any of the four directions. At that time there will not be anyone to help, and this is also a certainty that there is a fixed time and there will not be one minute more. The boat will leave from one's hand, and again you will not understand when in the sea of rebirth you will be plunged. The horrible torture of the endurance the birth and death will occur.

अमृत-कण
Amrit-Kana

2

धन से तुम्हारा अभ्युदय और कल्याण सम्भव नहीं; इसलिये लक्ष्मीपति भगवान को अपनाओ और लक्ष्मी की चिंता छोड़ दो ।

Your progress and welfare is not connected with financial wealth; for this reason possess Lakshmipati Bhagwan (the god Vishnu, husband of Lakshmi) and let go thinking of Lakshmi (the goddess of wealth).

भौतिकवाद का जितना विकास होता जायगा, संसार, सुख-शांति से उतना ही दूर होता जायगा ।

However much development there is of materialism, of worldliness, that much further away will be happiness and peace.

विश्व में शान्ति स्थापनार्थ भौतिकवाद का खण्डन बहुत ही आवश्यक है ।

The argument of materialism - that peace is to be found in the world - is fundamentally disproved of.

स्वतंत्र बुद्धिवाद से नहीं शास्त्रवाद से कल्याण होगा ।

Not by uncontrolled intellectualism but from an exposition of *Shastra* will happiness be found.

आज अध्यात्मवाद का अतिक्रमण करके भौतिकवाद प्रबल हो रहा है और बुद्धिवाद के आगे शास्त्रवाद गौड़ हो रहा है ।

Today materialistic arguments are becoming prevalent in violating discussion of spiritual texts, and intellectual debate is being put before the teachings of the *Shastra*.

भौतिकवाद् में सुख की बिडम्बना मात्र है इसी लिये भारत में भौतिकवाद् को कभी भी सुख शांति का आधार नहीं माना गया। यहाँ सदैव अध्यात्मवाद् की ही प्रधानता नही है।

In materialism happiness is merely mimicked, therefore, in India there is no support for materialistic peace and happiness. Here spiritual discourse is not always exactly excellent.

पूर्ण ब्रह्म परमात्मा ही अपार आनन्द का अनादि श्रोत है।

The revelation is of the perfect boundless infinite pleasure without beginning is indeed Paramatma (the Supersoul).

काष्ठ में अग्नि सर्वत्र व्याप्त है किंतु इस परोक्षज्ञान से कोई काम नहीं चल सकता। धर्षण द्वारा अग्नि को प्रकट कर लेने पर ही उससे कुछ काम लिया जा सकता है।

Fire is pervading everywhere in wood, but because of absence of knowledge someone cannot make use of it. Clearly this is disrespect to Agni (fire) but really from that some work can be done.

परमात्मा सर्वत्र चराचर में व्याप्त है केवल इस परोक्षज्ञान से दुख की सर्वथा निवृत्ति नहीं हो सकती।

Paramatma is pervading everywhere, in the animate and the inanimate. Only from this knowledge, of That which is beyond the sight, or else trouble may not altogether disappear.

उपासना द्वारा परमात्मा को प्रत्यक्ष प्रगट करके उसका अपरोक्ष ज्ञान कर लेने से ही समस्त दुखों की निवृत्ति और अतिशय आनन्द

की प्राप्ति सम्भव है ।

By the direct appearance of Paramatma through the way of
upasana (worship, meditation etc.) it is possible for all troubles to
disappear and to derive very great bliss.

केवल बीजक के अध्ययन से कोई धनी नहीं बन सकता । जब
तक बीजक के अनुसार खनन करके धन प्राप्त न कर लिया जाय ।

From only studying the inventory nobody can be made wealthy.
Until mining work is done according to the list, wealth is not
gained.

वेद और शास्त्र परमात्मा की प्राप्ति के लिये बीजक के समान हैं ।
वेद शास्त्रों की आज्ञानुसार जप ध्यान आदि के द्वारा परमात्मा को
प्रत्यक्ष करना ही निधि का खनन करना है ।

The *Vedas* and *Shastras* are similar to a list for the gain of
Paramatma. According to the injunction of the Vedic *Shastra*, do
japa (the silent repetition of a *mantra*), do *dhyaana* (meditation)
etc this is really the way for mining the treasure to discover
Paramatma (the Supersoul).

ज्ञान विज्ञान के समन्वय से ही सुख शान्ति की प्राप्ति होगी ।

Indeed by connecting knowledge and wisdom, happiness and
peace will be gained.

धर्मानुकूल आचरण नास्तिको के लिये भी सुख एवं शान्ति क देने
वाला है ।

Moreover by regular favourable conduct, even the unreligious are
granted happiness and peace.

प्रत्येक ब्यक्ति का आचरण होना आवश्यक है जिससे पारस्परिक
प्रेम की वृद्धि होकर समाज में शान्ति और सुव्यवस्था की स्थापना हो

सके।

The growth of mutual love in society can be established in peace
and orderliness from the good conduct of each and every
individual.

धर्म के दस लक्षण ऐसे हैं हो संसार के प्रत्येक मनुष्य के लिये
लाभ-दायक हैं चाहे वह किसी भी देश या समाज का हो। येतो
नास्तिकों के लिये भी सुख एवं शान्तिप्रद हैं।

The characteristics of a land of righteousness are that the land or
community desires to advantage every single person. These then
also give peace and happiness for those who are unreligious.

जो देश भौतिकवाद में बहुत आगे बढ़े हुये उनमें कलह और
अशांति के नित्य नये निमित्त उपस्थित होते रहते हैं।

But that country which grows more materialistic, in them
quarreling and constant restlessness become the new phase.

जब सुख की छाया के सान्निध्य से इतने आनन्द का अनुभव होता
है तो अनन्तानन्दमय परमानन्द आनन्दस्वरूप परमात्मा की प्राप्ति
के आनन्द का तो अनुमान ही नहीं लगाया जा सकता।

For others who experience happiness and peace it is but a mere
glimpse of peace. We accept that our real purpose is to give
knowledge of the existence of happiness.

When there is a shadow on the happiness then only so much
ananda (bliss) becomes experienced and then you really cannot
become connected with the idea of gaining the blissful form of
Paramatma's blissful soul, of being possessed of limitless bliss.

संसार में वस्तुओं की प्राप्ति से हमें सुख का जो अनुभव होता है,
वह क्षणिक ही होता है परन्तु उसके वियोग में होनेवाला दुःख

अधिक समय तक होता है।

The pleasure that we experience from acquiring things of the world, that really is only transitory but because of this comes a state of disunity, a time of greater suffering.

संयोग में क्षणिक सुख और वियोग में चिर दुख के सिवाय भौतिकवाद में और रक्खा ही क्या है।

The transitory connection with happiness and the pain of loss lasts a long time besides, so why hold onto materialism?

इसीलिये दुनिया के सारे देशों को भौतिकवाद के पीछे पागल बने हुये दौड़ते देखकर भी भारतीय उनसे प्रभावित न होकर वास्तविक सुख-शांति-प्रद अध्यात्मवाद का ही आश्रयण करते हैं।

Therefore India should not be influenced by countries of the world which have become crazy for materialism. Resort to the real giver of happiness and peace, the happiness that belongs to spirituality.

ग्राह ने जब गज को पकड़ा उस समय गज सर्वथा निराधार हो गया, उसे कहीं कोई सहायक नहीं दिखा। संसार की आशा छोड़कर, सर्वथा दीन होकर उसने भगवान् को पुकारा उसी समय दीनदयालु भगवान ने अपनी दयालुता का परिचय दिया।

On occasion when an alligator seizes an elephant, the elephant is completely without assistance, for there is no one seen there to help. Renounce dependence on the worldly existence, that is the time when you have become altogether needy to call out to Bhagwan Dinadayalu (who is merciful to the needy) - thus introducing your own pitifulness.

द्रौपदी चीर-हरण के समय दीन हो गई थी। कोई भी उसका रक्षक नहीं रह गया था, उस निस्सहाय दीनावस्था में उसने भगवान

को पुकारा-दीनदयालु भगवान ने उस पर दया की ।

Draupadi became pitiable at the time of the seizing of the cloth (her sari). Nobody was coming to rescue her. In her helpless plight she called out Dinadayalu Bhagwan ('Merciful-to-the-needy Bhagwan') and Bhagwan showed compassion on her.

जब तक संसार की आशा नहीं छूटेगी तब तक दीनावस्था नहीं आवेगी और दीन हुए बिना दीनदयालु भगवान की दयालुता के पात्र नहीं बन सकते ।

दीनावस्था में प्राणी को केवल एकमात्र परमात्मा का ही आधार रह जाता है ।

Until such time as attachment to worldly existence is abandoned you cannot receive the charity of Merciful-to-the-needy Bhagwan. Paramatma is the only one to support those who are living in a plight.

दीन, परमात्मा के प्रति अनन्य होता है । और अपने अनन्य भक्तों के लिये भगवान् को भी अनन्य होना पड़ता है क्योंकि उनकी प्रतिज्ञा है ।

"ये यथा मां प्रपद्यन्ते तांस्तथैव भजाम्यहम् ।" (श्री गीता)

भगवान् कहते हैं कि जो जिस प्रकार मुझे भजता है मैं भी उसी प्रकार से उसे भजता हूँ ।

The needy one becomes a reflection of the unbounded Supersoul, and for devotees the unlimitedness of the unlimited Bhagwan occurs, because of the promise!

"ये यथा मां प्रपद्यन्ते तांस्तथैव भजाम्यहम् ।"

"ye yatha mam prapadyante tamstathaiva bhajamyaham."
[*Bhagavad Gita* 4:11]

Bhagwan says that, 'However you worship Bhagwan then in that
way you will be served'.

वास्तव में संसारी मनुष्य यदि कुछ देर भगवान् का भजन करे तो
कोई बड़ी बात नहीं क्योंकि कर समय वह किसी न किसी को तो
भजता ही रहता है - स्त्री, धन, पुत्र, मित्र, शत्रु आदि सभी का वह
स्मरण करता है, स्मरण करना ही भजन है ।

In truth if some worldly people have been tardy in their worship
of Bhagwan then do not talk it because that time none can come
again, so in this time remain worshipping - woman, finances, son,
friend, adversary etc are all remembered, recollect only the
worship.

परमात्मा को अन्धा मत बनाओ । वह अन्तर्यामी है, सब के सब
कर्मों को जानता है । उनकी दृष्ट बचाकर कोई कार्य नहीं किय जा
सकता ।

Paramatma makes the blind not blind. That Almighty is he who
knows all actions. Their sight which nobody else could save.

ऐसा मत सोचो कि हमारे इस कार्य को कोई नहीं जानता ।
जिसके हाथ में सत्कर्म, दुष्कर्म, का लेख है वह तुम्हारे भीतर बाहर
की हर बात जानता है ।

So don't suppose that this work of ours is not known by anybody.
In whose power is the taking of all right and wrong doings, your
every inner and outer intention is known.

जो ठीक मार्ग लेकर भगवान् का भजन करने लगेगा वह दुराचारी

रह ही नहीं सकता ।

Whoever is on the true path adhering to the worship of Bhagwan
definitely cannot do wickedness.

अपने इष्ट को व्यापक-सर्वत्र देखो यही अनन्यता है ।

One's own *ishta* who is infinite sees everywhere and sees this
very place.

विष्णु, शंकर, देवी, सूर्य गणेश में कोई बड़ा छोटा नहीं है । यह
सभी अपने उपासक का पूर्णरूप से कल्याण करने में समर्थ हैं ।

Vishnu, Shankara, Devi, Surya and Ganesh are beings who are not
just a little great. We are capable of utterly good fortune from
becoming a devotee of all.

जैसे जैसे भगवान की उपासना करोगे वैसे वैसे शान्ति संतोष का
अनुभव होगा ।

In the manner that we worship Bhagwan, like that we will
experience peace and happiness.

अपने अधिकारानुसार सद्गुरु से प्राप्त मन्त्र का जप करने से पाप

नष्ट होते हैं ।

To the best of your ability obtain a *japa mantra* and by practicing,
sin is destroyed.

यदि मन को वश में करना है तो उपयुक्त ध्यान का प्रकार
समझकर नित्य-थोड़ा थोड़ा अभ्यास करो ।

कागज की नीव पर बैठकर समुद्र पार नहीं किया जा सकता ।
संसारि वस्तुओं से प्रेम करना कागज की नीव पर बैठना है । वह

स्वयं गल जायगी और बैठने वाले को डुबो देगी ।

If the mind has the desire then constantly do a suitable method of *dhyaana* (meditation) - little by little do some practice. Seated on the support of paper you cannot go to the other side of the ocean. Having love of worldly things is having paper support. That water will go up to the neck and the seated person will be immersed into the water.

यदि अच्छा बनना चाहते हो तो अच्छे लोगों का साथ करो ।

If you desire to be made good then be with good people.

यदि बुरा नहीं बनना चाहते तो बुरे लोगों के सम्पर्क से बचो ।

If you desire not to be made bad then avoid the contact of bad people.

अमृत-कण
Amrit-Kana

3

जो काम करो विचार कर करो।

विश्वामित्र अपने तपोबल से चाहते तो साक्षात् भगवान् में लीन हो जाते, परन्तु उन्होंने केवल ब्राह्मण कहलाने के लिये तप किया -

लोक वासना में फँसकर मनुष्य अपना बहुत समय व्यर्थ खो बैठता हैं; अन्त में यही हाता है कि 'खोदा पहाड़ निकली चुहिया'

If you wish, then consider.

Viswamitra (*guru* to Rama) absorbed himself in the presence of Bhagwan to fulfil his desire for having the power acquired by religious austerities, in spite of this he also did devotions, for he was impatient for Brahman -

One's own time is indeed squandered as a human being entrapped in worldly desire; for in the end the limitation is in this very place - '[From] a huge hollowed mound emerges a small mouse'.

विद्वानों को चाहिये कि जिस परमात्मा को उन्होंने वेद शास्त्र से पढ़कर जाना है उसको प्राप्त करने के लिये विधिवत उपासना करें।

You should gain understanding from learned scholars of the *Vedas* and *Shastras*, about how to worship properly.

अविश्वास करने की आदत मत डालो। हीरा भी मिल जाय और अविश्वास करके कांच मान लो तो उसका मिलना भी व्यर्थ ही,

जायगा । परन्तु ऐसा भी विश्वास मत करो कि बालू में चीनी की भावना हो जाय

Don't dispense with the habit of discernment. If a diamond has to be got be suspicious too that it might also be of no use, being glass. But also do not trust the feeling that there is sugar when there is sand.

मन को संसार में लगाओ; पर इतना ही जिससे परमार्थ न बिगड़े ।

Apply the mind in mundane existence; but only so much as salvation is not spoiled.

अन्न-वस्त्र का प्रबन्ध करना आवश्यक है किन्तु अन्न-वस्त्र की अधिकता से विश्व में सुख-शान्ति की स्थापना हो जायगी, यह आशा करना भूल है ।

It is inevitable that one has to make arrangement for food and clothing but hoping that increased happiness will come from increase in food and clothing, this expectation is made in error.

अन्न-वस्त्र का स्थूल शरीर से सम्बन्ध है और अपनी सूक्ष्म शरीर में होती है । इसलिये अन्न-वस्त्र का ढेर लगा देने से या भौतिक सामग्री की अधिकाधिक प्रचुरता होने से ही विश्व में शान्ति नहीं हो सकती ।

यदि किसी को प्राण दंड को आज्ञा हो जाय तो उसके मन में घोर अशांति और चिन्ता हो जायगी ।

क्या उसके शरीर का श्रृंङ्गार करने और शब्द, स्पर्श, रूप 'रस' गंध आदि इन्द्रिय उपभोग की भौतिक सामग्री से उसकी अशांति हटाई जा सकती है?

निश्चय है कि अशान्ति का स्थान सूक्ष्म शरीर है। और जब तक सूक्ष्म शरीर का उपचार, नहीं किया जायगा तब तक अशान्ति मिट नहीं सकती।

Food and clothing are connected with the gross body. One is in a subtle body. Therefore by giving attachment wholly to the accumulation of food, clothing or plenty of material articles you cannot find happiness and peace.

If the command of the *"prana danda"* ('breath stick' – a punishment of death) will come to any then there will be terrible unrest and anxiety in the mind. What can love of the body or the enjoyment of material goods through the senses of sound, touch, image, taste, scent etc do to remove the anxiety? Undoubtedly the subtle body is the place of anxiety. And until whatever time the subtle body is treated, the anxiety cannot be erased until then.

सेंसार की कोई वस्तु साथ नहीं जायगी इसलिये यहाँ की किसी वस्तु के लिये परेशान मत रहो।

Any worldly person cannot go [die] with anything therefore be not be troubled by any possession here.

अपने किये हुए कर्म ही साथ जाते हैं:-

"कर्मानुगो गच्छति जीव एकः"

इसलिये पुण्य कर्म ही करो जिससे आगे की यात्रा अच्छी हो।

We go with the consequence of the actions that we have done -

"कर्मानुगो गच्छति जीव एकः"

"karmanugo gachchati jiva ekah"

'Going with it's *karmas* the soul goes alone'

Therefore do virtuous *karma* so that the journey beyond will be
good.

धर्म कर्म और परमात्मा से विमुख होने से ही विपत्ति आई है और
उसी के अपनाने से जायगी ।

Perform virtuous action and by Paramatma become indifferent
even if misfortune comes and [the effect of] that which one has
done will go.

जितना दूसरों के दोषों के जानने की चेष्टा करते हो उससे आधी
भी चेष्टा यदि अपने दुर्गुणों को जानने को करो तो मनुष्य से देवता
बन जाओ ।

However much you come to know of the sinful actions of others,
together with that perplexity know of one's own defective actions,
then make a god out of the human being.

धर्माचार्यों का आदेश थोड़ा-थोड़ा भी मानते चलो तो कल्याण हो
जाय ।

Go and accept some *acharya's* instruction in righeous conduct
then become happy.

यदि कोई अपमान करे तो यही विचार करो कि यह मलमूत्र का
शरीर अपमान ही करने योग्य है, इसी का अपमान किया जा रहा है
- यथायोग्य ही काम हो रहा है - कोई अप्रसन्नता की बात नहीं ।

If you are disrespectful then right away consider this body of urine
and excrement body is actually qualified to do this insult, having
done this insult become desirous that no offence has been taken
from your speech.

जो धर्म कर्म कर लोगे वही आगे साथ देगा ।

If you behave righteously [towards others] the very same people
will give the same [treatment back to you] as well.

अपने मन में दृढ़ता तो रखो परन्तु मन का पूरा विश्वास मत
करो ।

अनर्थकारी प्रसङ्गों को बचाओ, जिससे मन को गड़बड़ाने का
अवसर ही न मिले ।

Strengthen the mind but do not have complete trust in the mind.
Avoid useless conjecture - this is an opportunity to avoid
confusion to the mind.

जिन्होंने अपनी मन रूपी बालू में परमात्मा रूपी सीमेंट का योग
दे दिया है, उनका मन इतना दृढ़ हो गया है कि फिर विषयों के प्रबल
प्रलोभन रूपी भूकम्प भी उसे नहीं डिगा सकते ।

The *yoga* of Paramatma gives *"cement"* to those whose minds are
similar to sand, their minds become so hardened that even things
which might create very great temptation do not swerve the mind
any more.

मन तो बिल्कुल बालू की दिवाल है, जरा बून्द पानी पड़ा कि
खिसकी ।

इसमें उपासना रूपी सीमेंट का थोड़ा योग दे दिया जाय तो यह
बहुत मजबूत हो जाती है

Mind then is a wall of sand, little drops of water move slowly.
Taking to this worship which is a little similar to the *yoga* of
adding *"cement"* [to form concrete] then you become very strong.

भगवान के नाम में बहुत शक्ति है पर यदि शक्ति का उद्घाटन हो
जाय तभी वह काम आयेगीं ।

अग्नि में सर्वस्य भष्म कर देने को शक्ति है; पर यदि अग्नि कमजोर है तो घृत के छींटे से भी बुझ जाती है ।

There is very great *shakti* (strength) in Bhagwan's name but if that *shakti* is gone then desires will come. In fire is the strength to turn everything into ash; but if the fire is feeble then even fine drops of *ghee* (clarified butter) can extinguish it.

भगवान का नाम अति शक्तिशाली और काम धुक है, पर उसी के लिये है जिसने उसकी शक्ति का उद्घाटन कर लिया है ।

From Bhagwan's name one possesses extra strength and keeness for work, but for him this is a release of energy.

बीज में वृक्ष की शक्ति अवश्य रहती है पर एक गज करोड़ों बीजों का भार उठा लेता है; किन्तु यदि एक बीज सुक्षेत्र में वपन कर दिया जाय और उसे प्रारम्भ में ऊपरी बाधाओं से बचाया जाय तो बढ़ कर वह महान् हो जाता है और उसी में अनेको गज बांधे जा सकते हैं ।

The strength of a tree certainly lies in the *bija* (seed), yet one elephant can take a load of tens of millions of seeds. But, if one pip is planted in an excellent field and is continuously looked after then it will grow to become great and you can chain many elephants to that [tree].

भगवन्नाम रूपी बीज सुक्षेत्र में ही जमकर पल्लवित पुष्पित और फलित होता है । ऊसर में डाल दिया जाय तो नष्ट हो जाता है ।

Possessed of the name of Bhagwan is actually [to plant] the *bija* (seed) in an excellent field for it to be assembled with green foliage, filled with flowers and to become fruit bearing. Casting it in fallow land and it becomes destroyed.

अपने अन्तःकरण को सुक्षेत्र बनाना चाहिए । अपने अधिकारानुसार वर्णाश्रमोचित कर्म करने से अन्तःकरण शुद्ध होकर

भगवान् को पाने का अधिकारी बनता है ।

One should make one's inner self to be an excellent field. One's
own occupation should be suited to the caste to which one
belongs; one's inner self should be untainted by such work and be
able to attain to Bhagwan.

जिनको विरक्त जीवन व्यतीत करना है उनको जड़ माया और
चैतन्य माया दोनों से दूर रहना चाहिये ।

Those who have become recluses - detached from worldly
existence – they should stay away from both *"jada maya"* and
"chaitanya maya".

जड़ माया है धन, पैसा, रुपया, मान, प्रतिष्ठा आदि और चैतन्य
माया है स्त्री ।

"jada maya" is wealth, *paisa*, *rupees*, dignity, honour etc and,
"chaitanya maya" is woman.

माया जहां है, जैसी है बनी रहे । न हमें उसकी निन्दा करना है न
प्रशंसा; केवल अपने को उससे अलग रखना है ।

Wherever *maya* is, similar is making. We do not blame ourselves
or praise; only set oneself apart from that.

यदि असंग नहीं रहोगे तो पतन की शङ्का पग-पग पर है ।

If you are not detached then you will falter in your steps and fall.

जड़ और चैतन्य माया से अलग रहने के नियम का विरक्तों को
कड़ाई से पालन करना चाहिये ।

To remain a recluse, separate from *jada* and *chaitanya maya*, you
should practice the fostering of rigid indifference.

देवियों को चाहिये कि कभी किसी साधू के पास अकेली न जायँ ।
कथा-वार्ता, सत्संग में जाना हो तो अपने पति, पुत्र या किसी
अभिभावक के साथ ही जायँ । यही मर्यादा है ।

Goddesses (ladies) should not go near any *sadhu* who lives alone.
For news and information, understand by mixing in the society of
good people - actually go with one's husband, son or anyone who
looks after you. Right here is the rule.

जिसको जो रुचे वह धर्म नहीं है । जो शास्त्र आज्ञा दे वही धर्म
है ।

Dharma is not according to taste. That which the *Shastras*
command, that is *dharma*.

अपना धर्म पालन करते हुए मर जाना भी कल्याणकारी है दूसरे
के धर्म को अपनाने से पतन होता है ।

Having done one's duty [in life] then understanding death is also a
blessing.

Another *dharma* is then which from owning becomes one's
downfall [i.e. *adharma*].

सन्यासी को रुपया पैसा, ब्रह्मचारी को पान तुम्बाखू और चोर को
अभयदान देने से दाता को भी नरक होता है ।

Paisas and *rupees* to the *sannyasi* - *pan* (betel leaf) and tobacco to
the *brahmachari* - and to give protection to a thief -
to the one who gives these there is also to be hell.

स्वधर्म और परधर्म दोनों को जानों । स्वधर्म जान कर उसका
पालन करो और परधर्म जानकर उससे बचो ।

Understand both your own *dharma* (duty) and that of others.
Foster an understanding of one's own *dharma,* and understanding

another's duty, refrain from that.

अपने धर्म के सम्बन्ध में समझना हो तो विद्वानों या महात्माओं से समझो जो वेद शास्त्र को मानते हो और उसके अनुसार चलते हों । जो स्वयं वेद-शास्त्र नहीं मानते उनसे अपना मार्ग पूछोगे तो वे यही चाहेंगे कि:-

- होउ पड़ोसी मोरी नाई -

From learned men or *mahatmas* become compliant with the *Veda Shastras*, understanding the relationship of one's own duty [with the *dharma* of others]. If you do not automatically accept the *Veda Shastra* enquire from them [learned men or *mahatmas*] the way for yourself, then right away they can sift [the Scriptures].

– 'The neighbour puts the head in the drain.' –

द्विजातियों को स्नान, संन्या, जप, होम, अर्चन पूजन और बलि वैश्वदेव नित्य करना चाहिये ।

The twice-born (*brahmans*, *kshatriyas* and *vaishyas*) should regularly do *snana* (ablution), *japa* (repetition of a *mantra*), *homa* (sacrifice), *archana puja* (worship) and *bali* (oblation).

शंकर, विष्णु (राम, कृष्ण), सुर्य, गणेश और देवी । इन पाँच देवताओं में से जो सबसे अधिक प्रिय हों, उनके मन्त्र का जप नित्य करना चाहिये ।

Shankar (Shiva), Vishnu (Rama, Krishna), Surya, Ganesha and Devi (goddess) - from these five gods all that is abundantly lovely occurs, you should regularly do *japa* of their *mantra*.

जप करने से पाप नष्ट होते हैं ।

'जपतो नास्ति पातकम्'

From the act of *japa* [the effects of] sins are destroyed.

"जपतो नास्ति पातकम्"

"japato nasti patakam"

'Sins are eliminated by reciting the name of God'

अपने इष्ट का मन्त्र और उनके ध्यान का प्रकार किसी अनुभवी
सद्गुरु से समझ कर नित्य कुछ न कुछ समय इष्ट मंत्र के जप और
ध्यान में अवश्य लगाओ ।

Understand from any experienced *sadguru* (true *guru*) the *mantra*
and meditation method of your *ishta* (desired god); regularly
spend some time at *ishta mantra japa* (repetition of *mantra* of the
desired god) and necessarily engage in meditation.

जप करने से सिद्धि होती है इसमें संशय नहीं ।

"जपात् सिद्धिर्जपात् सिद्धिर्नसंशयः"

'There is no doubt that *siddhi* comes from doing *japa*.'

'जपात् सिद्धिर्जपात् सिद्धिर्नसंशयः'

"japat siddhirjapat siddhirnasamshayah"

'*japa, siddhi japa, siddhi* from *japa* there is no doubt'

संसार छोड़ कर जीव जब जाता है तो उसके साथ केवल उसका
किया हुआ धर्म कर्म ही जाता है । इसलिए धर्म-कर्म करके आगे के
लिये अच्छा साथी बनाओ ।

When you let go of worldly existence then you become alone and
you really do the work of *dharma*. Therefore for further dutiful
work make a good friend [Paramatma].

उपेक्षा बहुत बड़ा अस्त्र है। कोई कटुवचन कहे या किसी रूप में अपमान करे तो उसकी उपेक्षा कर दो अर्थात् उसकी ओर से अपना ध्यान हटा लो।

Indifference is a very big *astra* (weapon). If anybody is uttering unpleasantness or being disrespectful in any way, then be indifferent to him, that is to say; withdraw one's own thought from his direction.

जब कोई किसी का अपमान करता है तो इसलिए करता है कि उसे कष्ट हो। यदि उसकी उपेक्षा कर दी गई और उस ओर ध्यान ही न दिया गया, तो उसका मनोराज्य विफल हो जाता है। यही उसकी हार है।

अन्याय से धन संग्रह करने का विचार मत करो।

Whenever anybody is contemptuous, then this action [of your indifference] will become distress for him. If you have given indifference and not even given heed to his direction, then he is unsuccessful in the fantasy [accusations]. He is defeated right there.

Don't even consider collecting wealth acquired unjustly.

मन से कभी किसी का अनिष्ट चिन्तन मत करो।

With the mind, never think of doing harm.

सावधान रहो कि शरीर से यथासाध्य कोई पाप न हो जाय।

Take heed not to commit any *paapa* (sin, crime or wickedness).

कभी किसी को कटुवचन मत कहो।

Don't make any unpleasant cutting remarks to anyone.

अमृत-कण
Amrit-Kana

4

जैसा संग होता है वैसे ही गुण-दोष आते हैं ।

यदि संसर्ग अच्छा न रहा तो वृत्ति का नीचे गिर जाना असम्भव नहीं ।

You are affected by those that you mix with and take on their qualities regardless whether they are good or bad. If the companionship is not good then consider it not unlikely that existence will sink down.

यदि सर्प को मारने के लिए बिल पर लाठी पीटी जाय तो क्या सर्प मरेगा?

सूक्ष्म शरीर के रोग (अशान्ति) दूर करने के लिए स्थूल शरीर सम्बन्धी उपचार किये जायँ तो क्या शान्ति मिलेगी?

If you don't go to an opening to beat the snakes, how else will they die? The sickness (anxiety) of the *"suksha sharir"* (subtle body) caused by past action is connected with the *"sthula sharir"* (gross body). Get to know the *"upachara"* (way of offering), for how else will you get peace?

उसी मार्ग को अपनाओ जिससे लोक-परलोक दोनों बने ।

You should make a path from this world to the next.

विश्व की अशान्ति अन्न-वस्त्र का ढेर लगाने से दूर नहीं होगी ।

Don't be attached to the world of anxiety, to accumulating material possessions.

जब तक परमानन्द स्वरूप परमात्मा की प्राप्ति नहीं होगी तब तक दुख की निवृत्ति नहीं हो सकती ।

If the highly blissful form of Paramatma has not been gained then this is the reason that troubles cannot disappear.

कोई किसी से प्रेम करता है तो अपने लिये करता है उसके लिये नहीं ।

Somebody is loving then it is not (obligatory) for oneself to do anything for them.

जैसे मार्ग में कंटक से बचते हो वैसे ही संसार में शब्द स्पर्श रूप रस गंध आदि विषयों से बचो ।

In the ways that you avoid a thorn, then like that altogether refrain from the worldly pleasures of sound, touch, shape, taste, scent etc, anything that is perceived by the senses.

ऊपर से मर्यादा पूर्वक जगत् का काम करते रहो और भीतर से भगवान् का नाम लेते रहो ।

Put the rules from above [the Scriptures] before acting according to the world of desire, and from within receive Bhagwan's name.

जहाँ रहो वहीं, जो कार्य करते हो, उसको करते हुये ही भगवान का भजन करते रहो ।

Wherever you are, whatever you do, actually do it as worship of Bhagwan.

वास्तविक राग परमात्मा में करो और बनावटी राग संसार में ।

तभी अपना जीवन सफल बना सकोगे नहीं तो अन्त में पछताना पड़ेगा ।

Have true attachment for Paramatma and feigned attachment for the material world, for if you might not be able to make your life fruitful then you would have regrets.

विषय लोलुपता छोड़ो और परमात्मा में मन लगाओ ।

Relinquish appetite for worldly pleasures and apply the mind to Paramatma.

परमात्मा में मन लगाओगे तो शांति और संतोष का अनुभव होगा एवं सब प्रकार की उन्नति होगी ।

You should apply the mind to Paramatma then you will experience *shaanti* (peace) and *santosha* (contentment), and there will be all kinds of benefit.

जब तक व्यक्तिगत रूप से लोगों के सूक्ष्म शरीर मन-का उपचार करके मन की मलिनता दूर न की जायेगी तब तक व्यक्तिगत अशान्ति की निवृत्ति संभव नहीं, और जब तक व्यक्तिगत अशान्ति नहीं जायगी तब तक विश्व-शांति की बातें केवल बातें ही हैं ।

As long as an individual's mind does not engage in *upachara* (offering) then the nastiness in the mind will affect the subtle body and cause *ashaanti* (anxiety) and until such time [as *upachara* is made] the anxiety will not go and any talk of peace will be just talk.

अविधिपूर्वक प्राणायाम करने से या पथ्य का उचित पालन न कर सकने के कारण प्राणायाम से अनेकों प्रकार के रोग हो जाते हैं । विचार-पूर्वक ही प्राणायाम का अभ्यास प्रारम्भ करना चाहिए ।

By going against the established rules of *pranayama* or by not

fostering the correct way of *pranayama*, there are going to be
many kinds of disorders. Indeed, consider carefully before starting
the practice of *pranayama*.

लोक-परलोक में सारी उन्नति मन के ऊपर ही रहती है। यदि मन
पवित्र है तो सर्वत्र उन्नति होगी और यदि मन अशुद्ध है तो
विवेकहीन होकर मनुष्य सदा पतन की ओर ही बड़ेगा।

In this world and the next all upward progress of the mind truly
lasts. If the mind is pure then advancement will be everywhere
and if the mind is impure then you will grow to be an absurd
human being, falling by the wayside.

शुद्ध मन परमात्मा से अनुराग करता है। परमात्मा का अनुराग
बढ़ने से विषय-वासनाओं से अरुचि हो जाती है, और विवेक का
उदय होता है। जिसके कारण मनुष्य शुभ संकल्पवान होकर सर्वत्र
उन्नति करता है।

Clear mind is love from Paramatma. From the growth of love for
Paramatma, desire for worldly pleasure becomes distaste (for
worldliness), and ascent of reason occurs. It is a good man who is
always determined to make improvement.

अशुद्ध मन विषयों की ओर दौड़ता है। विषयानुराग का फल दुख
और पतन होता है।

The impure mind runs in the direction of worldly pleasure.
Attachment to the fruits of worldly pleasure are trouble and
ruination.

शुद्ध मन में अविहिताचरण (धर्म-विरुद्ध आचरण) की भावनायें
नहीं उठतीं और अनाचार, दुराचार, पापाचार, भ्रष्टाचार आदि
पतनकारी प्रवृत्तियों के अभाव में सदाचार, सद्विचार, सत्यनिष्ठा, क्षमा
दया आदि दैवी प्रकृति के लक्षण की प्रधानता हो के कारण

मनुष्यलोक में सदा सुख शान्ति का अनुभव करता है ।

Of a clear mind, with no feelings for unlawful conduct (contrary
to *dharma*), neglect of religious observances, wicked, sinful
conduct, depraved behaviour etc, tendencies towards destructive
behaviour, deficiency in morality - true discernment, truthfulness,
tenderness etc are excellent indications of a divine nature, to
constantly experience peace and happiness in the world.

जो शास्त्रानुकूल पुरुषार्थ है वही पुण्य है और वही अभ्युदय
अर्थात् लौकिक उन्नति और मोक्ष का देनेवाला है ।

Who so labours in accordance with the *Shastras,* his work is
sacred and such work comes into existence as world advancement
and is the bestower of *moksha* (final liberation).

शास्त्रों के विरुद्ध पुरुषार्थ मत करो, पाप से बचो और पुण्य करो
यही उन्नति का प्रकार है ।

Don't do labour that is contrary to the *Shastras*, escape from
wickedness and in this very place progress in a holy manner.

संसार इतना स्वार्थी है कि यदि मनुष्य का चमड़ा भी काम में
आता होता तो चमड़ी खिंचवाकर चिता पर भेजता ।

The mundane existence is so very self-interested that if a human
being of hide comes together with desire, then the skin is caused
to be filled, be warned.

इसमें लेशमात्र भी सन्देह नहीं है कि जब तक लोगों का स्वार्थ
सिद्ध होता है तभी तक सब मान सम्मान और अनुराग दिखाते हैं ।

In this there is not a shadow of doubt that when people's self-
interest has become perfect it is upon this account all measure of
respect and affection are shown.

अमृत-कण
Amrit-Kana

5

व्यवहार के सहारे ही परमार्थ का मार्ग चलता है इसलिए व्यवहार को भद्दा मत होने दो । सबके साथ मर्यादापूर्ण व्यवहार रखो ।

To go the way of *paramartha* (highest wealth) is to assist worldly business, therefore don't be clumsy in the business. Perform your everyday business matters in complete accordance with the rules.

प्रारब्ध सबको भोगना पड़ता है ज्ञानी को भी भोगना पड़ता है । इसलिए सम्पत्ति विपत्ति जब जो सामने आये अपनी ही चीज समझ कर धैर्यपूर्वक भोगना चाहिये ।

All have to endure their fate, even the wise also have to undergo [fate]. Therefore whether you face prosperity or adversity you should endure it with courage understanding it to be your own.

मनुष्य जीवन की सफलता भगवान की प्राप्ति में है, किसी लौकिक कार्य के पूरा होने में नहीं ।

The fruitfulness of human existence lies in gaining Bhagwan, not in the completion of any earthly task.

संचित कर्मों को ज्ञानाग्नि से दग्ध करो, प्रारब्ध को धैर्यपूर्वक भोग कर समाप्त करो, और क्रियमाण कर्मों को भगवान को अर्पण कर दो, इस तरह कर्म करते हुए कर्मबन्धन से मुक्त हो जाओगे ।

Burn accumulated actions with the fire of knowledge, courageously experience the pleasure or pain of destiny, and offer

up your actions to Bhagwan. Having acted in this manner know
that you will be liberated from the bondage resulting from one's
deeds.

भगवान का भजन हो जीवन में मुख्य है । और भगवत भजन में
सुविधा रहे इसी के लिए स्वधर्म-पालन का उपदेश है ।

The worship of Bhagwan is the most important thing to do in life.
Also it is of benefit to know that by the worship of the Deity one's
own *dharma* (duty or religion) is tended.

अपने जीवन को धर्म के नियन्त्रण में रक्खो ।

Live one's own existence by fixed rules and follow them.

स्वधर्म पालन की स्वतन्त्रता तो कल्याणकारी है परन्तु
परधर्मावलम्बन की स्वतन्त्रता से पतन ही होता है ।

The freedom to live by one's own *dharma* (duty or religion), that
is happiness, but by freely resorting to living the *dharma* of
another is to fall into decline.

एकान्त स्थान में अपनी माता, पुत्री और बहिन के साथ भी न
बैठो - क्योंकि इंद्रियों का वेग प्रबल होता है, बुद्धिमानों को भी
विचलित कर देता है ।

Sit in a place alone without one's mother, daughter or sister -
since [in company] the senses quickly become prevalent, learned
ones are likewise given to becoming unsettled [in such company].

यदि धर्म का खण्डन करना है तो खण्डन करने के पहले समझ तो
लो वह क्या वस्तु है । बिना समझे किसी का खण्डन करना मूर्खता
ही नहीं असभ्यता भी है ।

If you deny *dharma* then first understand what this denial is.
Without any understanding, to deny [the need for *dharma*] is not

just outright ignorance but it is also uncivilised.

देश, काल, वय, परिस्थिति, बुद्धि और शक्ति का निदान करके गुरु शिष्य को उपदेश करता है तभी उससे लाभ होता है ।

To acquire wisdom and strength about solving problems related to country, era, age, and environment, one should take advantage of the instruction of a *guru* by becoming a *shishya* (student).

प्रातःकाल उठकर सबसे पहले पृथ्वी को प्रणाम करो, फिर माता को प्रणाम करो, फिर पिता को प्रणाम करो, फिर गुरु या आचार्य को प्रणाम करो, इनमें से जो निकट न हों उनके चित्र को प्रणाम करो, और यदि चित्र भी नहीं है तो उनका स्मरण करके मानसिक प्रणाम करो ।

Rise at daybreak and first do *pranaam* (salutation) to the earth, then do *pranaam* to mother, then do *pranaam* to father, then to *guru* or religious instructor do *pranaam*, if they are not close then do *pranaam* to their picture, and if their is no picture of them then do mental *pranaam* to their memory.

जो भक्ति करता हुआ भगवान से कुछ मांगता नहीं उस पर भगवान जल्दी प्रसन्न होते हैं ।

If you have faith in Bhagwan, Bhagwan is quickly pleased with him who does not make demands.

विषय भोग की इच्छा है तो शास्त्र-मर्यादानुसार विषयों को भोगो ।

[If you] desire to experience the worldly experiences of pleasure and pain, then undergo them according to the rules of *Shastras*.

सच्चे जिज्ञासु को संसार में कुछ भी अच्छा नहीं लगता । उसे किसी भी वस्तु की इच्छा नहीं रहती । वह अपने इष्ट की प्राप्ति के

प्रयत्नों में लगा रहता है ।

For the genuine seeker it is not good to be attached to anything in
the material existence. It is not good to remain desirous of any
thing. One remains attached in the effort of gaining one's own
ishta.

अपने-अपने धर्म से विमुख होने के कारण ही लोग आजकल
दुखी और अशान्त हैं । सब लोग अपने-अपने धर्म का पालन करने
लगें तो अभी सुख-शान्ति का अनुभव होने लगे ।

The real reason that people are indifferent to their *dharma* is that
people now a days are sorrowful and restless. All people should
apply themselves to looking after their own *dharma* then right
now they will be applying themselves to the experience of
happiness and peace.

पेट के लिए धर्म मत छोड़ो ।

Don't let go of the stomach (capacity) for *dharma* (good action).

जनता को चाहिये कि सरकार की बातें माने परन्तु धर्म विरुद्ध
बातें न माने ।

Folk should speak of the government but not with discussion that
is contrary to the meaning of *dharma*.

असत्य भाषण से यज्ञ का फल, घमण्ड करने से तप का फल,
ब्राह्मण की निन्दा करने से आयु और दान करके कह देने से दान का
फल नष्ट हो जाता है ।

The fruits of *yagya* (religious sacrifice) are destroyed by untrue
speech, the fruits of *tapas* (penance) are destroyed by behaving
arrogantly and it is said that for scorning a *brahman* the effects of
a lifetime of charitable behaviour goes to be destroyed.

कैसे जानें कि हमारा मन शुद्ध हो गया?

जब मन में कोई विकार न उत्पन्न हो तो समझना चाहिये कि हमारा मन शुद्ध हो गया। जब किसी की निन्दा और विरोध करने की इच्छा न रह जाय तो समझना चाहिये कि मन पवित्र हो गया।

How do we know that our mind has become pure? We should understand that our mind is pure when no *vikara* (disorder) can be born in the mind. You should understand the mind has become pure when you do not desire to scorn or be antagonistic.

भगवान का भजन करते हो तो झूठ, चोरी, दगाबाजी, परनिन्दा, चालाकीं आदि से बचो नहीं तो गज स्नान हो जायेगा। हाथी स्नान करके अपने शरीर को साफ तो करता है परन्तु फिर अपने ऊपर धूली डाल लेता है।

By worshipping Bhagwan but doing falsehood, theft, treacherousness, reviling others, fraud etc you will not be saved, but will become like an elephant bathing. The elephant cleans the body then again flings dust and dirt over itself.

औषधि का सेवन करो तो कुपथ्य से बचौ तभी पूरा लाभ होगा। सत्संग करो तो कुसंग से भी बचो। भगवान का भजन-पूजन करते हो तो जिसको तुम बुरा समझो उससे दूर रहो।

Make use of the *aushadhi* (herb or medicine) then avoid having an unwholesome diet and you will take complete advantage. Take *satsang* (meeting with the good) and then refrain from the evil company. Worship and do *puja* to Bhagwan then whoever you understand to be bad [company] keep your distance from.

अमृत-कण

Amrit-Kana

6

जैसा सौदा हो वैसा ही दाम चुकाओ। क्षणभंगुर सांसारिक व्यवहार में क्षणभंगुर तन और धन को लगाओ। मन तो सदा साथ रहने वाली स्थायी वस्तु है परलोक में भी साथ ही रहेगा। इसलिए इसके साथ स्थायी वस्तु का सम्बन्ध जोड़ो।

परम स्थायी चराचर में रमा हुआ, परमात्मा ही है; उसके साथ मन का सम्बन्ध जोड़ो।

Repay the price in accordance with the negotiation. In worldly business lasting only a very short time apply your body and your wealth. The mind is a lasting thing, always remaining with you, and even existing with you in the other (next) world. Therefore to this [mind] make a link to something permanent.

Attract the most permanent thing in this world of animate and inanimate existence, verily Paramatma; rejoin the mind's connection with That.

यदि मन को धन से सन्तोष हो जाय या पुत्र अथवा स्त्री से सन्तोष हो जाय तो वह फिर दूसरी जगह क्यों जायगा? किन्तु मन कभी भी एक पदार्थ में नहीं टिकता। इससे स्पष्ट है कि मन को कोई भी सांसारिक पदार्थ अच्छे नहीं लगते। किसी पदार्थ को मन अच्छा मानकर उसके निकट जाता है परन्तु थोड़ी देर में हट जाता है।

- - -

संसार में मन को कोई को नहीं चाहता और मन भी किसी संसारी वस्तु से सन्तुष्ट नहीं होता ।

न मन संसार के योग्य है न संसार ही मन के योग्य है ।

- - -

मन जब परमात्मा को पा जाता है तो वही स्थिर हो जाता है फिर कहीं किसी दूसरी वस्तु की इच्छा नहीं करता । इसी से मालूम होता है कि मन के योग्य परमात्मा ही है और कुछ नहीं ।

स्मरण रखो कि जिस मन को संसार में कोई नहीं चाहता वही मन परमात्मा के निकट पहुँचाने में काम आता है ।

इसलिए संसार की बाजार में तन और धन से व्यापार करो और मन को परमात्मा की ओर लगाओ तो संसार का व्यवहार भी चलता जायगा और परमार्थ का मार्ग भी साफ होता जायगा ।

If the mind becomes satisfied with wealth or is satisfied with a wife or son then why does it go elsewhere? The mind seldom sustains [interest] in any one thing. From this it is clear that it is good that the mind does not get attached to anyone or anything in the world. The mind goes to get a good appreciation of anything but after a little while it shifts on.

In the mundane existence nobody desires your mind, and the mind is not satisfied with anything worldly.

The mind is not suitable for the world, and the world is not suitable for the mind.

Whenever the mind goes to attain Paramatma then it becomes calm, then does not desire anything from anywhere. From this it is understood that Paramatma is indeed suited to the mind and nothing else is.

Remember that the mind which is without desire for the mundane
existence, the same mind comes to desire to reach near to
Paramatma. Therefore, in the bazaar of *samsara* (worldliness and
transmigration) and with wealth, do your job and apply your mind
in the direction of Paramatma, then *samsara's* business will also
proceed and the way of *parmartha* (highest wealth, salvation) will
also become clear.

भली प्रकार छानबीन करने के उपरान्त एक बार सद्गुरु प्राप्त हो
जाय तो फिर उसके वाक्यों को मूल-मन्त्र मानकर चलने की
आवश्यकता है । फिर तो कल्याण हो ही जायगा ।

Using a good method to find a *sadguru* then of his words it is
necessary to appreciate the *"mula mantra"*. Afterwards your
welfare will be improved.

[*"mula mantra"* means 'root *mantra*' but it can also mean
'essence of advice'.
Moola Mantra is also the name of the following verse;
'*AUM sachchidananda parabrahma purshottama* Paramatma *shri
bhagavati sameta shri bhagavate namah*'
'OM, Truth-Consciousness-Bliss Supersoul, the highest being,
Supreme Soul, Blessed Female Principle joined with Blessed
Male Principle, I bow down'.]

अस्थिर चित्त, छिछली श्रद्धा और पौरुषहीनता से परमार्थ तो क्या
स्वार्थ सिद्धि भी नहीं हो सकती ।

An unsteady mind, faith [that is coming and going] like the play
of ducks and drakes, and by unmaniliness how can there be
parmartha (the highest attainment, salvation) or even fulfilment of
self-interested desires?

यदि सारा संसार भी साधक की श्रद्धा को बिगाड़ना चाहे तो भी
उससे विचलित न होते हुए असीम दृढ़ता, धैर्य और लगन के साथ
साधनारूढ़ रहना चाहिए ।

If you wish to be a faithful spiritual seeker and destroy all worldliness then don't be unsteady, be immeasurably strong, you should grow accomplished at being very tolerant.

गुरु के बताये हुए मार्ग में जितनी दृढ़ श्रद्धा होगी उतनी ही तीव्रता के साथ चित्तवृत्तियाँ साधन में एकाग्र होगी ।

The *guru* has told of the path. You must really have so much resolute faith and then you will be undisturbed by the activity of the *chitta vrittris* (activities of the mind).

सर्वकल्याणकारी धर्म और सर्वशक्तिमान! भगवान की अवहेलना करके कौन सुख-शान्ति का अनुभव कर सकता है?

Neglecting all friendly righteous action and Omnipotent Bhagwan, who can experience happiness and peace?

हमने अपने जीवन के धार्मिक पहलू को छोड़ दिया है इसी से अशांति, असन्तोष और अनेकों दुःखों को भोग रहे हैं ।

If we let go of the religious aspect of existence, we are suffering unrest, dissatisfaction and many other problems.

इष्ट मित्र कुटुम्बी आदि सब अपनी आवश्यकताओं की पूर्ति चाहते हैं, आपके मन को कोई नहीं चाहता ।

तन और धन से इनकी आवश्यकताओं की पूर्ति करते रहो, मन से परमात्मा का चिन्तन करो ।

Beloved friends and relatives etc are needed in order to fulfil the necessities of one's life, but the mind does not need anybody. With body and resources accomplish the necessities, with the mind think of Paramatma.

इष्ट मित्र कुटुम्बीजन जो तुमसे व्यवहार में सहायता चाहते हैं उनको कुछ सहयोग न देकर केवल यह कहो कि मन से हम आपको बहुत चाहते हैं; तो वे यही कहेंगे कि 'अपना मन आप अपने पास रखिये हमारी तो आवश्यकताओं को पूरा कीजिए।'

संसार में कोई भी तुम्हारा मन नहीं चाहता। यहाँ सभी तुम्हारे तन और धन के ही ग्राहक हैं। मन तो तुम जबरदस्ती दूसरों के गलें लगाते हो।

जिसकी जहाँ जरूरत है उसको वहीं लगाना बुद्धिमानी है, योग्यता-नुसार वस्तु का उपभोग न हुआ तो व्यवहार कुशलता नहीं कही जा सकती।

A beloved friend or relative desires you to help in their business don't give help only say that you have a great need for your mind; then they will straightaway say 'You ought to put your mind to one side then help complete our needs'. In the material world nobody desires your mind. Here, all are only customers for your body and wealth. To embrace others you do injustice to the mind. Apply intelligence only when needed, without enjoyment of something suited to one's abilities one's business skills cannot go anywhere.

जो संसार यहीं छूट जाने वाला है उसमें यहीं छूट जाने वाले तन और धन को लगाना चाहिये।

You are a clever person if you get remission from the material existence, you are a clever person who understands that in this place you should apply your body and your wealth.

मन जब तक शंकाशील रहता है तब तक उसकी शक्ति बिखरी रहती है और साधन अच्छी तरह चल नहीं पाता।

Whilst the mind remains inclined towards doubt then its energy
continues to be scattered and does not achieve a good kind of
sadhana.

जब तक मनुष्य पाप करने से नहीं डरेगा और पुण्य कर्म में
उसकी प्रवृत्ति नहीं होगी तब तक सुख-शान्ति का यथार्थ अनुभव
नहीं होगा ।

Whilst the person is not frightened of doing wicked deeds and is
not inclined to holy deeds then they will not have an accurate
perception of happiness and peace.

जब तक मनुष्य पाप पुण्य को पहिचानेगा नहीं तब तक समाज में
भ्रष्टाचार, दुराचार, पापाचार बन्द नहीं होंगे, शासन सत्ता की ओर से
इसके लिये चाहे जितने निरोधक विभाग खोल दिये जायें ।

Until a person is familiar with [the difference between] sin and
virtue, not locked in the company of those who are wanton and
wicked, however much the power of government doesn't want
this they are given to create a department to repress [such
behaviour].

जेल और पुलिस आदि विभागों में सरकार करोड़ों रुपया खर्च कर
रही है परन्तु जेलों का काम ही न पड़े ऐसा काम नहीं किया जा रहा
है ।

Tens of millions of *rupees* are spent on the *"jail"* and *"police"*
departments but they are not lessening the need for jails.

जब तक छोटी उमर में ही बालकों को पाप पुण्य का स्वरूप नहीं
समझाया जायगा और उसके फल का बोध नहीं कराया जायगा - कि
पुण्य से सुख और पाप से दुःख होता है - तब तक समाज में दुराचार
बन्द नहीं हो सकता ।

Until the difference between sin and virtue is explained to young
boys, and they are caused to know the effects - that from virtue
comes happiness and from sin comes suffering - until then they
will not be freed from keeping wicked company.

धर्मिक शिक्षा के द्वारा ही बालकों को पाप पुण्य का बोध हो
सकता है ।

Religious instruction is indeed the way that boys can sense the
difference between *paapa* (sin) and *punya* (virtue).

यह अधार्मिक शिक्षा का ही फल है कि पापाचार भ्रष्टाचार करने में
लोगों को तनिक भी हिचक नहीं होती ।

The effects of unrighteous instruction are that people do not
hesitate in behaving in a depraved or wicked way.

मन का प्रधान कार्य परमात्मा का चिन्तन रक्खो और अप्रधान
कार्य व्यवहार रक्खो तो दोनों हाथ लड्डू रहेंगे ।

Thinking of Paramatma is the principal task of the mind and
setting it to *vyavahara* (everyday business) is the secondary task
then [in] both hands will be *laddu* (sweetmeats).

व्यवहार चलाने के लिये पूरा मन फँसाने की आवश्यकता नहीं ।

In order to fulfil your employment it is not necessary for the mind
to become entrapped completely.

मन के थोड़े सहयोग से ही व्यवहार चल सकता है ।

With a little assistance from the mind you can do your everyday
business.

जिस प्रकार कृपण (कंजूस) मनुष्य सभी व्यवहारिक कार्य करते
हुये भी मन के द्वारा प्रधान रूप से धन का चिन्तन करता रहता है

उसी प्रकार मन के द्वारा प्रधान रूप से भगवान का चिन्तन करते हुए, व्याव-हारिक कार्य करते रहो ।

He is a miser who is in the habit of using his mind just to make money. Thinking principally of Paramatma is the way, make a habit of doing this.

जीव जन्म-जन्मान्तरों से कर्म करता चला आ रहा, कर्म करने का इसका अभ्यास बहुत पुराना है, इसलिये मन का थोड़ा सहयोग देकर कार्य प्रारम्भ कर देने से उसी प्रकार कार्य होते रहते हैं जिस प्रकार इंजन किसी डिब्बे को धक्का देकर ढकेल देता है तो फिर डिब्बा बहुत दूर तक ढकिलता चला जाता है ।

The soul is working the *karma* of its lives, the habit of doing this work is very old, therefore a little help is needed to assist the mind at the beginning, the method is like giving a railway wagon a push with the engine, and the wagon soon goes away at a furious pace.

आवश्यकता इस बात की है कि मन के प्रयोग में प्रधान अप्रधान का विभाग कर लिया जाय, मन के लिये प्रधान कार्य परमात्मा का चिन्तन माना जाय और अप्रधान रूप से मन का व्यवहार में भी थोड़ा सहयोग देकर कार्य किया जाय ।

This statement is indispensible, that it is necessary to divide the use of the mind into that which is of primary and of secondary importance. For the mind the thinking of Paramatma is most important and some co-operation of the mind is also needed to deal with the subordinate aspect of dealing with everyday business matters.

व्यवहार संचालन में प्रधान रूप से तन और धन तथा अप्रधान रूप से मन को लगाओ ।

In running a business firstly apply your body and resources, and secondarily apply the aspect of the mind.

मन जब प्रधान रूप से परमात्मा में लग जाता है तब परमात्मा
को कृपा प्राप्त होती है। परमात्मा सर्वशक्तिमान है उसकी थोड़ी भी
कृपा जीव का पूर्ण रूप से कल्याण कर सकती है।

When the mind is applied principally to Paramatma then
Paramatma's kindness is gained. Paramatma is Omnipotent, a
little of His kindness can give a soul complete happiness.

वेद शास्त्र तो भगवान की इस प्रतिज्ञा को प्रमाणित करता ही है
कि 'जो अनन्य भाव से मेरा चिन्तन करता है उसका आवश्यक
व्यवहार भी मैं संचालन करता हूँ' परन्तु भक्तों दे अनुभव भी
भगवान की इस प्रतिज्ञा को प्रमाणित करते हैं।

In the *Veda Shastra* Bhagwan made this vow which is
authentically proven that; 'I manage the business of whoever is
reflecting my endless being', but also *bhaktis* (devotees)
authentically prove this promise.

अपने मन की दरिद्रता हटाओ।

पत्ते खाकर रहो परन्तु पेट के लिये पाप मत करो।

Remove the poverty of one's own mind, eat foliage and don't
have the stomach (capacity) for wickedness.

ब्राह्मण तो हिन्दू समाज को आगे बढ़ाने के लिये इंजन के समान
हैं। आज इंजन बिगड़ जाने के कारण ही गाड़ी रुकी पड़ी है। कोई
भी पथ-च्युत हो परन्तु ब्राह्मणों को तो स्वप्न में भी स्वधर्मनिष्ठा से
विमुख होने की बात नहीं सोचनी चाहिये।

A Brahman who promotes the Hindu Samaaj (community) is
similar to an engine. Today the understanding is spoken that the

reason the train has stopped is because of the engine. Others too
have spoilt the way but if Brahmanas are also in a dream they
should not consider talking about the calamity of one's own
religion.

मत भूलो कि तुम उन महर्षियों की सन्तान हो जो बन के फल
फूलों को खाकर तृण की कुटियों में निवास करते थे । परन्तु चक्रवर्ती
राजा भी उनके चरणों में धक्के खाते थे ।

Don't be mistaken, those *maharishis* of old dwelt in grass huts
and ate the fruits and flowers of the woodlands. But Raja
Chakravarti also ate of that [dust] shaken from their feet.

अपने इष्टदेव में अनन्य भक्ति रक्खो, अनन्य हुए बिना इष्ट दर्शन
कठिन है ।

Have endless devotion in one's own *ishtadeva* (one's chosen
deity). Without *darshan* of the *ishta* there is endless difficulty.

सर्व शक्तिमान भगवान की प्रतिज्ञा है कि:-

अनन्याश्चिन्तयन्तो मां
ये जना पर्युपासते ।
तेषां नित्याभियुक्तानां
योगक्षेमं वहाम्यहम! ॥
(गीता)

अर्थात! जो मुझे अनन्य भाव से भजता है जिसके लिये योग
(अप्राप्त वस्तु की प्राप्ति) और क्षेम (प्राप्त वस्तु का लक्षण) का प्रबन्ध
मैं ही करता हूँ ।

जब सर्वशक्तिमान भगवान समस्त व्यवहार संचालन का भार
अपने ऊपर लेने को तैयार हैं तो भी मनुष्य व्यवहार के पीछे परेशान

रह कर मन को सदा व्यवहार में लगाये रहकर परमार्थ से वंचित रहे इससे अधिक अज्ञानता और मूर्खता क्या हो सकती है?

भगवान की जब यह प्रतिज्ञा है तब तो यह प्रश्न ही नहीं हो सकता कि मन को प्रधान रूप से भगवान में लगा दें तो व्यवहार कैसे चलेगा। मन जब भगवान में लग जायगा तो व्यवहार जो आवश्यक होगा वह अधिक उत्तम रीति से चलेगा यही उपनिषद् और गीता का सिध्हान्त है और यही भगवान के भक्तों का अनुभव भी है।

All-powerful Bhagwan's promise is that:-

"अनन्याश्चिन्तयन्तो मां
ये जना पर्युपासते।
तेषां नित्याभियुक्तानां
योगक्षेमं वहाम्यहम! ॥"

"ananyashchintayanto mam
ye jana paryupasate.
tesham nityabhiyuktanam
yogakshemam vahamyaham!.."
[*Bhagavad Gita* 9:22]

That is to say that, 'For the person who worships me with unbounded feeling, I make arrangements for their *yoga*, acquisition of needed items, and *kshema* – I preserve their belongings'.

When Almighty Bhagwan is ready to accept the burden of running one's life's business then isn't cheating salvation, by attaching one's mind to business, exceedingly stupid and ignorant?

When Bhagwan has made this promise, then afterwards with the mind attached to Bhagwan there is really no question of how the everyday business will proceed then. When the mind will be connected with Bhagwan then gaining the requisites of living in abundance will occur. Right here devotees of Bhagwan have also experienced this doctrine of *Upanishad* and *Gita*.

अमृत-कण

Amrit-Kana

7

दुष्कर्मों से बचो और परमात्मा का चिन्तन करते चलो तो लोक परलोक दोनों बनेंगे ।

Get away from sinners and think of Paramatma, then both this world and the next will be prepared.

गंगा स्नान से पाप नष्ट होते हैं यह गंगा की कृपा नहीं उसका स्वभाव ही है कि जो उसके जल में अवगाहन करे उसके पाप नष्ट हों । वैद्य यदि रोगी को औषधि दे तो यह उसकी कृपा नहीं कर्तव्य ही है । धर्माचार्य स्थान-स्थान पर जाकर जनता को सन्मार्ग पर लाने के लिए धर्मोपदेश करें तो वह उनकी कृपा नहीं कर्तव्य ही है ।

Bathing in the Ganga River destroys sins. This is not Ganga's *kripa* (forgiveness) but is only nature, that those who immerse themselves have their sin destroyed.

If a *vaidya* (physician) gives *aushadhi* (herb or drug) to an ill person then his *kripa* (pity) is not necessary. If a religious *guru* goes to different places and introduces the populace to the path of virtue, instructing in religious matters, then their *kripa* (kindness) is not really necessary.

लोक परलोक दोनों बनाओ ।

लोक पर ही दृष्ट रखना और परलोक के सम्बन्ध में उदासीन रहना बुद्धिमानी नहीं है ।

वर्तमान में सुख मिले और भविष्य अन्धकारमय बने ऐसी प्रवृत्ति मूर्खों की ही होती है ।

Make both this world and the next world. It is not prudent to hold on to the world that is seen and be sad in relationship to the next world.

It is foolish to meet with contentment in the present. And to make a gloomy future is an altogether foolish tendency.

अर्थ उसे ही मानो परम अर्थ (परमार्थ) की ओर ले जाय ।

Wealth to him who has gone in the direction of *parmarth* (salvation) regards that to be really wealth
(*param* = highest *arth* = wealth).

अनर्थ सम्पादन करो ।

अधर्माचरण करना ही अधर्म का स्वरूप है ।

Edit *anartha* (misfortune). *Adharma charana* (immoral behaviour) is really a form of *adharma* (unrighteousness).

धर्म राष्ट्र का रक्षक है ।

dharma (virtue) is the protector of the state.

धर्म की अवहेलना करना भारी भूल है ।

To neglect *dharma* is a massive mistake.

आहार शुद्धि पर सदा ध्यान दा ।

Always give thought to the purity of food.

परलोक के लिए अभी से कुछ प्रबन्ध कर चलो ।

Right now go make some arrangements for the other world.

धर्म मर्यादा की रक्षा से ही सद्गति सम्भव है।

Only by protection of the rules of *dharma* salvation is possible.

मनुष्य को सतर्क रहना चाहिये कि कहीं ऐसा कार्य न हो जाय जिसके परिणाम में पाप का संग्रह हो और परलोक बिगड़े।

A person should remain careful to not do such actions as will result in the accumulation of sin, and will damage the next world.

प्रत्यक्ष में अभी सुख मिले और भविष्य के लिए दुःख की सामग्री बढ़े तो यह रोजगार घाटे का होगा।

शास्त्रानुसार कर्म करोगे तो ऐसा नहीं होगा।

It appears that to be happy, right now materials are accumulated (which makes for future suffering). Then this life will belong to a business wharf. Work done according to the *Shastras* will not be like this.

परधन और परस्त्री प्रत्यक्ष में सुख का साधन होते हुए भी, संग्रह के योग्य नहीं है क्योंकि शास्त्र कहता है कि इससे पाप होता है और परलोक बिगड़ता है।

It appears that another's wealth and another's woman are necessary in order to realise pleasure. But this grasping is not suitable, for as the *Shastras* tell, that from this comes sin and the next world is spoiled.

व्यवहार करो, परन्तु ऐसे ढंग से कि परलोक भी उत्तम बने।

Do everyday business, but in such a way that the best is also made for the next world.

अर्थ संग्रह करो, पर इस प्रकार से कि वह अर्थ, (परम अर्थ),

परमार्थ का विरोधी न हो ।

जो परमार्थ में बाधक हो, जिससे पाप का संग्रह हो वह अर्थ नहीं अनर्थ है ।

Collect wealth, but in such a way that the *artha* (wealth), is not contrary to *parmartha* (*parmartha* is salvation, *param artha* is highest wealth). If it hinders *parmartha*, then from that collection will not come *artha* (wealth) but *anartha* (great loss).

कमाया हुआ धन तो यहीं रह जायगा किन्तु उसके साथ कमाया हुआ पाप आगे भी साथ जायगा और उसका फल अकेले ही भोगना पड़ेगा -

इसलिए ऐसे ही कार्य करो जो सुख के साधन तो हों परन्तु निरय (नरक) के उत्पादक न हों ।

If you have earned then right here will be the wealth but together with the earnings any sin will also go with you and alone you will suffer the effects - therefore do work that makes for happiness but not that which creates hell.

जो सुख का साधन हो पर निरय का उत्पादक न हो, अर्थात नरक की ओर ले जानेवाला न हो वही धर्म है ।

Who realizes happiness and does not create hell; that is to say, that the clever person does not go in the direction of hell, that is *dharma*.

धर्म करने से पुण्य और अधर्म करने से पाप होता है ।

To do the work of *dharma* is *punya* (holy) but from the work of *adharma* comes *paapa* (wickedness).

पुण्य का फल सुख और पाप का फल दुःख होता है ।

The fruit of virtue is happiness and the fruit of *paapa* is to be
suffering.

किसी कर्म के करने से पुण्य और किस कर्म के करने से पाप होता
है इसका निर्णय शास्त्र ही करता है ।

To settle which work is good *karma* and which brings sinful
karma, act upon the *Shastra*.

शास्त्र त्रिकालज्ञ महर्षियों के वेदनानुसारी अनुभव है ।

Shastra trikalagya (The Sacred knowledge of past, present &
future) is the *maharishis'* perception according to the *Vedas*.

शास्त्रानुसार कर्म करने से ही लोक परलोक में सुख-शान्ति की
प्राप्ति सम्भव है ।

According to the *Shastras* it is possible to do action to gain
happiness in this world and the next.

भगवान श्रीकृष्ण ने गीता में स्पष्ट कहा है -

यः शास्त्रि!वधि मुत्सृज्य,
वर्तते कामकारतः ।
न स सिद्धि मवाप्नोति,
न सुखं न पराङ्गतिम ॥

तस्माच्छस्त्रं प्रमाणन्ते,
कार्याकार्योंव्यवस्थितौ ॥
ज्ञात्वा शास्त्रविधानोक्तं,
कर्म कर्तुं मिहार्हसि ॥

अर्थात! जो शास्त्रविधि का उल्लंघन करके स्वेच्छानुसार मनमाना

व्यवहार करते हैं उनको न सम्यक सिद्धि होती है न सुख मिलता है न परमगति-मोक्ष - की ही प्राप्ति होती है। इसलिए कौन सा कार्य करने योग्य है और कौन सा करने योग्य नहीं है इसके निर्णय के लिए शास्त्र का प्रमाण ही मानना चाहिये। शास्त्र का विधान जान कर ही कर्म करने योग्य है।

Bhagwan Shri Krishna clearly said in the *Gita*:-

यः शास्त्रविधि मुत्सृज्य,
वर्तते कामकारतः ।
न स सिद्धि मवाप्नोति,
न सुखं न पराङ्गतिम ॥

"yah shaastravidhi mutsrijya,
vartate kaamakaratah.
na sa siddhi mavaapnoti,
na sukham na paraangatima.."
[*Bhagavad Gita* 16:23]

तस्माच्छस्त्रं प्रमाणन्ते,
कार्याकार्योव्यवस्थितौ ॥
ज्ञात्वा शास्त्रविधानोक्तं,
कर्म कर्तु मिहार्हसि ॥

"tasmaachchastram pramaanante,
kaaryaakaaryovyavasthitau..
gyaatvaa shaastravidhaanoktam,
karma kartu mihaarhasi.."
[*Bhagavad Gita* 16:24]

That is to say that, 'Whoever contravenes the knowledge of the *Shastra*, doing work according to free-will - that which is pleasing to the mind - they will not meet with complete success, not meet with happiness, nor will the final beatitude - *moksha* - be really gained. Therefore, for resolving which work is suitable and which work is unsuitable, you should accept the authority of the *Shastra*. Know the laws of *Shastra* as to which work is suitable.'

'सत्वात्संजायते ज्ञानं'

परमात्मा सर्वत्र विराजमान है, परन्तु नेत्रहीन होने के कारण अनुभव नहीं होता। इसलिए नेत्र बनाने की आवश्यकता है।

परमात्मा कि पहचानने का नेत्र बनता है स्वधर्माचरण से और भगवान की उपासना से।

'सत्वात्संजायते ज्ञानं'

"satvaatsanjaayate gyaanam"
'From purity arises knowledge'
[*Bhagavad Gita* 14:17]

Paramatma is shining everywhere, but is not perceived, without the eye. Therefore it is necessary to make the eye. Paramatma's eye of discrimination is made from one's own religious conduct and by the worship of Bhagwan.

शास्त्रानुसार कर्म करना कठिन नहीं है, बिना जाने ही लोग कठिन मान लेते हैं।

अशुभ वासनाओं को शुभवासनाओं द्वारा दबाओ और शुभ वासनाओं से किये हुये विहित कर्मों के फल को भगवदर्पण कर दो तभी आवागमन के के चक्कर से छूट सकोगे।

According to the *Shastra*, performing *karma* is not difficult, but without understanding this people are accepting a weight of difficulty. Restrain from the way of good and bad desires and from the fruits of those actions performed from auspicious desires. Give the fruits to God and at the same moment get freedom from the coming and going of the wheel of transmigration.

स्मरण रखो कि, आदि की बिगड़ी तो बन जाती है परन्तु अन्त की बिगड़ी नहीं बनती - इसलिए ऐसा प्रयत्न करना चाहिये कि अन्त न बिगड़ने पावे ।

प्रसिद्ध ही है "अन्त मती सो गती"

सिद्धान्त है कि -

यं यं वापि स्मरन्भावं,
त्यजत्यन्ते कलेवरम ।
तं तमेवेति कौन्तेय,
सदा सद्भाव भावितः ॥

अन्त में प्राणी जिस भावना से शरीर त्याग करता है उसी के अनुकूल उसका अगला जन्म होता है । अन्त में उत्तम भावना से शरीर त्याग हो और जीव की सद्गति हो इसीलिए भगवान ने कहा है-

'तस्मात! सर्वेषु कालेषु मामनुस्मरयुद्ध च'

यहाँ युद्ध का अर्थ है स्वधर्मानुष्ठा करना । अपने-अपने अधिकारानुसार कार्य करो और सदा परमात्मा का स्मरण रक्खो । शरीर से विहित कार्य करो और मन से परमात्मा का चिन्तन करो ।

ऐसा करने से लोक परलोक दोनों बनेगा ।

Apply the memory, first about what is to be damaged and then to that which is to be made. But spoiling of the end is not to be made - such effort should be made that the end is not spoilt. Renowned indeed is:-

"अन्त मती सो गती"

"anta mati so gati" -
'You proceed according to the last thought'
Of the established truth:-

"यं यं वापि स्मरन्भावं,
त्यजत्यन्ते कलेवरम ।
तं तमेवेति कौन्तेय,
सदा सद्भाव भावितः ॥"

"yam yam vaapi smranbhaavam,
tyajatyante kalevarama.
tam tameveti kaunteya,
sadaa sadbhaava bhaavitah.."
[*Bhagavad Gita* 8:6]

In the end as the body is relinquished, whatever feeling there is for
any living being, that is coinciding to the following birth.
Abandoning the body at the end, emancipation of the *jiva* comes
from the greatest emotion, therefore Bhagwan said:-

'तस्मात् सर्वेषु कालेषु मामनुस्मरयुद्ध च'

"tasmaat sarveshu kaaleshu maamanusmarayuddha cha."
'Therefore at all times remember Me only and fight.'
[*Bhagavad Gita* 8:7]

Here the meaning of *'yuddha'* (fight, conflict, battle) is to perform
one's own religious duties. Do one's work and constantly
remember Paramatma. With the body do the arranged work and
with the mind think of Paramatma. Work done in this way will
both be the making of this world and preparation for the next one.

दुराचार से बचो किन्तु केवल सदाचारी होना ही पर्याप्त नहीं।
सदाचारी होकर भगवान में निष्ठा बढ़ाओ तभी कल्याण है।

Refrain from wickedness, but only being righteous is not enough.
Happiness is to be righteous and to grow in faith for Bhagwan, at
the same time.

शास्त्र का सिद्धान्त है कि निन्दा करने वाला जिसकी निन्दा करता
है उसका पाप बांट लेता है ।

The *Shastras* doctrine is that the one who speaks ill of another
takes a share of the *paapa* (sin) of the one they speak ill about.

किसी की निन्दा मत करो और जो तुम्हारी निन्दा करे, उसको
अपना पारमार्थिक हितचिन्तक समझो, वह तुम्हारी निन्दा करके
तुम्हारे पापों को स्वयं अपने ऊपर ले रहा है ।

Don't speak ill of anyone and whoever speaks ill of you,
understand him to be a benefactor of your salvation, that speaking
ill of oneself is to take one's wickedness upon himself.

किसी की निन्दा मत करो और जो तुम्हारी निन्दा करे, उसको
अपना पारमार्थिक हितचिन्तक समझो, वह तुम्हारी निन्दा करके
तुम्हारे पापों को स्वयं अपने ऊपर के रहा है ।

Don't do *ninda* (speaking ill, blaming, scorning) and if you are
spoken ill of, understand him to be well-wishing of one's own
salvation, that speaking of you, he takes your sins on himself.

दूसरों को दुःख न पहुँचाकर, दुर्जनों से सम्बन्ध न रखकर, और
स्वधर्म मार्ग का उल्लंघन न करके थोड़ा भी धन मिल जाय तो उसको
बहुत समझो । धनार्जन का भारतीय प्रकार यही है ।

Do not transmit suffering to others, don't associate with wicked
people, and do not violate the way of *swadharma* (one's duty).
Having gained a little wealth too - understand a lot. Right here is
the Indian method of acquiring wealth.

धन से व्यवहार तो चल सकता है परन्तु मोक्ष नहीं खरीदा जा सकता। मोक्ष के लिये तो स्वयं साधन करना पड़ेगा।

From wealth everyday business can go on but you cannot buy *moksha* (redemption). For *moksha* you must reach Self-realisation.

धन कमाने में कोई पाप न हो जाय इससे सावधान रहो।

Be heedful not to get any sin from earning wealth.

अविहित उपायों से धन संग्रह करोगे तो धन तो यहीं रह जायगा परन्तु उसके लिये किया हुआ पाप साथ जायगा और परिणाम में नरक की यातनायें अकेले भोगनी पड़ेंगी।

Amassing wealth from forbidden means, then the wealth will be coming here but the guilt of the doing will go with you, and consequently you will suffer hell's torture alone.

जो स्वयं वासनायुक्त है वह तुम्हें वासना मुक्त कैसे कर सकता है?

गुरु ऐसा ढूंढ़ो जिसे कोई लौकिक वासना न हो।

If of one's own accord one is immersed in desire then how can you be liberated from desire? Secure a *guru* and from doing that no earthly desires will any longer be.

सुख चाहते हो तो परम सुखी परमात्मा को ढूंढ़ो।

You want to be happy, then secure to the best happiness - Paramatma.

निश्चय रखो कि कार्य कभी समाप्त नहीं होंगे। सन्तोष कर लेना ही अच्छा है। सांसारिक वासनाओं को कम करते चलो और भगवान से मिलने की एक वासना को मजबूत बनाओ।

Have the determination never to leave any work unfinished. Have

few worldly desires and make one strong desire to meet with
Bhagwan.

सांसारिक व्यवहार में विहित प्रयत्न करते चलो । जो हो जाय उसी
में सन्तोष करो - जो न हो उसके लिए परेशान मत हो ।

Make effort in arranging worldly business. Get satisfaction in
doing that - if not, do not be troubled.

ऊपर से व्यवहार करो और भीतर से परमात्मा में राग बड़ाओ ।

From the outside do the everyday business and from within
expand love in Paramatma.

मृत्यु का वारन्ट, गिरफ्तारी का वारन्ट होता है - एक क्षण को भी
मोहलत नहीं मिलेगी । आगे के लिए जो तैयारी करना है अभी से
कर चलो ।

The *"warrant"* of death, is like a *"warrant"* of arrest, you will
not encounter one moment of extra leisure. Right now make
preparation for the future.

अपने वर्णाश्रम धर्म का पालन करो और भगवान का भजन करते
चलो ।

Cherish the *dharma* of the caste to which you belong and worship
Bhagwan.

थोड़ा-थोड़ा नित्य भगवान के भजन का अभ्यास करो । बूँद-बूँद से
घड़ा भरता है ।

Little by little do constant practice of the worship of Bhagwan.
Drop by drop an earthenware water pot is filled.

संसार की सुन्दरता ऐसी है जैसे ससुराल की गाली । गाली तो

गाली ही है पर उसमें अच्छी भावना कर ली गई है। संसार में कुछ सुन्दर है ही नहीं पर इसे सुन्दर मान लिया गया है।

The beauty of the material world is like abuse of the house of your father-in-law, Abuse is indeed abuse but you have taken good feeling in that. There is not much beauty in the material world but you have gone and accepted it.

जैसे पिता स्वयं पुत्र की सब प्रकार से रक्षा करता है; पुत्र को कष्ट निवारण के लिए पिता से प्रार्थना नहीं करना पड़ता उसी प्रकार अपना इष्ट अपनी सब प्रकार से रक्षा करता है। उससे प्रार्थना नहीं करनी पड़ती।

In the manner that a father gives all kinds of protection to his son on his own accord; the son does not request the prevention of suffering, in this way one's *ishta* protects us from all manner of things. From him we don't make any requests.

एक इष्ट पुष्ट कर लो तो कभी अनिष्ट नहीं होगा।

Take one *ishta* to strengthen, then *anishta* (calamnity) will not occur.

बलि वैश्व देव नित्य करो।

Constantly do *'vali vaishwa deva'* (offerings of food to various beings, including a portion for animals, birds etc.)

नित्य नैमित्तिक कर्मों को करते हुए भगवान का स्मरण करते रहो। निश्चय रक्खो कि यहाँ का कुछ भी साथ नहीं जायगा।

Remember Bhagwan whilst doing all kinds of activities. Put your trust that nothing [of *adharma*] will go with you.

भवसागर से पार होने के लिये ही मनुष्य शरीर रूपी नौका मिली

है । ऐसा करो कि पार हो जाओ ।

The human being has acquired a boat, in the shape of a body, to cross to the other side of the *bhavasagara* (sea of birth). Thus go and cross over to the other side of the sea.

जैसा अन्न खाओगे वैसा मन बनेगा । विहित उपायों से कमाया हुआ अन्न खाओगे तो मन बुद्धि शुद्ध रहेगी ।

So you will eat such that the mind will be made. Having earned from arranged means you will eat food then the mind's thinking stays clear.

अविहित उपायों से धन कमाकर खाओगे तो बुद्धि और भी मलिन होगी और अधिक अनाचार पापाचार करोगे ।

Earning a living from unlawful schemes and you will eat, then the mind will be more filthy and [lead to] greater neglect of religious observances and sinful living.

सत्संग करो परन्तु कुसंग से अधिक बचो ।

Do *satsang* (take company of the pious) but also escape from evil company.

कहीं किसी दुराचारी पापाचारी से व्यवहार में काम पड़े तो उससे इसी प्रकार मिलो जैसे पाखाने में जाते हो - काम किया और हटे - वहाँ अधिक रुकने की आवश्यकता नहीं ।

Anywhere, if any desire for wicked sinful behaviour occurs then this is the way, to go in the latrine - had the desire and got out of the way - it is not necessary to refrain more than that.

ज्ञान और भक्ति में परस्पर कोई भी विरोध नहीं है ।

There is no antagonism between *gyaan* (knowledge) and *bhakti* (faith/belief).

भगवान जगत में सर्वत्र है यह दृढ़ विश्वास हो जाना ही ज्ञान है और उनके स्वरूप को जानकर उनकी सेवा-पूजा करना ही भक्ति है ।

Bhagwan is everywhere in the world, you are really to know this resolute belief is *gyaan* and to know their *swaroop* (true nature), their service and *puja* is indeed *bhakti*.

किसी देवता की उपासना करो तो उससे कुछ माँगो मत । माँगने वाले को कोई अपनाता नहीं । बस इतना ही करो कि उसके हो जाओ और उसको अपना बना लो ।

Do worship of any god then don't demand from them. The one who asks does not get to own. This is enough to do, go and make them your own.

किसी को अपना शत्रु मत मानो । यदि कोई विपरीत कार्य करके हानि पहुँचाने की चेष्टा करे तो यही समझो कि हमारे दुष्कर्मों का फल इसके द्वारा आ रहा है । यही मानों कि यह हमारे दुष्कर्मों का वाहन है । उसी पर चढ़कर हमारे दुष्कर्मों का फल हमारे समीप आ रहा है । जो हमारे ही कर्मों का फल वह हमारे पास ला रहा, उससे द्रोह मानना उचित नहीं ।

Don't consider anybody to be one's enemy. In case someone behaves in a hostile manner then understand it to be the way our wicked actions are coming (back to us). Right here is the vehicle carrying the weight of our sinful *karmas*. This really is the rising of the fruits of our sinful *karmas* coming near us. Who brings the fruits of our actions, it is not proper to assume ill-will from him.

राष्ट्र के चरित्र बल की वृद्धि के लिए और हर तरह राष्ट्र की उन्नति के लिए देश में धार्मिक शिक्षा की अत्यन्त आवश्यकता है ।

The strength of a country's custom is for the advancement and religious instruction in the country, it is indispensible for the advancement of every land.

धर्महीन शिक्षा से इन्द्रिय लोलुप और उत्तम-विचारहीन समाज का सृजन हो रहा है ।

Without spiritual instruction the senses are greedy and you are creating company with those without discernment.

दर्शन और धर्म के सिद्धान्तों से अवश्य ही बालकों को परिचित कराना चाहिए, तभी देश सुखी, शान्त और समृद्धशाली हो सकता है ।

It is certain that young lads should be caused to be acquainted with the doctrines of *darshan* and *dharma*, on account that a happy land, peace and great prosperity can exist.

लक्ष्मीपति भगवान को अपनाओ तो लक्ष्मी तुम्हारे पीछे फिरेगी ।

स्मरण रक्खो कि यदि भगवान को नहीं अपनाया और लक्ष्मी की उपासना करके उसको प्राप्त करने की चेष्टा की तो भगवान को असंतुष्ट करोगे और भगवान सन्तुष्ट नहीं रहे तो लक्ष्मी भी तुमसे सन्तुष्ट नहीं रह सकती । ऐसी परिस्थिति में यदि वह आई भी तो तुम्हारी बुद्धि भ्रष्ट करके चली जायगी ।

Possess Lakshmipati (the god Vishnu, husband of Lakshmi) then afterwards Lakshmi (goddess of wealth) inclines towards you. Remember this that in case you do not possess Bhagwan and act as if you worship Lakshmi (wealth) then Bhagwan will be dissatisfied and [if] Bhagwan is not satisfied then Lakshmi also cannot satisfy you. So if that is your situation then your mind will also become defiled.

अमृत-कण

Amrit-Kana

8

जैसा व्यवहार दूसरों के द्वारा तुम चाहते हो वैसा ही व्यवहार दूसरों के साथ करो।

According to the way you wish others to behave, do such business with others.

जो अपने समान ही समस्त प्राणियों को देखता है उसी का देखना, देखना कहा जा सकता है। वही वास्तव में नेत्रवान है।

Whoever sees himself in all living beings can be said to be seeing. The same is in the possession of the eye of truth.

जब तुमको कोई गाली देता है या कटुवचन कहता है तो तुमको कष्ट होता है, इसी प्रकार जिसको तुम कटुवचन कहोगे उसको भी कष्ट होगा।

When anybody has abused you or said cutting words then you are distressed. In the same way, whoever you speak harsh words to will also be suffering.

ऐसा सोच कर, कभी किसी को ऐसी बात मत कहो, जिसको दूसरों के द्वारा तुम स्वयं सुनना पसन्द नहीं करते।

Having reflected thus, don't use such speech as you don't like others using to you.

जितने मत-मतान्तर हैं, सब सनातन समुद्र को तरंगे हैं ।

जब तरङ्ग समुद्र से बाहर जाती है तब कुछ न कुछ कूड़ा करकट संग्रह कर ही लेती प्रकार संग्रहीत कूड़ा करकट ही हैं ।

However much there are different beliefs and opinions, all are
waves on the eternal sea. When a wave comes up from the sea
then do not collect any rubbish (flotsam and jetsam). Indeed,
collecting rubbish is really the method of one given to collecting
rubbish and sweepings (a dustman).

इतिहास पुराणों में तपस्वियों के पतन का जो कहीं-कहीं स्पष्ट उल्लेख किया गया है उसका तात्पर्य उनकी निन्दा करना नहीं है; किन्तु भावी सन्तान को सचेत करने के लिये ही ऐसे प्रसंगों का उल्लेख किया गया है - जिससे साधक समझ लें कि काम क्रोधादि के द्वारा किसी रीति से साधकों का पतन होता है ।

जब तक यह न जानोगे कि किस रूप से पतन होता है तो पतन के मार्ग से बचने का उपाय कैसे करोगे ।

In the tradition of Puranas (old tales of Hindu mythology) there
are clear references to the downfall of ascetics. The gist of them is
not about scorn or blame; only that the topic is mentioned for
future generations to be attentive of. That one understands that for
the *sadhaka* (one devoted to spiritual practise), any kind of lust,
anger etc. is the *sadhaka's* downfall.

Without knowing this aspect of becoming ruined, then how can a
plan be made to avoid such downfall?

पौराणिक कथाओं को पढ़कर लोग कहते हैं बड़े-बड़े महात्मा गिर गये; परन्तु बड़े-बड़े महात्मा नहीं गिरते, साधक गिरते हैं । विद्यार्थी ही फेल (अनुत्तीर्ण) हो सकता है पण्डित नहीं, जो मार्ग में है वही

भटक सकता है लक्ष्य पर पहुँचे हुए के लिये गिरने का प्रश्न ही नहीं
आता ।

यदि भर्जित (भुने हुए) बीज में अंकुर निकला हो तो सिद्धों का
गिरना माना जा सकता है ।

People having read old Purana stories are telling of very great
mahatmas (great souls) who have fallen; but great *mahatmas* have
not fallen, it is *sadhakas* (seekers) who fall. A student can fail, but
not a *pandit*. If there is a route you can lose the way, but when you
come to a sign there is no question of falling from the path.

If the sprout in the seed has been roasted and then *siddhas* (saints)
cannot fall.

हर हालत में परमात्मा में मन को लगाओ । यह मत सोचो कि
भजन करते इतने दिन हो गये अभी कुछ नहीं हुआ ।

सन्देह मत करो कि भगवान का भजन कभी व्यर्थ जायगा ।

In all circumstances apply the mind to Paramatma. Don't consider
the day for worship has gone, and so just now not be doing any.
Don't doubt the worship of Bhagwan that sometimes it will go to
no purpose.

सब कुछ व्यावहारिक कार्य करते हुए भी परमात्मा का स्मरण करते
रहो जिसमें भगवान के भजन की ही जीवन में प्रधानता रहे ।

Doing all usual work also remember Paramatma. Doing
Bhagwan's *bhajan* (worship) is most important in life.

भगवान का भजन सदा करते रहोगे तो अन्त समय में भी
भगवान का ही स्मरण होगा और भगवान का कहना है कि -

अन्तोकाले च मामेव

समरन्मुत्त्वा कलेवरम! ।
यः प्रयाति त्यजन्देहं
स याति परमां गतिम! ॥

If you will be constantly worshipping Bhagwan then at the final
time (of death) you will be remembering Bhagwan too, Bhagwan
Krishna tells:-

"अन्तोकाले च मामेव
समरन्मुत्त्वा कलेवरम!"

*"antokaale cha maameva
samaranmuktvaa kalevaram!"*
'And whosoever, leaving the body,
goes forth remembering Me alone!'
[*Bhagavad Gita* 8:5]

यः प्रयाति त्यजन्देहं
स याति परमां गतिम!

*"yah prayati tyajandeha
sa yati paramam gatim"*
'He who departs leaving the body, he attains the Supreme Goal!'
[*Bhagavad Gita* 8:13]

जिसको आप बुलाते हैं वह समीप में आता ही है । यदि भगवान
को बुलाओगे तो ऐसा नहीं हो सकता कि वह न आयें ।

Whoever you call, indeed they come near to you. If you will call
to Bhagwan then it cannot be that he won't come.

बुलाने का विधान समझकर बुलाओगे तो अवश्यमेव परमात्मा
निकट आयेगा इसमें सन्देह नहीं ।

To understand the arrangement to call, you shall call, then there is
no uncertainty that Paramatma will necessarily come near.

मन का स्वभाव है लगना । विषयों में लगाया जाता है तो वहीं
लग जाता है । भगवान में लगाया जायगा और कभी भगवान के
दिव्य स्वरूप का रस मिल गया तो फिर वहीं चिपक जायगा ।
इसलिए मन को भगवत भजन में लगाना चाहिये ।

The nature of the mind is to be attached. Having become
connected to anything perceived by the senses then to that it
becomes attached. He who will have been connected to Bhagwan
and got a taste for Bhagwan's celestial form, then to that he will
cling. Therefore the mind should apply itself to worship of
Bhagwan.

अभ्यास करते चलो । मन भागे तो भागने दो, तुम मत उसके
पीछे भागो ।

Go practice. If the mind goes away, then let the mind go away -
you are not thereof - escape beyond.

मन को परमात्मा में लगाने का प्रकार है भगवान के मन्त्र का जप
और स्वरूप का ध्यान करना ।

'तज्जपस्तदर्थं भावनम'

The method to join the mind to Paramatma is *japa* of Bhagwan's
mantra, and *dhyaana* (contemplation / meditation) of *swaroop*
(true nature of the Supreme Being).

'तज्जपस्तदर्थं भावनम'

"tajjapastadartha bhavanam"
'The purpose of that *japa* (repetition of mantra) is contemplation.'
[*Patanjali's Yoga-Darshanam* 1:28]

शिव, विष्णु, शक्ति सूर्य गणेश सभी भगवान के ही रूप हैं, इनमें
से किसी के भी नाम का जप करो और उसी मन्त्र के अनुरूप उसके

स्वरूप का ध्यान करो - यही भगवान के भजन का प्रकार है ।

Shiva, Vishnu, Shakti, Surya, Ganesha are actually all forms of
Bhagwan. Do *japa* of the names of any of these too and do
dhyaana (contemplation / meditation) of the *swaroop* (true nature)
of that fit *mantra* - right here is the method of Bhagwan's *bhajan*
(worship).

केवल जप करोगे तो मन यहाँ-वहाँ भागेगा ।

ध्यान करने से मन बंधता है इसीलिये जप और ध्यान साथ-साथ
चलाना चाहिये ।

If you will do only *japa* then the mind will flit here and there. By
doing *dhyaana* (contemplation/meditation) the mind is bound.
Therefore, you should set in motion both *japa* and *dhyaana*
together.

ऊपर चढ़ने के लिये सोपान (सीढ़ी) का सहारा लेना आवश्यक
होता है । सोपान को त्याग कर कोई ऊपर नहीं जा सकता । इष्ट का
साक्षात्कार करने का सोपान है, गुरुपदिष्ट (गुरु के द्वारा उपदेश किया
हुआ) मार्ग ।

For climbing aloft it is necessary to acquire the aid of stairs.
Forsaking steps nobody can go [up]. The staircase for meeting the
ishta is by way of the *guru's* instruction.

कोई इक्षु दण्ड (गन्ने का टुकड़ा) पानी में डाल कर धोये और
आशा करे कि पानी मीठा हो जायगा, तो यह कैसे होगा । जल को
मीठा करने के लिये इक्षुरस निकाल कर पानी में डालो ।

विधान से जो काम किये जायेंगे उन्हीं से इच्छा की पूर्ति होगी ।

Having dropped a piece of a stick of sugar-cane into water you
ought to wash it and then hope the water will become sweetened.

But how will this be?

To make the water sweet, pour sugar-cane juice into the water. By this arrangement the wish will be fulfilled.

अध्यात्मवाद की बातें किसी को भुलावा देने के लिये काल्पनिक, मन गढ़न्त बातें नहीं हैं। केवल साधन सम्पन्न न होने के कारण सिद्धि होने में देर लगती है।

साधक को प्रमाद रहित होकर सावधानी के साथ अपने मार्ग पर आगे बढ़ना चाहिये।

Any discussion of spiritual knowledge gives unsubstantial deception, minds are not structured in words. Only, the *sadhana* is not being accomplished but is delayed. The *sadhaka* (seeker) should be cautious not to make mistakes in order progress further.

जैसे भोजन के एक-एक ग्रास में तुष्टि, पुष्टि और क्षुत! निवृत्ति (क्षुधा की निवृत्ति) का अनुभव होता है, वैसे ही अभ्यास करने वाले साधक को नित्य अपने साधन में आगे बढ़ने का अनुभव होता है।

In the manner that you are satisfied by a few mouthfuls of a meal, the feeling of hunger disappears, so if one constantly practises in own *sadhana* perception grows further.

प्रति दिन इस बात का ध्यान रक्खो कि पुण्य कार्य अधिक से अधिक हों और पाप कम।

Every day keep this instruction of the holy task of *dhyaana* more and more. And sin less.

पाप मनुष्य के सूक्ष्म शरीर का मल है।

Wickedness of a person is a blemish of the subtle body.

जैसे मल की सफाई के लिये घर में प्रति दिन झाड़ूदी जाती है वैसे ही अन्तःकरण के पाप रूपी मल की सफाई के लिये सन्ध्या वन्दन आदि नित्य कर्म बताये गये हैं ।

In the manner in which the sweeper daily goes to clean the dirt in the house, like that for cleaning the filth of wickedness from the inner self we are instructed to do evening *vandana* (obeisance) etc and *nitya karma* (sacred daily duties).

जिनका यज्ञोपवीत संस्कार हो चुका है, उन्हें प्रमादरहित होकर नित्य सन्ध्या वन्दन करना चाहिये । सन्ध्या वन्दन करने के बाद जो इष्ट मन्त्र का जप किया जाता है उसका फल विशेष होता है ।

Those who have completed the *yagyopavita* (investiture with the sacred thread), without fail should constantly do evening *vandana*. Who has done *mantra-japa* of the *ishta* after evening *vandana* [obtains] special reward.

विद्यार्थी स्वयं अपना पाठ्यक्रम निर्धारित नहीं कर सकता और अपने मन की पुस्तकें पढ़ेगा तो पंडित नहीं हो सकता ।

A student cannot determine the syllabus for himself but then studying the volumes of one's own mind cannot make one a *pandit*.

साधक अपनी उपासना का विधान स्वयं नहीं बना सकते और पुस्तकों में लिखे हुये उपासना विधानों को स्वयं चुनकर यदि उपासना करेगा तो अन्ततः सफल नहीं हो सकता ।

A *sadhaka* (seeker) cannot construct his own method of worship and if one picks a method of how to worship out of books then this worship may not be efficacious.

सिद्ध के निकट ही साधक को सिद्धि होती है ।

Close to *siddha* (completion) is the *sadhaka* who becomes *siddhi*.

लिखा है:-

'छाया भूतौ वसेद् गुरौ'

गुरु के निकट योगाभ्यासी शिष्य को ऐसे रहना चाहिये जैसे अपने निकट अपनी छाया सदा रहती है ।

It is written:-

'छाया भूतौ वसेद् गुरौ'

"chaya bhutau vased gurau"
'He should live in the shadow of the *guru*'

A disciple who practices *yoga* close to the *guru* thus should constantly stay in his shadow.

गुरु शिष्य को विघ्नों से बचाते हुये और उसके अनुभवों के आधार पर उसका साधन पथ निष्कंटक बनाते हुये उसको आगे बढ़ाते हैं ।

Having escaped obstacles by *guru-shishya* (relationship of *guru* and student) he also experiences more support of his *sadhana*, further enhancing of the path, making it free of from trouble.

सद्गुरु वही है जो ज्ञान विज्ञान सम्पन्न हो अर्थात! जो वेद-शास्त्रों के रहस्य का ज्ञाता हो और जिसने स्वयं साधन सम्पन्न होकर भगवान का साक्षात्कार कर लिया हो ।

The *sadguru* is the one that is possessed of learning and knowledge, one who knows the secret of the *Veda Shastras* and has finished his *sadhana* for the meeting of Bhagwan.

सद्गुरु का एक लक्षण यह भी है कि उसे संसार के प्रति राग नहीं रहता ।

ऐसे सद्गुरु को प्राप्त करके उसके बताये हुये मार्ग पर श्रद्धा विश्वास के साथ चलकर सिद्धि प्राप्त की जा सकती है ।

Also, one characteristic mark of the *sadguru* is this, that every desire of the material world does not remain. From the *sadguru* can be gained information of the ways to proceed with faith and trust, to achieve success.

अमृत-कण

Amrit-Kana

9

कार्य की सिद्धि के लिये उचित प्रयत्न आवश्यक है केवल इच्छा करने से कार्य की सिद्धि नहीं होगी ।

For the *siddhi* (success) of work a reasonable effort is required, *siddhi* will not come from wishing alone.

सुख शान्ति चाहते हो तो सुख शान्ति का मार्ग - अपनाना होगा । इच्छा मात्र से सुख शान्ति की प्राप्ति असम्भव है ।

If you want happiness and peace then you must possess the way of happiness and peace -. It is impossible to gain peace and happiness from a mere desire.

जो जिसके मिलने का प्रकार है वह उसी प्रकार से मिलेगा ।

That method for connecting, you will be connected by that very method.

शान्ति चाहते हो तो -

निदान करो, कि अशान्ति का क्या कारण है और शान्ति का स्थान कहाँ ।

If you want *shaanti* (peace) then make a diagnosis. What is the cause of *ashaanti* (unrest) and where is a place of peace?

शान्ति और अशान्ति दोनों सुक्ष्म शरीर (मन) में होती है ।

Both *shaanti* and *ashaanti* exist in the subtle body (mind).

यदि मन को ऐसा बना लो कि अनुकूल प्रतिकूल सभी परिस्थितियो में वह सदा एकरस रह सके, तो सदैव शान्ति का अनुभव कर सकोगे ।

If the mind is made comfortable then whether you are in favourable or unfavourable surroundings, always it can be similar. Then always you can have the perception of *shaanti* (peace).

जापर कृपा राम की होई, तापर कृपा करै सब कोई ।

All are merciful to him to whom Rama is merciful.

भगवान का सहारा लोगे तो फिर और किसी के सहारे की आवश्यकता न पड़ेगी । फिर चाहे सारा संसार विमुख हो जाय तो भी कुछ बिगाड़ नहीं सकेगा ।

If people support Bhagwan then afterwards there will not be a need for support.

एक साधारण राजा जिस पर कृपा करने लगता है उसे राज्य भर के लोगों का सहयोग प्राप्त होने लगता है । जो जगन्नियंता सर्वशक्तिमान परमात्मा की ओर झुकता है, उसके अनुकूल जगत! के सभी लोग हो जाते हैं और प्राकृतिक शक्तियाँ भी उससे सहयोग करने लगती हैं ।

If one ordinary *raja* (king) is kind, all the people of the kingdom are helped. Those who bow in the direction of the Almighty Omnipotent Supersoul, all people go to have a favourable world and natural energies, as well as help from him.

भगवान की प्रतिज्ञा है कि -

अपने भक्तों के लिये मैं सब कुछ करने को तैयार हूँ।

Bhagwan has promised that:-

'For my own devotees I am completing all their work.'

आजकल लोग साधारण (अल्पज्ञ, अल्प-शक्तिमान और स्वयं दुखी) मनुष्यों का तो विश्वास कर लेते हैं परन्तु सर्वज्ञ, सर्वशक्तिमान और परमानन्द-स्वरूप भगवान के शब्दों पर विश्वास नहीं करते।

भगवान की प्रतिज्ञा पर विश्वास करके भगवद् भक्त बनो तो लोक परलोक में सर्वत्र सदा सुखी रहोगे।

Nowadays there is trust put in ordinary people but on the words of the appearance of the All-knowing, Omnipotent Blissful Soul there is not trust.

Become devoted to God and trust the promise of Bhagwan then in this world and the next world everywhere will be constantly happy.

शास्त्र की आज्ञानुसार विषय भोग भी मोक्ष मार्ग में सहायक हो सकते हैं - और शास्त्र की आज्ञा के विरुद्ध जप तप भी मोक्ष मार्ग में बाधक है।

According to injuctions of the *Shastra* deeds and experiences on the paths to *moksha* may be helpful – and the *japa* and *tapa* which is contrary to the *Shastra* is also an obstacle to *moksha*.

सर्वशक्तिमान भगवान का भक्त दुःखी नहीं रह सकता।

The devotee of Bhagwan cannot suffer.

कुटुम्बियों की अश्रद्धा होने के पहिले ही भगवान की ओर झुक

जाओ ।

Before expressing contempt for relatives bow in the direction of Bhagwan.

भगवान का भक्त होकर जीव कभी नहीं दुखी रह सकता । यह हमारा अनुभव है ।

The life of the devotee of Bhagwan can never be sorrowful. This is our experience.

हमने घोर जंगलों में रहकर भगवान की सर्वज्ञता और सर्वशक्तिमत्ता का अनुभव किया है ।

जहाँ कोई भी लौकिक प्रपंच नहीं होता वहाँ भी भगवान के भक्तों के लिये समय पर सब आवश्यक प्रबन्ध हा जाता है ।

Living in dense jungles we experienced Bhagwan's Omniscience and Omnipotence. Wherever there is someone who is not deluded by the mundane, all requisite arrangements are also made there for Bhagwan's devotees.

भगवान सर्व समर्थ है उनका भक्त त्रैलोक्य में कहीं भी रहे आनन्द से रहेगा ।

भला जो सर्वशक्तिमान है वह अपने भक्त को कैसे दुःखी देख सकेगा ।

Bhagwan is completely capable [of ensuring that] Their devotees anywhere in the three worlds (heaven, earth and the lower regions) will remain blissful. If the Omnipotent is good to the devotees how would they be able to experience sorrow?

अपनी श्रद्धा, भक्ति और विश्वास के द्वारा भगवान के प्रति अनन्य होकर एक बार भगवान की कृपा प्राप्त कर लेने की आवश्यकता है,

फिर तो भगवान स्वयं सब देखभाल रखते हैं उनसे प्रार्थना करने की
आवश्यकता नहीं पड़ती ।

One's own reverence, belief and trust is a door to the infinite. It is
necessary one time to gain Bhagwan's *kripa* (grace), then
afterwards Bhagwan is searching to see everything. It is not
necessary to make a request from Them.

सुख शान्ति का उपाय बताते हुए भगवान श्री कृष्ण ने गीता में
कहा है - कि शास्त्रानुसारी कर्मों के करने से ही सुख शान्ति की प्राप्ति
हो सकती है ।

यः शास्त्र विधि सुत्सृज्य -
वर्तते काम कारतः ।
न स सिद्धि मवाप्नोति
न सुखं न परांगतिं ॥

मन में जो अशान्ति आई है उसके लिये ऐसा उपचार करना
चाहिये जो मन पर असर डाले ।

Information of the means to happiness and peace. Bhagwan Shri
Krishna said in *Gita* - that according to the *Shastras* from doing
actions happiness and peace can be gained:-

यः शास्त्र विधि सुत्सृज्य -
वर्तते काम कारतः ।
न स सिद्धि मवाप्नोति
न सुखं न परांगतिं ॥

"yah shastra vidhi sutsrijya -
vartate kama karatah.
na sa siddhi mavapnoti
na sukham na paramgatim.."

'He who, having set aside the rules of the Scriptures, acts
impulsively out of desire, does not attain perfection, nor happiness
nor the Supreme Goal.'
[*Bhagavad Gita* 16:23]

If *ashaanti* (unrest) comes in the mind you should do *upachara*
(service) if you are to be rid of the effects upon the mind.

मन की शुद्धि के जो प्रकार शास्त्रों में बताये गये हैं उन्हीं को
कार्यान्वित करना चाहिये ।

मन की शुद्धि के लिये आवश्यक है कि -

(१) आहार शुद्धि पर ध्यान दिया जाय ।

(२) अपने अधिकारानुसार नित्य नैमित्तिक कर्म किये जायँ ।

(३) सत्य, अहिंसा, अपरिग्रह आदि दैवी-सम्पद् के लक्षणों को
व्यवहारिक जीवन में घटाया जाय ।

(४) सत्संग किया जाय ।

(५) कुसंग से बचा जाय ।

(६) भगवान का विधिवत भजन, पूजन, चिंतन नित्य कुछ न कुछ
अवश्य किया जाय ।

For purification of the mind the instruction of the *Shastras* should
be implemented. Essential for the purity of the mind is:-

(1) Consideration is to be given to purity of food.

(2) Regular fortuitous action is to be done according to one's own
suitable profession.

(3) Reduce habitual traits in life for being honest, non-violent,
charitable etc which are the characteristic marks of divine

fulfilment.

(4) Do *satsang*.

(5) Avoid evil company.

(6) Regularly worship Bhagwan, perform *puja*, constantly reflect, certainly, at least sometimes.

सत्संग में जो कुछ सुना जाय, उस पर मनन करना चाहिये ।

मनन करने से बात मन में बैठ जाती है और जो बात मन में बैठ जाती है वही समय पर व्यवहार में काम देती है ।

Having heard something in *satsang*, reflect upon that. Sit and reflect on the words in your mind and having sat thinking of the talk, desire that in your business/behaviour.

भगवान के नाम, रूप और लीलाओं का मनन करने में समय लगाया जाय । तो भगवान के प्रति प्रेम बढ़ेगा ।

'प्रेम तें प्रकट होय मैं जाना ।'

Take time in reflecting on Bhagwan's *naam* (name), *rupa* (appearance) and *leelas* (plays). The likeness of the *prem* (love) of Bhagwan will grow; 'By means of *prem* (love) I become clear'.

निदिध्यासन ईश्वर को प्रकट करने के लिये सुदृढ़ सोपान की अन्तिम सीढ़ी है,

निदिध्यासन में लगे हुए साधक का मुख्य कार्य ध्यान की प्रगाढ़ावस्था ही समाधि है ।

समाधि के दीर्घकालीन अभ्यास से ही जीवन्मुक्ति की सहजावस्था का उदय होता है । और इस अवस्था में - 'यत्र यत्र मनोयाति तत्र –

तत्र समाधयः।' जहाँ-जहाँ मन जाता है वहाँ वहाँ उसे समाधि का ही अनुभव होता है। यही स्थिति आत्मनिष्ठा की पराकाष्ठा है।

Remembering Ishwar again and again is clearly a very powerful step on the staircase to 'The End', applying himself in remembering again and again. The *sadhaka's* primary task, the serious job of meditation, is really *samadhi*. With long time practice *samadhi* progresses to be the natural condition of *jivan mukti* (freed from bondage of human life). And in this condition:-

'यत्र यत्र मनोयाति तत्र – तत्र समाधयः।'

"yatra yatra mano yati tatra tatra samadhayah"
'Wherever the mind goes it experiences *samadhi*.'
[*Drigdrishya Vivekah* 30]

Indeed here is the state of the highest degree of subjective [experience].

ब्राह्मणों को रमानुरागी (लक्ष्मीभक्त) न होकर रामानुरागी होना चाहिये।

Brahmans should not be lovers of Lakshmi (wealth).

शास्त्र विरुद्ध पुरुषार्थ से पतन होता है। शास्त्रानुकूल आचरण से ही सद्गति सम्भव।

From labour contrary to *Shastra* is ruination. Good conduct is indeed possible by conduct in accordance with the *Shastras*.

मनुष्य शरीर का मूल्य है भगवत्प्राप्ति जब तक की प्राप्ति नहीं हुई तब तक जीने की आशा ठीक है।

The value of a human body has not been gained until whatever time God is gained, until then it is a life of good hope.

नैतिकता का स्तर उठ नहीं सकता जब तक भगवान के अस्तित्व पर विश्वास नहीं होगा ।

There cannot be a standard of morality whilst you do not trust in the existence of Bhagwan.

अमृत-कण

Amrit-Kana

10

सुख की इच्छा से राजा, रईस, मिनिस्तर गवर्नर आदि का सहारा
ढूँढते फिरते हो; समझते नहीं कि ये स्वयं ही परेशान रहते हैं और
कुछ विशेष कर भी नहीं सकते। जो स्वयं दुखी है वह दूसरे को क्या
सुख पहुँचा सकता है।

For the desire of happiness you attempt to enlist the support of
raja, rich man, governor, minister etc. They do not understand and
they stay troubled and cannot do something specific. He who is
himself sorrowful, what can he do to cause happiness for another?

पहले तो अपने भाग्य पर विश्वास रक्खो; और यदि किसी का
सहारा चाहते ही हो तो उसका सहारा लो जो सर्वशक्तिमान है।

Firstly then, put the trust on one's own destiny; but if there is any
real desire for assistance, then obtain the assistance of the
Omnipotent.

किसी को प्रसन्न करना चाहते हो तो सर्वशक्तिमान परमात्मा को
प्रसन्न करो, जिसकी एक बार कृपा की दृष्टि फिर जाने से आयाच्य
और निर्भय हो जाओगे।

अयाच्य अर्थात! वह जिसे किसी से कभी कुछ याचना करने की
आवश्यकता नहीं पड़ती।

If there is any desire to please, then please the Omnipotent

Supersoul, whose grace once given, in future know that you will be fully satisfied and fearless then. Fully satisfied, that is to say that from which there will be no need to ask anything at anytime.

जिसने सूर्य, चन्द्र, नक्षत्रादि को बनाया है, जिसने पदार्थ के अणु, परिमाणु को भी अचिन्त्य शक्ति सम्पन्न बनाया है, उस सर्वशक्तिमान परम पिता परमात्मा का स्मरण करो तो कभी भी दुख का अवसर न आयेगा ।

Whoever made the sun, the moon, the planets etc, who made the atom, who is also possessed of unthinkable measure of strength, remember him, the Omnipotent Supreme Father, then there will never come a moment of trouble.

'आये थे हरिभजन को, ओटन लगे कपास' ।

माता के गर्भ में यह प्रतिज्ञा की थी कि हे परमात्मा! किसी तरह से इस घोर नरक से बाहर निकालो । बाहर निकल कर सदा तुम्हारा

ही ध्यान, भजन, पूजन किया करेंगे । किन्तु बाहर आकर भगवान को तो भुला दिया और संसार के शब्द, स्पर्श, रूप, रस, गन्ध आदि के चक्कर में पड़ गये ।

स्मरण रक्खो कि समय पूरा होने पर माता के गर्भ में जाकर वही नरक फिर भोगना पड़ेगा । ऐसा कुछ करो कि फिर वह नौबत न आये तो अच्छा है ।

'They had come to pray to Hari (Vishnu), attaching the *otan* (appliance for cleaning cotton) to the cotton-plant'. In mother's womb was this declaration; *"He* Paramatma!*"* 'Oh God!' By any means let [me] outside from this terrible hell. Actually to let [me] outside you shall have done *dhyaana*, *bhajana* and *puja*. But to come outside then you have forgotten Bhagwan and gone in the wheel of the sound, touch, shape, taste, smell etc of *samsara* (worldliness and transmigration). The whole time remember that you will undergo the suffering of the very same hell of the mother's womb. So do something so that again this condition does not come, then this is good.

अपना कोई इष्ट न बना सकने के कारण ही लोग दुःख और दरिद्रता की चक्की में पिसते रहते हैं ।

जैसे पिता के रहते हुए बच्चा कभी अनाथ नहीं होता बिना कहे ही पिता स्वाभाविक रूप से पुत्र की कठिनाइयो का निवारण करता है, वैसे ही इष्ट भी अपने उपासक की सदा ही रक्षा करता रहता है ।

The *ishta* (beloved) does not make people remain being ground by the mill-stone of suffering and poverty.

In the manner that the father does not sometimes make the child an orphan, without his being asked it is the father's natural condition to prevent difficulties for the son, so indeed the *ishta* also constantly protects his own devotee.

उपासना की विधि अनुभवी गुरु से पूछना चाहिए । प्रायः लोग पुस्तकों को पढ़कर, माहात्म्य देख कर जैसी-तैसी उपासना प्रारम्भ कर देते हैं । महीनों उपासना करने पर जब कोई फल नहीं दिखाई देता तो साधन छोड़कर बैठ रहते हैं और कभी-कभी तो अपना विश्वास भी खो बैठते हैं ।

साधन के सम्बन्ध में यह नहीं भूलना चाहिये कि अविहित साधनों से प्रायः अनिष्ट हो जाता है, कोई भी कैसी भी साधना हो बिना गुरु से समझे हुए प्रारम्भ नहीं करनी चाहिये ।

For the method of *upasana* (worship) the *guru* should be asked. Mostly people study books, and in the beginning see great value of *upasana*. Months of *upasana* but when it does not yield any effects for somebody then they give up their *upasana* and sometimes also lose their faith. In connection of *sadhana* you should not make this mistake, mostly undesired [results] are from unprescibed *sadhanas*. You should not begin any *sadhana* without understanding from the *guru*.

मायापति भगवान के अनुकूल हो जाने से माया के क्षेत्र की समस्त शक्तियाँ अपने अनुकूल बर्तने लगती हैं ।

From understanding what is favourable to Mayapati (Lakshmi's husband - Vishnu) arrange oneself as a favourable vessel of all the energies of the strength of *maya* (Lakshmi).

वैसे तो मनुष्य स्वतन्त्र है, अपनी बुद्धि के अनुसार जो ठीक समझे वह कर ही सकता है (स्वतन्त्रकर्ता) - उचित कार्य करके वह अपनी, अपने समाज और देश की उन्नति कर सकता है और अनुचित कार्य करके स्वयं पतन के गर्त में गिर सकता है और अपने समाज और देश को भी कलंकित कर सकता है ।

शास्त्र के द्वारा उचित या अनुचित समझ लो और जो ठीक समझो वही करो ।

So then, a person is free, according to one's intelligence one can understand that if one does suitable work, one's company and land can be improved, but doing improper work you may fall into the pit of ruin and your companions and land may be tainted too.

Understand well what is proper and what is improper [through] the door of *Shastras*.

जैसा कर्म करोगे वैसा ही फल मिलेगा बबूल का बीज बोने से आम खाने को नहीं मिलेगा, काँटे की चुभेंगे ।

According to our *karma* so too will be the fruits we will meet with. From sowing the seeds of the acacia tree you will not get mango fruits, instead thorns will pierce you.

मनुष्य अल्पज्ञ है, उसे एक क्षण भी आगे की बात का पता नहीं कि क्या होने वाला है; इसलिये क्या उचित है और क्या अनुचित यह मनुष्य अपनी बुद्धि के अनुसार निश्चित नहीं कर सकता। उचितानुचित और कर्तव्याकर्तव्य का निर्णय शास्त्र से ही प्राप्त किया जाता है।

वेद शास्त्रानुसारी बुद्धि ही मान्य हो सकती है। स्वतन्त्र बुद्धि का कोई मूल्य नहीं।

The human being is ignorant, to him he has no information of what lies ahead, even one moment. Therefore, in order to determine what is proper and what is not, man's own intelligence cannot do. Indeed in order to settle what is proper and what is not he gains this [information] from the *Shastras*. Intelligence in conformity with the *Veda Shastras* can indeed be considerable. Anybody's independent mind is of no value.

वेद शास्त्र बदलते नहीं हैं और मनुष्य की बुद्धि क्षण-क्षण में बदलती रहती है।

भौतिक विज्ञान (साइन्स) के सिद्धान्त मनुष्यों की बुद्धि की उपज होने के कारण सदा बदलते रहते हैं। बदलते हुए सिद्धान्तों के आधार पर जीवन चलाया जायगा तो धोखा ही धोखा है।

अपौरुषेय सनातन वेद और वेदानुसारी शास्त्रों के आधार पर ही, सत्यासत्य और उचितानुचित का निर्णय किया जा सकता है।

शास्त्रानुसारी मार्ग पर जीवन की गाड़ी चलाने से ही मनुष्य लक्ष्य तक पहुँच सकता है।

The *Veda Shastra* does not change but human beings change their minds from moment to moment. [From] the standpoint of science,

the reason man's mind is productive is because it constantly shifts.
On the basis of theories of change, life will be driven is deception,
really deception. Divine eternal *Veda* and *Shastras*, in comformity
with and in support of the *Vedas*, [in that] one can truely go to
resolve what is proper and what is improper.
According to the *Shastras* man is really a vehicle set going on the
road of existence until he can reach the goal.

शिक्षा संस्थाओं के सूत्रधारों के हाथ में देशवासियों की सुख-
शान्ति निर्भर है ।

जैसी शिक्षा होती है वैसा ही देश का मस्तिष्क निर्माण होता है ।

In the hands of the chiefs of teaching establishments lies the peace
and happiness of natives. Such teaching produces the brains of the
country.

शिक्षा ऐसी होनी चाहिये कि बालकों का मस्तिष्क इस प्रकार का
बने कि अनुकूल प्रतिकूल सभी परिस्थिति में उनका मानसिक
सन्तुलन न बिगड़ने पाये ।

ऐसा होने पर ही देश स्थायी सुख-शान्ति का अनुभव कर
सकेगा ।

Teaching should be of a method so the heads of children are
prepared in favourable surroundings, so that the mental balance is
not spoiled by unfavourable surroundings.

On becoming thus, the country can experience permanent
happiness and peace.

जगत् की परिस्थितियाँ तो प्रारब्धानुसार बनती बिगड़ती रहेंगी ।
परिस्थितियों पर नियन्त्रण करना कठिन है । किन्तु अपने मन को
ऐसा बना लेना अपने अधिकार की बात है कि वह सभी परिस्थितियों
में एकसा रहे ।

यह तभी सम्भव है जब मन व्यवहार में अधिक फँसा न रहकर परमात्मा के प्रति झुके ।

The world of surrounding will be made or be damaged according to destiny. About surroundings it is difficult to fix a rule and follow it. But the instruction is to make one's mind able to [see] all surroundings as similar.

When for this reason the mind is not excessively entrapped, then to bow again to Paramatma.

संसार के सभी पदार्थ नष्ट हो जानेवाले हैं । इनका वियोग निश्चित है, जिसका वियोग हो जाना ध्रुव है, उसके द्वारा स्थायी सुख-शान्ति की प्राप्ति की आशा करना और उसकी प्राप्ति के लिए अहर्निश प्रयत्नशील रहना मूर्खता ही है ।

Be knowing that everything of the material world is destroyed. Sunderance from these is certain, understand this loss to be fixed, thereof is the promise of the gain of lasting happiness and peace, and making effort day and night for profit is ignorance indeed.

सूर्य के उदय होने पर प्रकाश और चन्द्रमा के उदय होने पर शीतलता बिना माँगे ही मिलती है ।

परमात्मा का उद्घाटन हो जाने के बाद सुख-शान्ति स्वाभाविक रूप से प्राप्त होती है ।

At the rising of the sun there is more light and on the rising of the moon there is coolness, acquired without demand.
From discussion about understanding how to uncover Paramatma a natural form of happiness and peace is gained.

परमात्मा तो हमारे निकट से निकट है, परन्तु काम, क्रोध, मोह, लोभ आदि का पदा पड़ गया है, इसीलिये उसे हम देख नहीं पाते ।

जीव और ब्रह्म को अलग रखनेवाले इस पर्दे को नष्ट करने के चार उपाय हैं - (१) सत्संग (२) वासना त्याग (३) अध्यात्म विद्या का विचार (४) प्राणायाम इनमें से एक को भी भली प्रकार पकड़ लो तो काम पूरा हो जायगा ।

We are very near to Paramatma, but are tormented by *kama* (lust), *krodha* (anger), *moha* (ignorance), *lobha* (greed) etc, therefore we do not obtain sight of him. The soul and Brahman are separated by a curtain which is destoyed in four steps - (1) *satsang* (good company) (2) letting go of longings (3) consideration of spiritual knowledge (4) *pranayama* (breathing exercise) - From amongst these seize a good method, then your desire will be fulfilled.

धर्महीन शिक्षा से भारत का सर्वनाश हो रहा है ।

From *dharma*-less teaching Bharat (India) is becoming totally destroyed.

सतर्क रहो कि इन्द्रियाँ मन को अविहित विषय भोग के लिये प्रवृत्त न कर दें ।

Be careful not to let the mind and senses be inclined towards forbidden sensual pleasure.

अपने विवेक को सदा जागृत रक्खो । यह न भूलो कि पाप का फल दुःख होता है । सदैव शास्त्र के आधार पर पुण्य पाप का निदान करो ।

Always be awake to one's own reasoning. Don't make the mistake of suffering the effects of sin. Always on the basis of the sacred *Shastras* make an end to *paapa* (sin).

पुण्य करो, पाप से बचो और अपने मन को व्यवहार में अधिक न फँसाकर परमात्मा में लगाओ ।

दिन भर बालू को पेरिये एक बूँद भी तेल प्राप्त नहीं हो सकता ।

महीनों जल का मन्थन किया जाय, कभी भी नवनीत नहीं निकलेगा ।

जहाँ से जो वस्तु निकल सकती है वहीं पर वैध प्रयत्न करने से अभीष्ट की प्राप्ति सम्भव होती है ।

भौतिकवाद् में कभी भी किसी को शान्ति का अनुभव नहीं हो सकता । शान्ति का आधार आध्यात्मिकता ही है, भौतिकता नहीं ।

भौतिकवाद् के सहारे शान्ति प्राप्त करने की आशा उसी प्रकार है जैसे तेल के लिए बालू को पेरना और मक्खन के लिए पानी का मन्थन करना ।

Do meritous action, refrain from sin and don't get trapped excessively in thinking about everyday business, stick to Paramatma.

All day long crushing sand and not one drop of oil can be gained. Months having stirred water, but at no time does butter appear. There are prescribed rules as to what result comes from any particular action.

In materialism there cannot be any experience of peace, not in materiality.

Hoping for the support of materialism in obtaining happiness is like crushing sand in order to find oil or stirring water to make butter.

संसार सागर से पार होने के लिए शरीर-रूपी नौका मिली है, यह नौका सदा अपने अधिकार में रहने वाली नहीं है । जब तक यह अपने अधिकार में है, तब तक ऐसा प्रयत्न करो कि इसके द्वारा

भवसागर से पार हो जाओ ।

Having got a body, it is a boat to get us to the other side of the
ocean of worldly existence. This boat does not stay in your
possession forever. Whilst it is in your possession then make an
effort to find a way to the other side of the sea of rebirth.

जब तक शरीररूपी नौका अपने हाथ में है तब तक इसका
सदुपयोग करो । यदि समय का मूल्य न किया तो जब इसके छोड़ने
का समय आयेगा तो निराधार होकर चारों तरफ रोते फिरोगे ।

उस समय कोई सहायक न होगा, और निश्चय है कि एक मिनट
की भी मोहलत नहीं मिलेगी; नौका हाथ से छूट जायेगी और फिर न
जाने कब तक संसार समुद्र में निराधार होकर डूबते उतराते हुए
जन्म-मरण की घोरातिघोर यातनायें भोगनी पड़ें ।

Whilst this body is in your possession then make good use of it. If
this time has not been valued then when the time comes to let go
of the body then you will be without support you will be turned
about weeping in all directions.

There will be nobody to help you at that time, and there will not
be one extra minute of leisure. The boat will go from one's hand
and you will not know when you will return again to the material
world. Without support you will be floundering in the sea of
rebirth suffering the horrible torment of birth and death.

शरीर से विहित कार्य करो, अविहित कार्य न करो ।

Do the arranged work with the body, and don't do actions that are
forbidden.

मन में अच्छे विचार लाओ और जिन्हें समझते हो कि बुरे हैं
उनसे मन को बचाओ ।

Apply the mind to good contemplation and avoid thinking of
those things that one understands to be bad.

मन के द्वारा सद्विचार और शरीर के द्वारा सदाचार का पालन
करो ।

The mind is the way to consider truth and by means of the body
foster morality.

इंद्रियों के उद्रेक को विचार के द्वारा रोको ।

Stop the way of excess of the senses.

अमृत-कण

Amrit-Kana

11

जिसको तिसको गुरु नहीं बनाना चाहिये । कहावत प्रसिद्ध है -

पानी पीजै छान कर, गुरु कीजै जान कर ।

Those who have no *guru* should make preparation. There is a celebrated proverb:-

"paani piijai chaana kara, guru kiijai jaana kara"

'Filter the drinking water, understand the action of the *guru*.'

शास्त्र द्वारा परमात्मा का स्वरूप जानने को ज्ञान कहते हैं और परमात्मा का प्रत्यक्ष अनुभव कर लेने को विज्ञान ।

ज्ञान विज्ञान सम्पन्न अर्थात् श्रोत्रिय, ब्रह्मनिष्ठ महापुरुष ही गुरु बनाने योग्य हैं ।

We relate knowledge for to know the way of the *Shastra* is a form of Paramatma and accept wisdom for perceiving the appearance of Paramatma.

Possessed of knowledge, one is wise who has thoroughly studied the *Vedas*, indeed a great personage possessing knowledge of the immortal Self is suitable to make a *guru*.

जो समय बीत रहा है वह फिर लौट कर नहीं आयेगा ।

The time that is passing will never return again.

बिना सद्गुरु के साधन फलवती नहीं होती ।

Without a *guru* the *sadhana* is not fruitful.

अनुभवी गुरु की खोज करो ।

Search for an experienced *guru*.

ऐसा करो कि अन्त समय में पछताना न पड़े ।

After this manner act so that in the end you do not fall to
regretting.

विश्व को स्वास्थ्य लाभ कराने के लिए अपने को जिम्मेवार मानने
वाले आयुर्वेद शास्त्र के प्रणेता चरक और सुश्रुत का मत है कि धर्म-
भावना की प्रखरता रहने से 'प्रकृति-साम्य' स्थापित रहता है । और
जब अधर्म भाव बढ़ता है तब प्रकृति वैषम्य' हो जाता है, अर्थात्
तीनों गुण विषम अवस्था में हो जाते हैं जिससे समाज में कलह,
विद्रोह, द्वेषभाव, अतिवृष्टि, अनावृष्टि, अकाल तथा नाना प्रकार की
व्याधियों द्वारा दुःख और अशान्ति बढ़ती है ।

Accept responsibility for causing the good health of all. The view
of the authors of the *Ayurveda Shastra* - Charaka and Sushruta - is
to stay with the feeling of *dharma* - resembling nature, natural -
and when the feeling of *adharma* increases then irregularity of
nature occurs. That is to say that the three *gunas* (qualities)
become uneven, so from that occurs quarrelling amongst
companions, malice, deluge, drought, famine, and various
illnesses, ways of anxiety and suffering grow.

एक बार अनन्य होकर भगवान को भज लो तो जन्म-जन्म की
दरिद्रता दूर हो जायगी, जीवन में सुख-शान्ति का अनुभव होगा और
यहाँ से चलकर भी आनन्द ही रहेगा इसलिए -

जगत् को मन से हटाओ और ईश्वर को अपनाओ ।

Worship Bhagwan to become unbounded, then the wretchedness
and many lifetimes will become distant. Happiness and peace will
be experienced in life and from here you will proceed and will
stay blissful. Therefore remove the mind from the world and
possess Ishwar (the Lord).

मोह-निद्रा के भंग होने पर ही जीव को अपने वास्तविक स्वरूप
का ज्ञान होता है ।

Verily, you live your life on a sleepy wave of ignorance, your own
true identity to comprehend.

सत्संग करते रहने से मोह छूट जाता है ।

By doing *satsang* freedom from ignorance comes.

गुलाब के पुष्प के सम्पर्क से क्यारी की मिट्टी भी गुलाब की सी
सुगन्ध देने लगती है । वैसे हा विषयी पामर लोग भी यदि
महात्माओं के सत्संग में रहे तो धीरे-धीरे उनमें भी विवेक और
भगवद्भक्ति जागृत होने लगती है ।

विवेक और भक्ति के जागृत होने पर माया-मोह का आवरण हटने
लगता है ।

From contact with the earth of the flower-bed, the rose produces a
similar scent. People that are base and licentiousness, if they are
having *satsang* with *mahatmas* then slowly, slowly reasoning and
devotion to God is awakened in them as well.
On being awake to reasoning and faith, the veil of ignorance of
maya is removed.

बादलों से तो स्वच्छ जल बरसता है पर भूमि का स्पर्श होते ही
मैला हो जाता है ।

गर्भ में जीव भगवान का भजन करने की प्रतिज्ञा करता है किन्तु बाहर निकलते ही माया में लिप्त हो जाता है ।

From clouds clear water rains upon the earth then and touching the earth it actually becomes dirty. In the womb the soul promises to worship Bhagwan but emanating outside it becomes smeared in *maya*.

जिसने विश्वनियन्ता परमपिता परमात्मा में अपने मन को लगा दिया, उसके लिए किसी प्रकार का भय नहीं रह जाता ।

विश्व का रक्षक जिसका रक्षक हो, भला उसका कौन कुछ बिगाड़ सकता है?

Whoever applies his mind to the All-governing Almighty Father, Paramatma, for him there is going to be no peril. All protection comes to those who defend Paramatma. Who can injure them?

रामनामरूपी अमृत जो पान कर रहा है उसको किसी प्रकार का कोई दुःख और व्याधि नहीं आ सकती ।

Who is possessed of the name of Rama, drinking the *amrita* (nectar), no manner of suffering and disease can come to him.

श्रद्धा विश्वासपूर्वक सच्चे हृदय से एक बार भी भगवान का नाम ले लोगे तो भवसागर से पार हो सकते हो, सांसारिक दुःख दरिद्रता का हटना तो साधारण बात है ।

From faith and trust, together with a sincere heart, once people take the name of Bhagwan then they can be on the other side of the sea of birth. 'To get out of the way of worldly suffering and wretchedness' is a well-known statement then.

निश्चय रखो कि भगवान का भक्त कभी दुखी नहीं रह सकता ।

भगवान का होकर कोई दुखी रहे यह हो ही नहीं सकता ।

Have certainty that the worshipper of Bhagwan can never be
sorrowful. Belonging to Bhagwan, truly, grieving cannot be.

अमृत-कण

Amrit-Kana

12

मत भूलो कि यहाँ से एक दिन अवश्य ही चलना है .... ।

जब रहना नहीं है तो यहाँ राग मत बढ़ाओ ।

व्यवहार में केवल शिष्टाचार करते चलो ।

Make no mistake that one day you are certainly to go from here.....! When you will not stay then don't let love grow for here. Proceed by really behaving properly in everyday business.

चाहे धोखा खा जाओ, पर किसी को धोखा मत दो ।

धोखा खा जाओगे तो भी भाग्य नहीं समाप्त होगा ।

किसी को धोखा दोगे तो बुद्धि भ्रष्ट होगी, यहाँ भी अशान्ति रहेगी और परलोक भी बिगड़ेगा ।

Go and live on needing deceit, but do not cheat anyone. If you will live on deception then also your destiny will not be fulfilled. If]you cheat anyone then your intelligence will be spoiled, you will remain here in anxiety and the other world (life) will also be spoiled.

सत्संग का प्रभाव उतनी जल्दी नहीं पड़ता, जितना कुसंग का

पड़ता है ।

कुसंग से बचने के लिए सतर्क रहो ।

The effect of *satsang* (good company) does not quickly drop, as much as *kusang* (bad company).

Be careful to refrain from evil company.

अभी तक लापरवाही से जो पाप हो गये सो हो गये, परन्तु अब आज से सतर्क हो जाओ ।

नित्यमपूर्वक भगवान का भजन-पूजन आरम्भ कर दो तो पिछले पाप धीरे-धीरे नष्ट हो जायँगे और बुद्धि शुद्ध होती जायगी; आगे भी पाप से बचोगे ।

If until now you have been doing sin, in spite of this from today now go and be careful. Commence doing *puja* to eternal Bhagwan then previous wickedness will slowly, slowly be destroyed and the mind will become clear. Refrain also from any further wickedness.

शक्तिशाली बनना चाहते हो तो सर्वशक्तिमान की शरण में आओ ।

If you desire to be made strong then come take shelter in the Omnipotent.

ऐसा मत सोचो कि हमारे इस कार्य को कोई नहीं जानता । जिसके हाथ में सत्कर्म दुष्कर्म का लेखा है वह सर्वज्ञ है और तुम्हारे भीतर बाहर की हर बात को जानता है ।

Don't suppose that our actions to anybody are not known. That All-knowing in whose hand is the records of all *satkarma* (virtuous actions) and *dushkarma* (wickedness) and knows inside out your every word.

जैसे-जैसे भगवान की उपासना करोगे वैसे-वैसे शान्ति सन्तोष का अनुभव होगा ।

In the manner that you will worship Bhagwan, like that you will be experiencing peace and happiness.

केवल बीजक के अध्ययन से कोई धनी नहीं बन सकता, जब तक बीजक के अनुसार खनन करके धन प्राप्त न कर लिया जाय ।

वेद और शास्त्र परमात्मा की प्राप्ति के लिये बीजक के समान हैं; और वेद-शास्त्र की आज्ञानुसार जप, ध्यान आदि के द्वारा परमात्मा को प्रत्यक्ष करना निधि का खनन करना है ।

From the mere listing of someone's schooling cannot make anybody wealthy, not until the list according to the mining work done is procured.

The *Veda* and *Shastra* are similar to a list for gaining Paramatma; and according to the command of *Veda Shastra*, *japa*, *dhyaana* etc are the ways to dig for the treasure of Paramatma.

ज्ञान विज्ञान के समन्वय से ही स्थायी सुख शांति की प्राप्ति होगी ।

The consequence of knowledge and wisdom is that truly you will gain permanent happiness and peace.

शास्त्रीय सिद्धान्तों को अपने आचरण में लाये बिना केवल वाचिक ज्ञान तो 'तोता-रटन्त' के समान है ।

Without bringing scriptural theories into one's own conduct is only verbal knowledge similar to memorizing parrot fashion.

ऐसा नहीं करना कि अपने लौकिक अर्थ के लिए कोई पाप कर बैठो ।

So for the purpose of one's own earthly purpose don't cling to doing sin.

शब्द ऐसे निकालो जो किसी को आघात न करें ।

Bring out the words in this way, do not attack anyone.

कोई भी कार्य करो, उचितानुचित विचार कर करो ।

Do some other work, consider properly.

इन्द्रियों पर नियन्त्रण रक्खो ।

On the senses, fix a rule and follow it.

रागी यदि जंगल में भी जाय तो वहाँ भी उसे फँसाने वाली वस्तुओं का अभाव नहीं होगा ।

मन पर अधिकार रखने वाला संयमी घर पर ही रहे तो वही उसके लिए तपोवन है ।

If a lover (of Bhagwan) has gone to the jungle, then to the one trapped there will be no deficiency of things. The one who lives self-restrained at home is entitled in thinking that this is the same as as living in a *tapovana* (a forest in which ascetics perform religious austerities).

अकेले मन पर अधिकार कर लो तो अलग-अलग इन्द्रियों पर अधिकार करने की झंझट ही मिट जाय ।

The mind has a right to be alone, then one is in possession of the separate senses, really the incumbrance becomes erased.

मन रूपी ड्राइवर (चालक) के अधिकार में (पाँच ज्ञानेन्द्रियाँ और पाँच कर्मेन्द्रियाँ रूपी) दस मोटरों। ड्राइवर जिस मोटर में बैठता है वही मोटर चलती है, बाकी बेकार खड़ी रहती हैं। ड्राइवर के अधिकार में है कि चाहे जिस मोटर को जब चाहे चलाये। ड्राइवर को अपने अधिकार में कर लेने से अपने अधिकार में दसों मोटरों आ जायँगी।

एकहि साधै, सब सधै' ।

Having a mind is like being a driver, with five organs of senses for knowledge, and five organs of action, ten motor cars. The driver who sits in the motor car proceeds in the same car, the [others] remaining stand idle. The driver has the right to desire when the motor car moves. The driver in accepting command, he himself is in command of ten cars to come and go.

"एकहि साधै, सब सधै ।"

"ekahi sadhai, sab sadhai"
'One accomplished, all finished'

संसार की चकाचौंध में पड़कर भूलो मत कि वह दिन आ रहा है जब यहाँ से चलना ही पड़ेगा।

Do not mistake the dazzling effects on the eyes of the mundane existence. That day is coming when verily you will go away.

जगत् से अलग होना असम्भव है। जगत् में रहते हुए ही इसके स्वरूप को समझ लेना चाहिये।

If it is impossible to be separate from the world. Staying in the world you should acquire a knowledge of the *swaroop* (true nature).

जगत् मदारी के बनाये हुये रुपये की तरह मिथ्या है ।

जिस प्रकार मदारी के बनाये हुये रुपये को देखकर कोई भी उसे उठाने की इच्छा नहीं करता उसी प्रकार क्षणभंगुर मिथ्या संसारी वस्तुओं से अपना लगाव मत रखो ।

The world has been built by a conjuror, designed with delusory wealth. Nobody wishes to rise up and see that it has been made by a kind of conjuror. Don't make a contract between yourself and worldly delusory transitory things.

संसार में व्यवहार करो पर उसे सत्य न मानो; भीतर मन में उसका स्थान मत बनाओ ।

In doing business do not assume him to be dishonest; don't make a place in the mind for this.

संसार में पदार्थ बाधक नहीं - ईश्वरीय सृष्टि बाधक नहीं - उसके साथ बनये हुए अपने सम्बन्ध बाधक हैं । इसलिये अपनी मानसिक सृष्टि मत बनाओ ।

In the material world there is nothing obstructing, the divine nature is not obstructing - it is one's own relationship having been made that is obstructing. Therefore don't make a fanciful world.

किसी वस्तु की इच्छा हो तो उसकी प्राप्ति के लिए विहित उपायों को अपनाओ ।

Anything you wish for, then arrange for the means of acquiring that.

क्षुद्र सिद्धियों के फेर में जीवन का बहुमूल्य समय न गँवाओ ।

Don't waste time. A costly life in return for insignificant success.

समस्त सिद्धि समूह अपने परम कल्याणकारी भगवत्प्राप्ति के मार्ग में बाधक है ।

The entire collection of *siddhis* obstructs ones own best welfare, the road to gaining God.

जब साधक के पास सिद्धियाँ आती हैं तभी यह निश्चय होता है कि उसका साधन मार्ग ठीक है और वह उन्नति कर रहा ।

When the *sadhaka* comes to the possession of *siddhis* it is certain that the way of *sadhana* is going well, and that it is progressing.

जिसके साधन में विघ्न न आयें और साधन करते करते जिसके पास सिद्धियां न आयें उसे समझना चाहिये कि उसके साधन विधान में कहीं कुछ कमी है ।

Whose *sadhana* has not become obstructed, and who is doing *sadhana* but *siddhis* have not come to him, he should understand thereof that there is a deficiency somewhere in the method of the *sadhana*.

सात्विक सुख की प्राप्ति में काम, क्रोध आदि आन्तरिक शत्रु ही बाधक हैं । विहिताचरण और भगवच्चिन्तन के द्वारा इन्हें दबाकर रखने से सात्विक सुख की अनुभूति होती है ।

Anger etc. are really the internal enemies to the desire of gaining pure happiness. By restraint is the way of arranging your behaviour and the study of God is the experience of *satvik* (pure) happiness.

गृहस्थों को इन्द्रियों का निग्रह करना चाहिये, क्योंकि उन्हीं के समीप विषय सामग्री रहती है ।

शास्त्रानुकूल विषय सेवन ही गृहस्थों के लिए इन्द्रिय निग्रह का

अभ्यास है ।

Householders should subjugate their senses, because near them,
that which is perceived by the senses exists as baggage.
Anything agreeable to the *Shastra* is indeed useful for
householders to practice subjugation of the senses.

ऐसे को गुरु बनाओ जो पक्षपात शून्य हों - वेद शास्त्रानुसार ही
जो उपदेश करते हों ।

Similarly you should take an impartial *guru* - who gives advice
according to the *Veda Shastras*.

गुरु का काम है शिष्य को भवसागर से पार करना ।

The wish of the *guru* is for the *shishya* (disciple) to cross to the
other side of the *bhavasagara* (pool of birth).

उपासक की अपने इष्टदेव में अनन्य भक्ति होनी चाहिए ।

The worshipper should worship his own *ishtadeva* (divine Adored
One, god) endlessly.

जिसको इष्ट बनाओ उसे सर्वत्र देखो ।

Take an *ishta* (beloved) and see him everywhere.

कोई भी स्थान ऐसा नहीं जहाँ तुम्हारा इष्ट न हो ।

There is not a place where your *ishta* is not.

जब तक इष्ट के प्रति अनन्य भावना नहीं बनेगी तब तक इष्ट
दर्शन कठिन है ।

Until the unbounded feeling of the likeness of the *ishta* has not
been made then *darshan* of the *ishta* will be difficult.

सन्यासी द्विजोत्तम होता है। द्विज अपने कर्तव्य से च्युत हो तो द्विजोत्तम का यह कर्तव्य है कि उसे स्वधर्मानुष्ठान में आरुढ़ करें।

Twice-born become *sannyasi*. It is the obligation of a twice-born that if a twice-born has become fallen it is imperative to do determined righteous duty to him.

किसी रोग को हटाने के लिए औषधि और पथ्य दोनों की आवश्यकता होती है।

मन की चंचलता रूपी व्याधि को नष्ट करने के लिए औषधि है अभ्यास, और पथ्य है वैराग्य।

For removing any sickness *aushadhi* (herb or medicine) and *pathya* (diet) both are indispensible. For destroying the disease which makes the mind unsteady, *abhyasa* (practice) is the *aushadhi* and *vairagya* (freedom from worldly worldly desires) is the *pathya*.

अपने इष्टदेव में मन को लगाना ही अभ्यास है।

इष्ट का चिंतन, उन्हीं का ध्यान, उन्हीं के सम्बन्ध में बात करना उन्हीं का चिन्तन निरन्तर करते रहना यही अभ्यास का स्वरूप है -

तत्कथनं तच्चिन्तनं,
अन्योन्यं तत्प्रबोधनम्।
एतदेक परत्वंच,
ब्रह्माभ्यासं चतुर्विधाः॥

उन्हीं का चिंतन करते रहो।

विषयों से उपेक्षापूर्वक भगवान का ध्यान स्मरण चिन्तन करना चाहिये।

Abyasa is application of the mind to one's own *ishtadeva* (beloved divine, god). Thinking of *ishta*, *dhyaana* (meditation) on them, talking about the connection with them, remaining thinking continuously about them is the abhyasa (practice) of *swaroop* (true nature of Self).

"तत्कथनं तच्चिन्तनं
अन्योन्यं तत्प्रबोधनम् ।
एतदेक परत्वंच
ब्रह्माभ्यसं चतुर्विधः ॥"

"tatkathanam tachchintanam,
anyonyam tatprabodhanam.
etadeka paratvamcha,
brahmabhyasam chaturvidhah.."
'Speaking only about That, thinking deeply only about That,
awakening each other by mutual conversation
and depending entirely on That, with no interest in anything else,
this is *Brahmabhyasa* (meditation on Brahman).'
[*Panchadasi* 7:106]

Be thinking of Them (*ishta*).

From previous failing due to perception of sense objects you should remember to meditate on Bhagwan.

औषधि खाओ और कुपथ्य करते जाओ तो लाभ कैसे होगा? भगवान का ध्यान चिन्तन कथन करना तो औषधि सेवन है और अनाचार, पापाचार, दुराचार आदि अविहिताचरण और विषयभोग की इच्छा इस मार्ग का कुपथ्य है ।

Take the *aushadhi* (medicine) but go and eat an unwholesome diet then what will be the advantage? Meditation, thinking and recital of Bhagwan then is useful *aushadhi* and neglect of religious observances, sinful conduct, wickedness etc., conduct forbidden by law, desire of sensual experience, this is the way of unwholesome diet.

विषयों की उपेक्षा ही वैराग्य है।

Indifference to anything perceived by the senses is *vairagya*
(freedom from worldly desires).

जब मन इष्ट में लग जाता है तो वैराग्य पीछे-पीछे फिरता है। इसलिए हम तो यही कहते हैं कि रागी बनने की आवश्यकता है। अर्थात् मन इष्ट के प्रति राग उत्पन्न करने की आवश्यकता है।

When the mind becomes attached to the *ishta* then afterwards
returns *vairagya* (freedom from worldly desires). Therefore we
right here are saying that it is necessary that we are made a lover
(a *bhakti*, a devotee). That is to say that it is indispensible that
love of the likeness of the *ishta* is gained.

मन से इष्ट का स्मरण कभी भूले नहीं, यही राग का लक्षण है। इष्ट में राग बढ़ेगा तो जगत् में विराग स्वाभाविक हो जायगा।

Never lapse in bringing recollection of the *ishta* to the mind, this
is exactly the sign of love. The love will grow in the *ishta* then
naturally you will come to have an absence of desire or passion in
the world.

यदि इष्ट में राग नहीं हुआ और जगत् से विरागी बनने लगे तो अशान्ति ही भोगनी पड़ेगी।

If you haven't love in an *ishta* and you are attached to being a
viragi (averse to worldly pleasure) then you will indeed suffer
ashaanti (anxiety).

बुद्धि शोधन के लिये प्रयत्न पहिले करो और पीछे धन-संग्रह के लिए।

For disciplining the mind firstly make an effort and afterwards collect wealth.

सन्तान का गर्भाधान संस्कार विधान से कराओ और बाकी संस्कार भी समय पर विधिपूर्वक होना चाहिये ।

Cause to be done the method of *samskara* (mental impressions) at the *garbhadhana* (ceremony of conception of progeny), and remaining *samskara* also on time should duly occur.

संतान की बुद्धि शुद्ध करने का ध्यान यदि प्रारम्भ से ही न रखा गया तो आगे चलकर पछताना ही हाथ रहता है ।

जैसा बीज बोओगे वैसा ही काटोगे ।

dhyaana (meditate) of the clear intelligence of the progeny, if from the beginning you haven't put (*dhyaana*) then in future you will regret indeed.

As you will sow the seeds, so will you reap.

मन की वृत्ति में ही महात्मापन होता है । जहाँ हो वहीं रहते हुए मन की धारा को बदलो, संसार का चिन्तन कम करो और परमात्मा का चिन्तन बढ़ाओ ।

In the condition of the mind is the greatness of a *mahatma* (great soul). Wherever you have been living, alter the flow of the mind, think less about *samsara* (worldliness and transmigration) and increase thinking of Paramatma.

मुख्य चिन्त्य (चिन्तन करने योग्य) परमात्मा ही है ।

Primarilly think really of Paramatma.

संसार में व्यवहार तो करो परन्तु यह निश्चय रखो कि वह चिन्त्य नहीं अचिन्त्य है ।

अचिन्त्य को चिन्त्य मान लिया गया है इसीलिए सुख-शान्ति का अनुभव नहीं हो रहा है ।

Do the everyday business in the material world but it is certain not to worry about the inconceivable. To surrender to concern about the inconceivable, then you are therefore not having the experience of peace and happiness.

प्राण का पोषण करो और उसे परमात्मा में लगाओ ।

यदि प्राणों का रक्षक केवल सांसारिक कार्यों और विषय-भोगों के लिए है तो वह लोहार की धौंकनी ही है ।

Cherish the *prana* (breath) and become attached to Paramatma. If you save the breaths for worldly work and experience of worldliness alone then actually that is to blow as the blacksmith's bellows.

अमृत-कण

Amrit-Kana

13

चरित्र ही मनुष्य का सबसे बड़ा धन है।

With all human beings behaviour is really the best wealth.

चरित्रहीन के लिए कहा जाता है - 'यतो भ्रष्टः ततो भ्रष्टः।' लोक में जो पतित हुआ वह परलोक में भी अधोगति को प्राप्त होता है।

For the characterless the saying goes –

"यतो भ्रष्टः ततो भ्रष्टः।"

"yato bhrashtah tato bhrashtah"
'From where one is fallen, from there one is fallen'

'In the world he who has become fallen gets misfortune also in the next world.'

उत्तम शिक्षा से ही उत्तम चरित्र निर्माण होता है।

From the best instruction is created the best behaviour.

कर्तव्य और अकर्तव्य का बोध धर्म-शास्त्र ही कराता है। धर्महीन शिक्षा के द्वारा लोगों को कर्तव्य-कर्तव्य का बोध नहीं हो रहा है, स्वेच्छाचारिता बढ़ती जा रही है और राष्ट्र का चरित्रबल गिरता जा रहा है।

The sense of what is proper, what is improper to be done, cause to be done only [according to] the *Dharma-Shastra*. The people who [learn] the way of *dharma*-less instruction are not perceiving what is proper to be done, arbitrariness is growing and the country's customs are becoming degraded.

धर्म यही सिखलाता है कि, किस कार्य को कैसे करें कि उसका फल अपने लिए और समाज के लिए लाभदायक हो ।

Dharma is right here to instruct what work is done by whom and about the reward for oneself and what is advantageous for the society.

स्वधर्म का ठीक बोध न होने के कारण ही स्वेच्छाचारिता और चरित्रहीनता की वृद्धि होती जा रही है ।

Proper understanding of one's own *dharma* is not brought about by arbitrariness and becoming characterless.

धर्महीन शिक्षा का ही फल है कि यह बुद्धि प्रायः लोप हो गई है कि पाप करेंगे तो नरक की यातनायें भोगनी पड़ेंगी । यही कारण है कि लोग प्रत्यक्ष में इन्द्रिय भोग सामग्री के साधन 'अर्थ' को ही सब कुछ समझने लगते हैं ।

The effects of *dharma*-less instruction are indeed that this intelligence probably becomes destroyed. If you will do wickedness then hell's torture will befall you. Right here is evidently the reason that people experience the sensory pleasure, that is the baggage of *sadhana*, indeed all understanding is attached to it as 'wealth'.

धर्महीन शिक्षा से राष्ट्र का चरित्रबल क्षीण हो रहा है ।

From *dharma*-less instruction the country's customs are becoming weakened.

ऐसा धन-संग्रह मत करो -

जिसके द्वारा जीवन में अशान्ति और परलोक में नरक हो ।

So, do not collect riches – [anyone] who does this will have
anxiety in this life and hell in the next world.

धर्मानुसारी अर्थ संग्रह ही कल्याणकारी होता है ।

To become happy, only amass legally acquired wealth.

रुपया पैसा सब यहीं पड़ा रह जायगा ।

You are going to leave all *rupees* and *paisa* right here.

संग्रह इस प्रकार होना चाहिये कि उससे सुख-शान्ति की प्राप्ति हो
सके ।

कहीं ऐसा न हो कि हमारा कमाया हुआ रुपया दुःख और
अशांति-प्रद हो जाय ।

The manner of collection should be that which can gain happiness
and peace for you. Nowhere in our work should the *rupee* become
the giver of suffering and anxiety.

अधर्म, असत्य और अनाचार, दुराचार आदि अविहित उपायों
द्वारा कमाये हुए धन का परिणाम दुःख और अशान्ति हो होता है ।

Unrighteousness, untruth and improper conduct, wickedness etc.,
scheming ways that are forbidden by law, wealth earned in this
way becomes the effect of unhappiness and anxiety.

जो धन सत्य और धर्म के आधार पर कमाया जाता है उसी के
द्वारा सुख-शान्ति का अनुभव होता है । इसलिए यदि धन के द्वारा
सुख चाहते हो तो धनार्जन में सत्य और धर्म का आधार लो ।

Who earns wealth by way of supporting truth and *dharma*
experiences happiness and peace. Therefore if you desire

happiness and peace then in earning wealth be a supporter of truth
and *dharma*.

जो अपनी वासनाओं की पूर्ति के लिए सच झूठ और न्याय-
अन्याय पर विचार नहीं करते और उसके फल की भी चिन्ता नहीं
करते, ऐसे ही लोगों के द्वारा समाज में अनाचार, भ्रष्टाचार फैलता
है ।

Who, in order to fulfill his own desires does not consider truth and
untruth, justice and injustice, and also does not think of the
consequences, thus improper conduct is the way of people in
society, extending to depraved behaviour.

जब तक मनुष्य में धर्मबुद्धि रहती है तब तक तो वह पाप करने से
डरता है और पुण्य करने की चेष्टा करता है । परन्तु जब उसको धर्म
का बोध ही नहीं है तब वह अपनी बुद्धि के ऊपर किसी का नियन्त्रण
ही नहीं मानता ।

Until whatever time the distinction between virtue and vice exists,
from then he dreads doing wickedness, and he works with a
virtuous spirit. But when he has no sense of *dharma* then
[decisions are based] upon one's own intelligence not on
accepting the fixed rule and following it.

सर्वकल्याणकारी वेद शास्त्र के अनुशासन को भूलकर मनुष्य
इन्द्रियों का गुलाम् होकर क्षणभंगुर विषय सुखों के लिये अनाचार,
भ्रष्टाचार आदि करता हुआ अपना भविष्य अन्धकारमय बना रहा
है । यही अपने हाथों अपने मार्ग में कण्टक बोना है ।

Slipping from the instructions of the all-friendly *Veda Shastra*,
becoming a slave to the senses, improper conduct of transitory
pleasures of the senses, doing depraved behaviour etc. is making
one's future gloomy. Right here one's own hands are scattering
thorns on the path.

जब तक मनुष्य को स्वधर्म और उसके द्वारा सद्गति का बोध नहीं होगा तब तक लाख उपाय करने पर भी फैलता हुआ भ्रष्टाचार नहीं रोका जा सकता ।

Whilst a human being does not [live] by the means of his own religion and will not have a sense of good conduct, then with a hundred thousand schemes you cannot go and stop the spread of depraved behaviour.

ऋषि-प्रणीत मर्यादा ही भारतीय जीवन शैली का अधिष्ठान है ।

The *rishi* has constructed the limits of Indian customs of living.

पाश्चात्य देशवासियों को अपनी सभ्यता पर भले ही गर्व हो पर, धर्मावलम्बी भारतीय उनकी आसुरी चकाचौंध से मोहित नहीं हो सकते ।

To Westerners, be proud of your own civilisation. Supporting *dharma* do not be deceived by their *asuri* (demoniacal) dazzling effects of light on the eyes.

जो माता, पिता और गुरुजनों के चरणों में श्रद्धा-भक्ति से नत-मस्तक होकर प्रातःकाल और सायंकाल अभिवादन अर्थात् प्रणाम करता है और जो वृद्ध जनों की सेवा का सदा ध्यान रखता है उसकी आयु, विद्या, यश (कीर्ति) और बल (शारीरिक बल) की वृद्धि होती है ।

If at day-break and dusk, with head bent, you worship with reverence the feet of mother, father and elderly people and do *abhivadana*, that is to say *pranaam* (salutation), and if one is constantly considering the service of aged people, ones longevity, learning, reputation and stamina grow.

दूसरे में नहीं,

अपने में दोष देखो तो कल्याण होगा ।

In accomplishing searches for defects in yourself, you will then
have happiness.

चरित्रवान मनुष्य ही लोक-परलोक में शान्ति का अनुभव कर
सकता है ।

A man of good moral character can experience *shaanti* (peace) in
both this world and the other world.

जो चरित्र भ्रष्ट है उसे लोक में ही शान्ति नहीं रहती, परलोक में
उसके लिए शान्ति की बात ही क्या?

Whose conduct has not fallen, he remains in peace in this world,
and so, what talk of peace in the other world?

अपने में ढूढो कि कौन-सी बुराई अभी तक बाकी है । जो हो उसे
हटाने का प्रयत्न करो ।

Don't look at the defects of others, trace your own flaws up to the
present and attempt to remove them.

पुरस्कार के योग्य का पुरस्कार और तिरस्कार के योग्य का
तिरस्कार करो ।

Respect those who are worthy of respect and reproach those who
are worthy of reproach

चरित्रहीन लोगों से कथा वार्ता सुनना, सत्संग करना वैसे ही है
जैसे वेश्या के मुख से गीत गोविन्द सूरसागर सुनना ।

To hear news tidings from people whose conduct is worthless and
to do *satsang,* is really like hearing the *Gita* of Govinda and the
Surasagara (the *Ramayana*) from the mouth of a *veshya* (whore).

गंगाजल पान करना है तो शुद्ध धारा से लो, नाबदान से गंगाजल
वह कर आये तो उसके पीने का विधान नहीं है ।

When drinking the Gangajal (the sacred waters of the River
Ganga), take from the clear current. Gangajal flows into the gutter
but we don't make arrangements to drink from there.

यदि उपदेशक चरित्रवान है तब तो उसको बात सुनो ।

चरित्रहीन के शब्दों में केवल राग-रागिनी में मुग्ध हो जाना
उसकी चरित्रहीनता को बढ़ाने में सहयोग देना है ।

If the preacher is of good character and conduct, then listen to his
speech. In the sounds of someone of worthless conduct one only
becomes ignorant of *raaga-raagini* (classical melodies), really
that is only giving help in promoting his characterlessness.

जो भगवान का भजन करता है उसका चरित्र उत्तम होना
चाहिये । यदि चरित्रहीन है तो समझ लो कि भगवान का भक्त नहीं;
लोगों को धोखा देने के लिए ऊपर से भक्ति का हाव-भाव दिखाता
है ।

ऐसे धोखेबाज लोगों से स्वयं बचो अपने सम्पर्क की भोली-भाली
धार्मिक जनता को भी बचाओ ।

He who sings the prayers of Bhagwan, his conduct should be the
best. If the conduct is vile then understand that he is not devoted
to Bhagwan. In order to deceive the people he displays the
temperament of a devotee. One should escape from people who
cheat, and help those in the community who are but innocent folk.

शक्तिशाली होकर सम्मानित जीवन व्यतीत करो । शक्तिहीन का
सर्वत्र अपमान होता है ।

To be full of strength, revere the lives of the departed. To be weak, to be disrespectful is to be always weak.

मनुष्य का शरीर मिला है पुरुषार्थ करके बलवान बनो ।

Having got the body of a human being, labour to make it powerful.

दूसरे के दोषों का चिन्तन करोगे तो उसको तो कोई लाभ नहीं होगा, उल्टे दूसरे के दोष तुम्हारे मन में घुसेंगे ।

If you will find fault with another then there will not be any advantage, your mind will enter the shortcomings of another.

ऐसा काम करो कि कम से कम अपनी रक्षा तो रहे । अपनी रक्षा का ध्यान न किया तो जैसी आँधी आयेगी उसी में उड़ जाओगे ।

So, little by little work for your own protection. If you have not considered protecting yourself then it is such that you will fly away when a gale comes.

नित्य सायंकाल विचार करो कि आज हम में कितने गुण आये और कितने दोष छूटे ।

अपने दोषों को देखने लगोगे तो फिर धीरे-धीरे दोष अपने आप छूटने लगेंगे ।

Invariably, of an evening think how many qualities came in the day and how many faults were discharged. If one looks at one's own faults again, then slowly, slowly your faults will be discharged.

दोषों के सम्बन्ध में पहले अपनी चिन्ता रखो; दूसरे की बात सोचना अपने लिए घातक है । पहले अपनी रक्षा करो बाद में दूसरे की चिन्ता ।

Of faults in a relationship, firstly think of oneself; consider talk of
another as the destroyer of one's self. Firstly protect yourself,
afterwards think of the other.

स्मरण रखो कि तुम उन्हीं महर्षियों की सन्तान हो जो संसार में
सब कुछ करने में समर्थ थे। अपने संकल्प से दूसरी सृष्टि रच देने की
सामर्थ्य उनमें थी उन्हीं की सन्तान होकर आज चारों तरफ से दुःख
और अशान्ति से घिर रहे हो।

अपने घर की निधि को भूल जाओगे तो फिर दरवाजे-दरवाजे
ठोकर तो खानी ही पड़ेगी।

You remember the *maharishis* of old, who were strong, doing
everything in the material world. In them of old was really given
the ability to create another world. Today, from four directions we
are becoming surrounded with suffering and anxiety.
You have lost the treasure in your own home, then you thump the
doors, then suffering occurs.

शेर यदि भेड़िये के झुण्ड में जाकर में-में करने लगे और उसी में
सुख मानने लग जाय तो यह उसके लिए कितनी लज्जा की बात
होगी।

If a tiger goes amongst a flock of sheep, and accepts that happilly,
then how much talk of dishonour will there be?

भारतीय यदि अपनी पुरानी आध्यात्मिक और आधिदैविक
सम्पत्तियों को भूल जायँ और ऊपरी शब्द, स्पर्श, रूप, रस, गन्ध
आदि की भौतिक सामग्री को प्राप्त करके ही सुख सन्तोष मान लें तो
यह उनका कितना बड़ा पतन है।

If an Indian forgets his own ancient spirituality and lapses into
affluence-bringing misery, and measures happiness and
satisfaction in taking the acquisition of the outward sound, touch,

form, taste, smell etc of material stuff, then how much is this their great downfall?

शक्तिशाली बनने के लिए अपने पूर्वजों के अनुभूत नुसखों से काम लो ।

For making oneself strong, take the actions tried and prescribed by one's ancestors.

सर्वशक्तिमान जगन्नियन्ता की शरण में आओ और अपनी आध्यात्मिक शक्तियों का विकास करो ।

Come into the shelter of the Omnipotent Almighty and develop one's own spiritual strength.

जगन्नियामिका चेतन सत्ता का अधिकार प्राप्त करो, तभी वास्तव में शक्तिशाली बन सकते हो और वही स्थिर शक्ति सत्ता होगी ।

Gain possession of the Almighty living being. In truth, at the same moment, one can one become strong and will have the very same permanent energy and power.

निश्चय रखो कि आज भी तुम त्रिकालदर्शी और तत्वविजयी होकर समस्त ब्रह्मांड की शक्तियों को अपने अनुकूल कर सकते हो ।

Of a certainty, today you can see the present, past and future also, and have mastery over the elements. All the energies of the universe can be favourable to yourself.

भारत में तुम्हारा जन्म हुआ है । तुममें अनन्त शक्तियाँ निहित हैं । प्रयत्न करके उनका उद्घाटन करो और शक्तिशाली होकर उन्नत मस्तक होकर रहो ।

Your birth has been in Bharat (India). In you are placed limitless energies. Make an effort to reveal them. And becoming strong, hold your head up high.

भगवान् का भक्त -

काल पर भी शासन करता है ।

The worshipper of Bhagwan - in time is also to command.

भगवद्भक्त को कौन जीत सकता है?

Who can be victorious over a devotee of God?

निन्दा करने से किसी का सुधार तो होता नहीं; व्यर्थ में उसे अपना शत्रु बना लेते हैं - - मूर्खतावश अपने ही पैरों में चुभने के लिये कण्टक वपन करते हैं ।

From scorn comes no improvement; it is useless to make him your
enemy -- indeed it is folly to sow the seeds for having thorns stuck
in one's own feet.

शास्त्रों में लिखा है कि निन्दक जिसकी निन्दा करता है उसके पाप ग्रहण करता है । भला कितनी बड़ी मूर्खता है कि पाप तो कोई और करे और हम उसकी निन्दा करके उसके पापों का संग्रह अपने लिये करें ।

जिसमें दूसरों का सुधार भी न हो और अपना बिगाड़ हो, ऐसा काम क्यों करते हो?

In the *Shastra* it is written that those who are abusive, those who
scorn, are seizing the wickedness. How much good is this great
folly then? If anybody does sin and we scorn them, then we are
collecting their wickedness.

In this way others are not corrected but we are injured. Why do
you desire to do this?

जिस पर भगवान की कृपा हो जाती है उस पर भगवान की

शक्ति-माया - की भी कृपा रहती है ।

On whom the grace of Bhagwan goes, on him is graced the
strength of Lakshmi too.

भक्त माया से अपना कोई सम्बन्ध नहीं चाहता और न माया की
शक्तियों की इच्छा करता है; वह तो अपने इष्ट भगवान के ही चिन्तन
में निमग्न रहता है । माया की शक्तियाँ ऋद्धि सिद्धि के रूप में आकर
सदा भक्त की इच्छा पूर्ण किया करती हैं और सदा उसको सब प्रकार
से रक्षा करती हैं ।

The devotee, with *maya* (Lakshmi), does not desire a relationship
with anybody and does not desire the energies of *maya*; then he is
drowned in thinking truly of beloved Bhagwan. The energies of
maya (Lakshmi) appear in the form of prosperity and success, the
worshipper's wishes are constantly fulfilled and he is protected
from all manner of things.

जो सर्वशक्तिमान का प्रिय भक्त हो जाता है । उसके अनुकूल सब
कुछ हो जाता है । शास्त्र से यही प्रमाणित है और भक्तों का भी यही
कहना है ।

The worshipper becomes beloved of the Omnipotent. Everything
goes comfortably. The *Shastra* is right here authentically proven
and devotees indeed tell this too.

भगवद्भक्त अजेय होता है । न वह किसी के द्वारा पराजित होता है
और न कोई उसको जीत सकता है ।

The devotee of God is invincible. There is no way of defeating
him nor can anyone gain mastery over him.

यहाँ तो धर्मशाले का निवास है; अपने मन को बहुत फँसाने
लायक नहीं साधारण रूप से काम चलाते चलो और दृष्टि आगे की

यात्रा पर रक्खो । धर्मशाले के प्रबन्ध में अपने को बहुत फँसा लेना मूर्खता ही है ।

This world is a *dharmashala* (a dwelling house for pilgrims). In this place it is not proper to involve the mind very much. The general way is to do the work and put your sight on the *yatra* (journey, pilgrimage). It is really a folly to ensnare oneself in the arrangement of this *dharmashala.* So, behave according to what a thing is.

चार दिन के जीवन में बहुत हाव-भाव करना अच्छा नहीं ।

In four days of existence, putting on a show of emotion is not good.

जब तक सांस चल रही है भगवान् का भजन करते हुये समय बिताओ ।

For as long as you are breathing, pass the time praying to Bhagwan.

मन में यदि व्यवहार घुस गया तो बार-बार इसी चौरासी के चक्कर में घूमना पड़ेगा । इसलिये बड़ी सतर्कता से काम करो ।

In everyday business proceed with proper behaviour. In case everyday business has intruded into the mind, then again and again there is a return to the eighty-four hundred thousand births, fallen and rolling in the wheel. Therefore, do work with great alertness.

व्यवहार में मन को अधिक फँसाओगे तो अन्त में व्यवहार ही याद आयेगा ।

अन्त में व्यवहार याद आया तो फिर जन्म लेना पड़ेगा ।

If the mind is very trapped with everyday business then in the end

you will just be remembering business. In the end if I have come
to remembering everyday business then again I will take birth.

जीवन भर जिसमें मन अधिक लगा रहेगा वही अन्त समय में भी
याद आयेगा।

यदि स्त्री का ध्यान रहा तो मरते समय स्त्री का ही स्मरण होगा
और फिर मरकर स्त्री होना पड़ेगा। यदि पुत्र का ध्यान रहा तो मरकर
उसका पुत्र होना पड़ेगा।

That which the entire life the mind has been connected with, the
very same will come to the memory. If you are contemplating a
woman then at the time to die he will remember and to die will
become a female. If you are considering a son then having died he
will become a son.

संसार में सद्गति चाहते हो तो सतर्क होकर व्यवहार चलाओ जहाँ
तक हो सके मन को बचाओ।

Desiring emancipation in the material world then proceed in
everyday business carefully, protect the mind wherever it may be.

धन और दूसरी संसारी वस्तुओं की प्राप्ति के लिये लोग कितना
अथक प्रयत्न करते हैं - दिन रात एक कर देते हैं, परन्तु जिस
भगवान की प्राप्ति से सब कुछ सहज सुलभ हो जाता है उसके लिए
उचित प्रयत्न नहीं करते। कितना बड़ा अविवेक छाया है!!

How much effort do people put into gaining wealth and other
worldly things? Day and night they are giving. But that Bhagwan
from whom everything comes to be gained naturally and easily,
for That no attempt is made! How much is desired
indiscriminately!?

इससे बड़ा आश्चर्य और क्या हो सकता है कि सुख शांति के

कारण सर्वशक्तिमान भगवान की ओर ध्यान न देकर तुच्छ संसारी वस्तुओं के लिए दिन रात परेशान रहे ।

From this is great surprise and what can be the [reason] for not giving *dhyaana* (meditation, consideration) in the direction of Omnipotent Bhagwan who is the cause of happiness and peace, troubling day and night for empty worldly things.

भगवान की अवहेलना करके अन्य वस्तुओं की प्राप्ति के लिए चेष्टा करते हो तो जो कुछ भी प्राप्त होगा तो वह इतना न होगा कि सन्तोष दे सके ।

Neglecting Bhagwan, busying oneself for the acquisition of other things, then the one who will be gaining something cannot be getting satisfaction.

छाया को भी पकड़ना चाहते हो तो असली रूप को पकड़ो । यदि रूप को छोड़कर छाया को पकड़ना चाहोगे तो कुछ भी हाथ नहीं लगेगा । इसी तरह यदि सांसारिक सुख चाहते हो तो भी भगवान का भजन करो । भगवान के भजन से लौकिक सुख और पारलौकिक शांति बोनो प्राप्त होंगी ।

जीवन में सबसे मूल्यवान वस्तु समय है, जिसना समय भगवान के भजन में लगाओगे उसका कई गुना मूल्य ब्याज सहित अदा हो जायगा ।

Who desires to catch the shadow catches hold of the original form then. If he lets go of the form and wishes to take hold of the shadow then the hand is attached to nothing. If you desire this kind of worldly happiness then also worship Bhagwan. By worshipping Bhagwan you will be gaining worldly happiness and sowing the seeds for peace in the next world.
With all precious things in life there is a time, he who applies that time in worship of Bhagwan, thereof is going to be many times

the cost, together with interest payment.

जो आया है सो जायगा, यहाँ किसी को रहना नहीं है ।

He who has come therefore will go, it is not for any to stay here.

मृत्यु का वारन्ट गिरफ्तारी का वारन्ट होता है, उसमें फिर अपील की गुञ्जाइश नहीं होती; तुरन्त सब कुछ छोड़कर चलना पड़ेगा; जो जहाँ है वहीं पड़ा रह जायगा ।

The death *"warrant"* is a *"warrant"* of arrest, for you there is no scope for appeal; quickly all is to be dropped and let go; wherever you are, there you will fall.

हर समय यहां से चलने के लिए बिस्तर बाँधे तैयार रहो न जाने किस समय वारन्ट आ जाय, पहले से तैयार रहोगे तो चलते समय कष्ट नहीं होगा ।

Every time you go from here have your bedding ready packed not knowing when the warrant will come. If from the first you will be ready then there will be no suffering when it is time to go.

जो हर समय संसार छोड़ने के लिये तैयार रहता है उससे कभी कोई पाप नहीं होता ।

Who stays ready to let go of mundane existence at any time, never will there be wickedness from him.

परलोक को भूल जाने से ही दुराचार पापाचार होता है ।

By doing wicked sinful conduct is indeed making a mistake to the next world.

यदि हर समय यह स्मरण रहे कि यह सब कुछ एक दिन छोड़कर चलना ही है तो फिर मनुष्य असत्य और अविहित आचरण को

कभी न अपनाये ।

Truly, if you always remember that one day you must go and let go of everything, then afterwards you will not be an untruthful person and will not behave contrary to the law.

कोई काम ऐसा न करो जिसके लिए बाद में पछताना पड़े ।

Do not do such work that you will later fall to repenting.

संसार में मनुष्य के लिए असम्भव कुछ नहीं है ।

In mundane existence nothing is impossible for a human being.

पुरुषार्थ हो और उचित अर्थात् वैध पुरुषार्थ हो तो कौन सा ऐसा कार्य है जो सिद्ध न हो जाय ।

You labour and labour in that which is reasonable and legal, then what is the work that cannot be accomplished?

जहाँ पुरुषार्थ है वही सफलता है ।

Wherever labour is, there is productivity.

प्रबल पुरुषार्थ के समक्ष प्रारब्ध भी घटने टेक देती है । इसलिये विहित ढंग से पुरुषार्थ करना ही अपना कार्य है ।

In order to be sufficient, take rest before commencing powerful labour. Therefore one's work is by labour of an arranged method.

यदि पुरुषार्थ करने पर भी कहीं सफलता न मिले तो भी कार्य को असाध्य नहीं मानना चाहिए ।

If you do not meet with success when doing work somewhere then you should not also assume that you are incapable of the work.

असाध्य कुछ भी नहीं है, यह हो सकता है कि बैल का भार बकरी

के लिए असाध्य मालूम पड़े परन्तु ऊँट के लिए वह असाध्य नहीं।

किसी पुरुषार्थहीन बलहीन मनुष्य के लिए कोई कार्य चाहे असाध्य लगता हो परन्तु पुरुषार्थवान सबल पुरुष के लिये संसार में असम्भव कुछ नहीं है।

Nothing is beyond one's reach. This may be the load of oxen which is known to be beyond the ability of a nanny goat, but a camel is not incapable.

One has a weak desire for any exertion that one is incapable of due to lack of energy or strength, but for a strong labourer nothing is impossible in the mundane existence.

अमृत-कण

Amrit-Kana

14

जब तक संसार के मिथ्यात्व का बोध नहीं होगा, तब तक भोगों से वैराग्य होना असम्भव है।

Whilst you do not perceive the falsehood of mundane existence, until [you do] then it is impossible to have *vairagya* (freedom from worldly desires) from the experience of pleasures and pains.

भगवान की निष्काम उपासना करो और विचार द्वारा राग-द्वेष को दूर करते चलो।

तुम्हारी श्रद्धा देख कर भगवान स्वयमेव कृपा करेंगे।

Free from any wish, pray to Bhagwan and by the means of consideration keep away from mental affliction and malice. Seeing your faith, Bhagwan of his own free will will give kindness.

भगवान की कृपा से तुम्हारा मोह-जनित अज्ञान दूर होकर उसमें दृढ़ अनुराग उत्पन्न होगा।

जब तक मन भोगों के लिए बेचैन रहता है तब तक गृहस्थधर्म का पालन करते हुए विहित भोगों को भोगो।

From Bhagwan's *kripa* (grace) your ignorance becomes distant' and resolute love will be born in you.
Whilst the mind remains restless for the experiences of pleasure or pain, then undergo the arranged *bhogon* (experiences of pleasure

of pain) whilst cherishing the *dharma* of the *grihastha* (householder).

यदि स्त्री में सुख मानते हो तो अपनी स्त्री में ही सन्तुष्ट रहो दूसरी ओर दृष्ट न दौड़ाओ ।

If you consider happiness in a woman then be satisfied in one's own wife, do not run for sight in another direction.

व्यवहार संचालन के लिए धन की आवश्यकता है तो सदाचार पूर्वक धन का उपार्जन करो ।

Wealth is indispensible for managing business, then together with morality acquire wealth.

अपना खान-पान पहिनाव अपनी आय के अनुकूल रखो तो कभी चिन्तित नहीं होना पड़ेगा ।

Have a suitable income for one's own eating, drinking and clothing then there will never be anxiety.

किसी को पीड़ा न देते हुए सात्विक परिश्रम द्वारा प्राप्त किये हुए धन का उचित उपयोग करो । इससे बुद्धि शुद्ध होगी और मन में शान्ति रहेगी ।

Not giving any annoyance, having acquired wealth by good honest endeavour, use it properly. From this will be clear thinking and the mind will be in peace.

सदाचार का पालन करते हुए जितना समय मिले सज्जनों और महात्माओं का संग करो ।

सदाचारी व्यक्ति ही दूसरों का कल्याण कर सकता है ।

However much you have been preserving a virtuous conduct meet

good people and associate with *mahatmas*. Indeed a righteous
individual can be the happiness of others.

स्वधर्म पालन एक ऐसी वस्तु है जो सबका सभी परिस्थितियों में
कल्याण कर सकती है ।

जो जहाँ जिस वर्णाश्रम में है उसी के अनुसार स्वधर्म पालन करे
तो उसका सब प्रकार से कल्याण होकर रहेगा ।

वह अपने जीवन-काल में शान्ति का अनुभव करेगा और परलोक
में भी उसकी सद्गति होगी ।

Cherishing one's own *dharma* is one such thing that all the
surroundings can be in happiness. Whatever *varnashrama* (caste)
you are, if you protect your *dharma* then the happiness of all will
continue.

He who in his own lifetime will be experiencing peace then in the
next world too he will have emancipation.

वेद शास्त्रानुसारी क्रिया-कलाप की यही विशेषता है कि इससे
इहलोक में व्यक्तिगत एवं सामाजिक सुख शान्ति मिलती है और
परलोक में भी सद्गति होती है ।

According to the *Veda Shastras* the occupation here is a
characteristic, [that if] from this present world, the individual and
the community meet with happiness and peace then in the next
world there will be emancipation also.

जो जिस वर्णाश्रम में हो वहीं अपने धर्म का दृढ़ता से पालन
करके देखो - सुख शान्ति का अनुभव अवश्य होगा ।

Who is of that caste, look to protect and strengthen one's own
dharma right there – he will surely be experiencing happiness and
peace.

जो कुछ धर्म का पालन कर लोगे, जो कुछ भगवान का भजन-
पूजन चिन्तन कर लोगे वही आगे साथ देगा और उसी के आधार
पर संसार में भी सुख शान्ति और समृद्धि की प्राप्ति होगी ।

People who do some protection of the *dharma*, people who do
some *bhajana* (worship), *puja,* and thinking in the future the
same, will give as well and be a supporter of, also will be gaining
happiness and peace in the material world.

भगवान के भजन में लाभ ही लाभ हैं - थोड़े दिन विधिवत्
उपासना करके देखो स्वतः अनुभव हो जायगा ।

यदि थोड़े दिन उपासना करने पर शान्ति सन्तोष में वृद्धि नहीं
होती तो समझ लो कि उपासना का प्रकार कुछ गड़बड़ है ।

Indeed there are advantages in the worship of Bhagwan - look,
regularly worshipping daily, you will spontaneously be
experiencing. If upon some daily *upasana* (worship) there is no
progress in peace and satisfaction then understand that there is
some kind of confusion in the method of *upasana*.

उपासना करने के लिए ऐसे को ही गुरु बनाओ हो वेद शास्त्र को
मानता हो और उपासना मार्ग का भी अनुभवी हो ।

Indeed for doing *upasana* (worship) take a *guru* who accepts *Veda
Shastra* and is experienced in the way of *upasana*.

भगवान का भजन नित्य कुछ समय अवश्य करो ।

Certainly take some time doing regular worship of Bhagwan.

हर समय रोटी-कपड़े की ही चिन्ता में मत पड़े रहो । चौबीस
घण्टों में कम से कम दस-बीस मिनट अवश्य ही भगवान् के भजन-
पूजन में लगाओ ।

Indeed, don't be all the time thinking about *roti* (bread) and clothing. In twenty-four hours, little by little, certainly even only ten, twenty minutes engage in *bhajan* and *puja* of Bhagwan.

यह समझ लो कि सब काम बीस पचास वर्ष तक ही, जब तक जीवन है तभी तक, के प्रबन्ध के लिए है, इससे आगे यह सब प्रबन्ध कुछ काम नहीं देगा ।

Understand this, of all work, even until twenty, fifty years, however long the life is, for this reason is the arrangement, from this forward, there is no arrangement given for some work.

कुछ ऐसा भी कर चलो कि जब यहाँ से चलना हो तो खाली हाथ न जाना पड़े ।

Go a little like this, so that when you proceed from here, then you don't go with an empty hand.

अपने समान दूसरे को भी मानो ।

Accept that others are similar to oneself.

इस बात के लिए सतर्क रहो कि तुमसे किसी का अपकार न हो जाय ।

Be alert for this statement, don't come to any harm.

कभी किसी को अपनी ओर से कष्ट देने की बात मत सोचो । जहाँ तक हो सके दूसरों की भलाई करो ।

At no time consider giving pain from your direction by what you say. Wherever you can, do goodness to others.

चार दिन का जीवन है, इसमें ऐसा करो, कि जहाँ तक हो सके दूसरों की भलाई हो । और यदि भलाई न हो सके तो कम से कम

किसी की बुराई तो न हो ।

Life is four days in this, so do goodness to others wherever you can. And if you cannot do goodness then little by little of badness don't do.

अपने द्वारा किसी का बिगाड़ हुआ तो अपने ही ऊपर उसका पाप पड़ेगा ।

If any damage has been done to one's way, then sin will occur upon oneself.

जहाँ तक हो सके शुभकर्म करो जिससे पुण्य का पलड़ा भारी रहे ।

पुण्य अधिक रहेगा तो लोक-परलोक में सर्वत्र आनन्द से रहोगे ।

Do pious action wherever you can, from that the balance of merit will be heavy.

The more merit that will exist this world, then the next world, everywhere will be of *ananda* (bliss).

"वर्तमान भौतिकवाद ने जीवन को जटिल बनाते हुए केवल उदर परायणता और काम वासनाओं की वृद्धि की है ।

You have been living a life of materialism made difficult, only attached to the stomach and the progress of work and desires.

रात-दिन पेट भरने की चिन्ता में लगे रहना और पेट भर कर इन्द्रियों के विषयों को भोगने में लग जाना और इन्हीं बातों में जीवन समाप्त कर देना मानव-जीवन का घोर दुरुपयोग है ।

Day and night being attached to thinking about filling the stomach and attached in undergoing a belly full of sensual enjoyments, and completing the life in talking about these [pursuits], man's existence is a horrible perversion.

तीर्थों में पापाचरण करने वाले की महान दुर्गति होती है ।

People doing sin in sacred places is a great catastrophe.

वेद-शास्त्र भगवान की आज्ञा है । यदि सुख-शान्ति चाहते हो तो उसकी आज्ञा का पालन करना तुम्हारा कर्तव्य है ।

Veda Shastra is the command of Bhagwan. If you desire happiness and peace then your task is to cherish his command.

भरण-पोषण करने का भार स्वयं ईश्वर के ऊपर है, इसीलिए उसे विश्वम्भर कहते हैं । उसी की शरण में जाने पर दुःखों से छुटकारा होगा ।

The *bhara* (load) of the work of cherishing and supporting is upon Ishwar, therefore we call him Vishwambhara (*vishwa* = universe). By going in his shelter troubles will be got rid of.

वेद-शास्त्र के अनुसार जीवन बनाना ही श्रेष्ठ पुरुषार्थ है ।

According to the *Veda Shastra,* labour is to make life really superb.

स्वरूपाकार वृत्ति होते ही सुख-दुख इत्यादि द्वन्द्व समाप्त हो जाते हैं ।

Really, by the activity of obtaining *swaroop* (the true Self) the pair of happiness and trouble etc. are terminated.

ठग लोग साधु वेष अपनाकर सच्चे साधुओं की बड़ी रक्षा करते हैं, जैसे गुलाब के पुष्पों को कण्टक रक्षा करते हैं ।

Thugs who dress in the clothes of hermits greatly protect true *sadhus*, in the manner that thorns protect the rose.

भारत भूमि में सद्गुरुओं की परम्परा कभी समाप्त नहीं हुई ।

पहचानने वाली आंखों न होने के कारण यदि ईश्वर भी तुम्हारे सामने आयें तो तुम्हारा कुछ कल्याण नहीं हो सकता ।

In the land of Bharat (India) the *parampara* (lineage) of *sadgurus* (genuine *gurus*) has sometimes been interrupted. The means is not in the eyes of the one who is distinguishing. If Ishwar would come face to face with you, even then you may not have any happiness.

अमृत-कण

Amrit-Kana

15

परमात्मा को सर्वत्र मानोगे तो फिर तुमसे कोई पाप कर्म नहीं होगा इसलिए परमात्मा को व्यापक मानते हुए चरित्रवान बनो। अपने आचरणों में पवित्रता लाओ, अपनी भावनाओं को शुद्ध बनाओ और स्वधर्मानुकूल व्यवहार करो तो अन्तःकरण पवित्र होगा। अन्तःकरण की पवित्रता बढ़ने से तुम्हारे संकल्प में बल आयेगा, कार्य भी अधिक सुदृढ़ होंगे और परमात्मा में भी निष्ठा बढ़ेगी। परमात्मा में निष्ठा बढ़ने से हर प्रकार का मंगल होगा। इसलिए ऐसा ही मार्ग अपनाओ जिससे सब प्रकार का मंगल हो - लोक परलोक दोनों बने।

Assume that Bhagwan is everywhere then afterwards you will not do any bad *karma*. Therefore, have wide acceptance to Paramatma, become of good moral character and conduct. Bring spirituality into one's own conduct, make one's own sentiments uncorrupt and do business favourable to one's *dharma,* then the conscience will be spotless. From the sanctity of the conscience growing your resolve will be strengthened, work will become very much stronger and also certainty in Paramatma will grow. From growth of certainty in Paramatma there will be every kind of auspiciousness. Therefore indeed, after this manner, possess the way. Every kind of auspiciousness there will be to make this world and the next.

परमात्मा सर्वज्ञ है - वह सबके कर्मों को जानता है, इसलिए कोई

पाप कर्म मत करो। ऐसा मत सोचो कि हमारे इस कार्य को कोई नहीं जानता। जिसको तुम्हारे कर्मों का फल देना है, जो फैसला करने वाला है वह बिना गवाही के ही सब कुछ जानता है। यदि किसी से डरना ही है तो पाप करने से डरो, कोई बुरा कर्म मत करो।

Paramatma is all-knowing - He knows of all *karmas*, therefore do not do any sin. Don't consider that any of our actions is not known. To whom you give the effects of your actions, who is judge even without evidence knows everything. If there is anything to fear then fear from sin, don't do any bad *karma*.

जो अपने समान ही समस्त प्राणियों को देखता है उसी का देखना देखना कहा जा सकता है। वही वास्तव में नेत्रवान है।

He who sees himself as similar to all beings can be said to see. Of the very same material is the possessor of the eye.

जब तुमको कोई गाली देता है या कटुवचन कहता है तो तुमको कष्ट होता है इसी प्रकार जिसको तुम कटुवचन कहोगे उसको भी कष्ट होगा, ऐसा सोच कर कभी किसी को ऐसी बात मत कहो जिसको दूसरों के द्वारा तुम नहीं सुनना चाहते। जैसा व्यवहार दूसरों के द्वारा तुम चाहते हो वैसा ही व्यवहार तुम भी दूसरों के साथ करो।

When someone gives abuse of cutting words to you then this is a kind of hardship to you. He to whom you make cutting remarks, he will also suffer. Reflect that you don't make any such remarks that you do not wish to hear by way of others. The way you wish to be treated in everyday business, indeed do such business with others.

कभी किसी की निन्दा मत करो। निन्दा करने से किसी का सुधार तो होता नहीं, व्यर्थ में उसे अपना शत्रु बना लेते हैं।

Don't ever do *ninda* (scorn, slander). From speaking ill of

someone then no improvement will be, to no purpose you make
him an adversary to yourself.

शास्त्रों लिखा है कि निन्दक जिसकी निन्दा करता है उसके पाप
ग्रहण करता है। भला कितनी बड़ी मूर्खता है कि पाप तो कोई और
करे और हम उसकी निन्दा करके उसके पापों का संग्रह अपने लिए
करें। जिसमें दूसरों का सुधार भी न हो अपना बिगाड़ हो, ऐसा काम
क्यों करते हो?

It is written in the *Shastra* that the one who censors others is
seizing the sin of the one who sins. How great a folly is the sin,
then if anybody else censures he is collecting sins to himself.
Wherein there is no improvement in the other there is injury to
oneself. Why do you do such action?

नदी जब तक समुद्र में नहीं मिल जाती तब तक वह पत्थरों और
पहाड़ों से टकराती रहती है। समुद्र में मिल जाने के बाद उसको
ठोकर देने वाला कोई नहीं रह जाता। इसी प्रकार जीव जब तक
परमात्मा से नहीं मिला है तभी तक उसे अनेकों आधि व्याधियों का
सामना करना पड़ता है।

परमात्मा के मिलने का मार्ग भगवान श्रीकृष्ण ने स्वयं बताया है।

तस्मात् सर्वेषु कालेषु मामनुस्मर युध्य च।

अर्थात् सदैव चलते-फिरते, उठते-बैठते, सोते-जागते,
स्वधर्मानुष्ठान में लगे रहो और मेरा स्मरण करते चलो।

Whilst the river has not met with the sea then the stones and the
hills are being dashed together. After meeting in the ocean it is not
bashing anyone. The kind of life, of encountering mental agonies
and encountering calamities, occurs whilst Paramatma is not met
with.

The way to meet Paramatma? Bhagwan Shri Krishna himself
pointed out:-

"तस्मात् सर्वेधु कालेषु मामनुस्मर युध्य च।"

"tasmaat sarvedhu kaaleshu maamanusmara yudhya cha."
'Therefore at all times remember Me only and fight.'
[*Bhagavad Gita* 8:7]

That is to say, 'Always come and go, rise, sit, sleep/manifest, be
connected with undertaking one's own *dharma* and proceed
remembering me'.

जिसकी जो ‘सीट’ है उस सीट पर उसको बैठना चाहिए। अपने-
अपने स्थान पर ही सब चीज अच्छी लगती है। महिलाओं को
चाहिए कि भगवान की भक्ति तो करें पर कहीं ऐसा न कर बैठें कि
भक्ति के पीछे अपने पतियों का त्याग कर दें। भावावेश में बहना
ठीक नहीं, काम वह करना चाहिये जा कुछ दिन चले। दूरदर्शिता से
काम लेना चाहिये। जिस प्रकार सद्गुरु के प्रसन्न होने पर इष्ट को
प्रसन्नता प्राप्त होती है उसी प्रकार पति के प्रसन्न रहने पर स्त्री पर देवी
देवता और भगवान भी कृपा करते हैं और हर प्रकार से मंगल होता
है। यही हमारे भारत का पुराना अनुभूत नुसखा है।

Whose *"seat"* that is, on that he should sit. All things should be
connected to their own place. To the ladies who wish to worship
Bhagwan then do not sit doing worship and afterwards abandon
the husbands. It is not proper to wander aimlessly in emotional
agitation. The work that should be done, go and proceed any day.
Prudently you must take care of the work. That method which is
favourable to the *sadguru*, to the *ishta* is happiness to be gained.
This manner on staying favourable of the husband, on the woman
is the grace of the *devi* (goddess), *devata* (god) and Bhagwan also,
and every kind of auspiciousness to be. Exactly here is the tried
prescription of our Bharat (India) of old.

हनुमान जी ने भगवान की हर प्रकार की सेवा की, पर उसके बदले में कुछ नहीं चाहा। दास्य भाव को अपनाते हो तो हनुमान को उदाहरण में लो। निष्काम भक्ति का यही स्वरूप है, इष्ट के निमित्त कार्य करो और उसके फल रूप में अपने लिये किसी वस्तु की याचना न करो।

Hanuman Ji did many kinds of service, but had no desire for recompense. As to possessing a temperament of servitude, take Hanuman as an example. Free from any wish, this is exactly the form of *bhakti* (devotion), do the task for the reason of the *ishta* and do not implore any fruits for oneself.

शास्त्रानुकूल पुरुषार्थ ही पुण्य है और वही अभ्युदय अर्थात् लौकिक उन्नति और मोक्ष का देने वाला है

Indeed, labour that is in accordance with *Shastra* is holy and prosperity that is earthy increases and is the giver of *moksha* (salvation).

इष्ट प्रीत्यर्थ काम करना चाहिये। इष्ट प्रसन्न रहे यही एक वासना हो। ऐसा नहीं कि शंकर जा को एक लोटा जल चढ़ाया और प्रार्थना में कहने लगे कि लड़के की नौकरी लग जाय, स्त्री की तबियत ठीक हो जाय या धन की कमी है रोजगार में वृद्धि हो जाय। इस प्रकार की संसारी वासनाओं को लेकर इष्टाराधन करते हो तो इष्ट भी घबराता है। क्योंकि याचक से सभी दूर भागते हैं।

Do the work for the sake of love of the *ishta*. Pleasing *ishta*, this is the one desire to have. So it is not of benefit to go with one small metal pot of water and in prayer having gone attached to ask for work for a youngster, having gone for a woman of good disposition or progress in trade if the wealth is in decline. From this kind of worldly desire to be adoring the *ishta* then the *ishta* will also be confused. Since they are running away all distance from a beggar.

जो काम जितने पुरुषार्थ से होने वाला है उतने ही पुरुषार्थ से होता है । जितने पुण्य से भवसागर से पार हो सकते हैं उतने पुण्य के बिना पार होना असंभव नहीं । किसी को एक सेर जल की प्यास लगी हो तो वह एक छटांक जल से कैसे बुझ सकती है ।

However much energy you have for work, that much is to be from labour. However much holiness can be from the extremity of *bhavasagara* (ocean of feeling), holiness without limit is not impossible to be. To any who is thirsty for a seer of water, how can that be quenched by one *chatamka* (one sixteenth of a seer) of water?

धार्मिक ग्रन्थों के पढ़ने से पुण्य अवश्य होता है । गीता रामायण आदि का पाठ पुण्यप्रद होता है परन्तु केवल पाठ से इतना पुण्य संग्रह नहीं होता जो भवसागर से पार कर दे ।

From studying religious books you surely become holy. The reader of *Gita, Ramayana* etc is given holiness, but by reading alone one does not collect so much who gives limit to *bhavasagara* (sea of feeling).

जब तक लोगों का स्वार्थ सिद्ध होता है तभी तक सब मान-सम्मान और अनुराग दिखाते हैं । भगवान आदि शङ्कराचार्य ने कहा है -

यावत् वित्तोपार्जन सक्तः
तावन्निज परिवारो रक्तः ।
पश्चाद्धावति जर्जर देहे
वार्ता कोऽपि न पृच्छति गेहे ॥

अर्थात् जब तक धन कमाने की सामर्थ्य है तभी तक अपने

स्वजन कुटुम्बी लोग भी अनुराग करते हैं। फिर जब बृद्धावस्था आती है और शरीर जीर्ण-शीर्ण हो जाता है तब कोई घर में बात नहीं पूछता।

Self-interested people [who wish] to be successful, exhibit respect and interest of their peers. Bhagwan Adi Shankaracharya said: –

यावत् वित्तोपार्जन सक्तः
तावन्निज परिवारो रक्तः।
पश्चाद्धावति जर्जर देहे
वार्ता कोऽपि न पृच्छति गेहे॥

"yavat vittoparjana saktah
tavannija parivaro raktah.
pashchaddhavati jarjara dehe
varta ko api na prichchati gehe.."
[*Bhaja Govindham* v5]

That is to say, that 'Whilst you have the ability to earn wealth, then for this reason one's own kinsmen and relatives too are interested. Then when the state of old ages comes and the body becomes ragged and withered then no one in the house will ask to speak with you'.

वशिष्ठ, विश्वामित्र, भारद्वाज, अत्रि, अंगिरा जमदग्नि आदि त्रिकालज्ञ सर्व समर्थ महर्षियों के नाम आप लोग आज भी बड़े गौरव के साथ लेते हो। उनके नाम पर अपने गोत्र बताते हुये गौरव का अनुभव करते हो। किन्तु वे सर्व समर्थ थे और आज उनकी सन्तान होकर आप लोग सर्वथा शक्तिहीन हो रहे हो। क्या कभी अपनी इस दीन दशा पर विचार भी करते हो? आज भी अपने पूर्वजों के मार्ग पर चलकर आप अपना उत्कर्ष साधन कर सकते हैं।

Vasistha, Vishvamitra, Bharadvaja, Atri, Angira, Jamadagni, etc

all names of capable Omniscient *maharshis* that you together take
pride in. Their names are sensed with pride as they signify one's
own race. But they were all strong and today their offspring are
people who are being altogether powerless. Do you consider
sometimes why you are in this poor condition? Today also one
can walk on the road one's own ancestors, you can do *sadhana* for
your own exaltation.

जिस सोपान का सहारा लेकर इन लोगों ने भगवान को प्राप्त
किया और इतना सामर्थ्य सम्पादन किया, उसी सोपान का सहारा
लेकर आप लोग चलोगे तो निश्चय है कि वही सिद्धि समाधि आपको
भी प्राप्त होगी । आज भी आप लोगों के शरीरों में उन्हीं का रक्त है
और पथ-प्रदर्शक वही प्राचीन गुरु परम्परा आज भी पूर्ववत् उपलब्ध
हैं । केवल अपनी ओर से कमी है ।

With the help of steps those people gained Bhagwan and
accomplished strength. Then by the support of the steps people
will move, then of a certainty the same *siddhi* and *samadhi*
respectively will also be gained. Today, the bodies of you people
are of their blood too and the one who shows the path is of the
same *guru parampara* (lineage) that was also formerly known.
Only from one's own side is the deficiency.

सन्तान के लिए धन संग्रह करने में आप लोग जितना प्रयत्न
करते हैं उसका आधा प्रयत्न भी यदि बुद्धि शुद्ध करने के लिए करें तो
बहुत लाभ हो ।

बुद्धि शुद्ध रही तो धन कम रहते हुए भी सन्तान सुख शान्ति का
अनुभव कर सकती है और यदि बुद्धि दूषित रही तो अनन्त धन
धान्य रहते हुए भी दुर्वासनाओं में पड़कर सन्तान दुःख और
अशान्ति ही भोगेगी । इसलिये बुद्धि शोधन के लिए प्रयत्न पहले
करो, पीछे धन संग्रह करो ।

सन्तान का गर्भाधान संस्कार विधान से कराओ और बाकी संस्कार भी समय पर होने चाहिए। द्विज वर्ण को अपने बालकों के विधिवत् उपनयन संस्कार कराने के बाद सन्ध्या गायत्री में अवश्य लगाना चाहिए। भगवान के जप ध्यान से ही बुद्धि की मलिनता दूर होती है।

However much effort you people do in amassing wealth for progeny, half the effort you will do if the intelligence is clear, then it becomes a great advantage.

Clear thinking then, having less wealth the progeny can also be experiencing happiness and peace but if thinking is corrupted then limitless *dhana* (wealth) remains *dhanya* (a very small measure). Also in desires which occur which cannot be fulfilled, the progeny will undergo trouble and anxiety. Therefore firstly make an effort to purify the thinking, afterwards amass wealth.

Cause to be arranged the *"garbadhana samskara"* (a Hindu ceremony relating to conception) and the remaining *samskara* ceremony should also be on time. To the twice-born *varna* (caste) the investiture with the sacred thread you should cause to be done for one's own children in accordance with the law. The evening afterwards you should certainly join in Gayatri (a RigVedic *mantra* which is recited daily by the twice-born). Indeed by *japa* meditation of Bhagwan, impurities of the thinking become distant.

सन्तान को बुद्धि शुद्ध करने का ध्यान यदि प्रारम्भ से ही न रखा गया तो आगे चलकर पछताना ही हाथ रहता है। जैसा बीज बोओगे वैसा ही तो काटोगे।

Consider the clear thinking of the progeny. If you have not done that from the beginning, then afterwards regrets will indeed remain. According to the seed you sow, so shall you reap.

चरित्रवान मनुष्य ही शान्ति का अनुभव कर सकता है। जो चरित्र

भ्रष्ट है उसे न तो लोक में ही शान्ति रहती है और न परलोक में ही ।
दूसरों की बुराइयाँ मत देखो, अपने में ढूँढो कि कौन-सी बुराई अभी
तक शेष है जो हो उसे हटाने का प्रयत्न करो । अपने में दोष खोज-
खोजकर निकालोगे तो कल्याण होगा ।

Indeed a person of good moral character can experience peace. If
the conduct is fallen then he does not remain in peace in this
world and not in the next world. Don't see the defects of others,
seek in oneself any similar badness that is remaining, making an
effort to remove that. Searching in oneself for faults to turn out,
then happiness will be.

कभी भी किसी के दोषों का चिन्तन मत करो । दूसरों में दोष
ढूँढने से अपना भी अन्तःकरण मलिन होता है । पाप कोई करे और
उसका चिन्तन हम करें यह तो हमारे लाभ की बात नहीं । जब हम
स्वयं पाप करने से डरते हैं तो दूसरे के पापो का चिन्तन करके अपने
मन को पापी क्यों बनायें?

Do not think of any defects. From seeking defects in others one
dirties one own inner self. It is no advantage for us to talk of sin
and to think about it. As we are frightened of doing wickedness
ourself then why make one's own mind evil thinking of the sins of
another?

मनमानी करना हो तो पहले मन को शुद्ध बनाओ मन को शुद्ध
बनाने के लिए सत्संग, जप, पूजा, पाठ भगवच्चिन्तन तथा
शास्त्राभ्यास उपयोगी माने गये हैं ।

To be acting agreeably, first make the mind clear. For making the
mind clear do *satsang*, *japa*, *puja*, reading and thinking of God.
So you are gone in useful practice of meaning of the *Shastras*.

प्राणायाम से भी मन की चंचलता दूर होकर मन पवित्र होता है ।

किन्तु इसका साधारण अभ्यास तो करने में कोई हानि कि शंका नहीं परन्तु यदि कुछ विशेष अभ्यास करना हो तो बिना किसी अच्छे योगी का सहारा लिये इस मार्ग में हानि की ही अधिक सम्भावना रहती है । अविधिपूर्वक प्राणायाम से अनेकों प्रकार के रोग हो जाते हैं । इसलिए विचारपूर्वक ही इसका अभ्यास करना चाहिये ।

By *pranayama* as well the activity of the mind becomes distant, the mind becomes pure. But in doing this common practice nobody should be at risk. If you are doing a special exercise, then without the assistance of a good yogi, in this way indeed remains more of a possibility of injury then. From *pranayama* against the established rules several kinds of disorders are possible. Therefore one should engage in such practice thoughtfully.

मन की शुद्धि के लिए आहार शुद्धि भी अत्यन्त आवश्यक है द्रव्य की कमाई का प्रकार उचित ही होना चाहिए । अविहित मार्गों से कमाये हुए धन के उपभोग से मनमलिन होता है ।

For the purity of the mind, the purity of the diet is also very much requisite, you should indeed be in the proper kind of profession. Earning by ways that are forbidden by law, enjoyment of such wealth sullies the mind.

अमृत-कण

Amrit-Kana

16

गुरु और गोरू शब्दों थोड़ा ही अन्तर है। गुरु की शिष्य के कल्याण पर दृष्टि रहती है और गोरू केवल अपनी भोजन-सुविधा से ही सम्बन्ध रखता है। जो गुरु शिष्यों से केवल अन्न-वस्त्र और भेंट-विदाई से ही सम्बन्ध रखते हैं, उनकी बुराइयों को दूर करने का प्रयत्न नहीं करते और उन्हें परमार्थ-दर्शन नहीं करा सकते वे शिष्यों के गुरु नहीं, गोरू ही हैं। शिष्यों को चाहिये कि अपने गुरुओं के चारा-पानी का प्रबन्ध तो अवश्य करें, किसी के लिए अन्न-वस्त्र का प्रबन्ध करना बुरा नहीं है; परन्तु अपने कल्याण का मार्ग उसी से लेना चाहिये जिसमें गुरु के सब लक्षण विद्यमान हों। लक्षण-सम्पन्न गुरु की खोज करनी चाहिये।

शास्त्र में गुरु के दो प्रधान लक्षण लिखे हैं: श्रोत्रियता और ब्रह्मनिष्ठता। लिखा है - "तद्विज्ञानार्थस गुरुमेवाभिगच्छेत् समित्पाणिः श्रोत्रियं ब्रह्मनिष्ठ" तत्पदवाच्य जो ब्रह्म है उसके जानने के लिए ऐसे गुरु के पास जावे जो श्रोत्रिय और ब्रह्मनिष्ठ हों; क्योंकि श्रोत्रिय अर्थात् वेद-वेदार्थ के जानने वाले होंगे तो शिष्य की शंकाओं का समाधान कर सकेंगे और ब्रह्मनिष्ठ होंगे तो तर्क अस्त होने पर यथार्थ बोध (तत्व का अनुभव) भी करा सकेंगे।

[The words] *'guru'* and *'goru'* sound only a little different. The *guru* sees to the happiness of the *shishya* (disciple) and the *goru* (cattle) are only connected with nourishment and comfort. If the *guru* sets a relationship to collect food, clothing and financial gifts from disciples, not making effort to dispel their defects and cannot offer any prospect of their salvation, they are not students of a *guru*, they are really *goru* (cattle). Certainly students should make arrangements for the fodder and water of one's own *gurus*, then certainly you will have to act, it is not bad to make arrangement for food and clothing: but one should receive one's own happiness from the way of a *guru*, with all signs of knowledge. You should investigate the signs of an accomplished *guru*.

In the *Shastra* it is written that there are two marks of a *guru*: *stotriyata* (one who has thoroughly studied the *Vedas*) and *brahmanishthata* (one possessing knowledge of the immortal Self, Brahman) –

"तद्विज्ञानार्थस गुरुमेवाभिगच्छेत् समित्पाणिः श्रोत्रियं ब्रह्मनिष्ठ"

"tadvigyanarthasa gurumevabhigachchet samitpanih shrotriyam brahmanishtha"
[*Manduka Upanishad* 1:2:12]

Who expresses about salvation and of Brahman, in words that can be understood, thus 'to go near a *guru* is go to one who will be *shrotriya* (one who has thoroughly studied the *Vedas*) and *brahmanishtha* (one possessing knowledge of the immortal Self)'; because *shrotriya*, that is to say that the one who will understand *Veda* and *Vedartha* (divine knowledge) then can reconcile the student's doubts and if he will be *brahmanishtha* (realized) then can have a good feeling of a hidden inference [of realisation].

किसान वही अच्छा माना जाता है जिसका स्वयं का हल-बैल हो और बोने के लिए घर में बीज भी हो; क्योंकि वही परती बंजर को ठीक से जोत कर क्षेत्र तैयार करके समय पर बीज वपन कर सकता है । यदि घर में बीज न हुआ तो बीज का प्रबन्ध करते करते जमीन फिर खराब हो जायगी । इसी प्रकार गुरु यदि केवल श्रोत्रिय हैं तो वे शिष्य की शंकाओं और तर्कों का समाधान तो कर देंगे, परन्तु यथार्थ

बोध नहीं करा सकते; क्योंकि उनको स्वयं तत्व-बोध नहीं है। इसलिए सफल गुरु वही है जो शिष्यों की शंकाओं का यथार्थ समाधान देकर उसके तर्कों का अन्त करके परम लक्ष्य का बोध करा सके। इसीलिए गुरु के लिए श्रोत्रियता और ब्रह्मनिष्ठता - दो प्रधान विशेषण कहे गये हैं।

A farmer is regarded as good who has a plough and ox and also has *bija* (seed) in the house for sowing; since it is proper that the place of uncultivated fallow land is ready on time for the act of sowing the *bija* (seeds). If there are no seeds in the house then make arrangements for *bija* else the soil will be poor again.

The kind of *guru* that has only studied the *Vedas*, then to the doubts of the student he only guesses at the answers, but cannot be very precise; because he does not have the knowledge of the truth. Therefore the fruitful *guru* is one who gives very precise answers to the doubts of the students, the guessing is at an end. This may be the best mark of knowledge. Therefore it has been said that the two principal signs of a *guru* are *shrotriyata* (one who has thoroughly studied the *Vedas*) and *brahmansihthata* (one possessing knowledge of the immortal Self).

आज कल लोग परमात्मा को ही अन्धा बनाते हैं। साधारण सांसारिक लोगों की आँख बचा कर कुत्सित कर्म करते हैं और सोचते हैं कि कोई नहीं जानता। सर्वान्तरात्मा जगन्नियन्ता भगवान तो सर्वत्र हैं, सभी के सब प्रकार के व्यवहारों को हर समय देख रहे हैं; उनको दृष्ट से बचाकर कभी कोई काम नहीं किया जा सकता। इसलिए यदि वास्तव में अच्छे बनना चाहते हो तो ऐसा प्रयत्न करो कि उनकी दृष्टि में कोई कुत्सित कर्म न आने पावे। संसारियों की दृष्टि में अच्छे बने रहना और चुपचाप कुत्सित कर्म करते जाना दूसरों को धोखा देना नहीं, अपने आपको धोखा देना है। इससे मनुष्यों का घोर पतन होता है।

Nowadays people are being made blind to Paramatma. Common worldly people escape seeing the vile *karma* and do not think to consider. The Universal Soul, the Almighty Bhagwan is everywhere then, looking to see all kinds of business every time; nobody can avoid their actions being seen. In reality therefore, if you desire to be made good, then make the effort not to do any vile *karma* in their sight. In the sight of the worldly people continue to make good but do not deceive others by silently doing vile *karma*, respectively deceiving oneself. From this people are falling horribly.

अनेकों इच्छाओं का संयम करके एक प्रबल इच्छा प्रवाहित करो । वह इतनी बलवती होगी कि उसकी गति को रोकने वाला (उसका बाधक) स्वयं उसमें बह कर उसका सहयोगी हो जायगा ।

Restraining many desires, flow with one desire. The condition of the one who stops [desire], obstructing the flow will be a help to oneself.

जैसी वासना धन के लिए है, पुत्र के लिए है, इष्ट मित्र और अन्न-वस्त्र के लिए है वैसे ही यदि परमात्मा के लिए हुई तो इतनी कमजोर वासना से परमात्मा कैसे मिलेगा? स्त्री-धन-पुत्र-इष्ट मित्रादि से परमात्मा बहुत विशिष्ट है; इसलिए उसको प्राप्ति के लिए उसी कोटि की उत्कृष्ट वासना उत्पन्न करना चाहिये ।

If it is similar to longing for wealth, for a son, for a beloved friend, for food and clothing. How will you meet with Paramatma with such feeble longings then? By comparison with a woman - wealth - son - beloved friend, Paramatma is very great; therefore for gaining Him you should produce longing of ten million [times more] excellence.

बछड़े का दुग्ध-पान का भाव व्यक्त होते ही वात्सल्य के कारण जिस गाय के सवाँग से आकृष्ट हो दुग्ध-स्तन में एकत्रित होकर उसे

प्राप्त होता है, उसी प्रकार भक्त के भावों से आकृष्ट होकर व्यापक परमात्मा की शक्ति प्रतिमा आदि में केन्द्रित होकर उसे प्राप्त होती है ।

देव प्रतिमा में देवत्व (दैवी-शक्ति) लाने के लिए और उसके द्वारा उपासकों के कल्याण के लिए चार बातें प्रधानतः आवश्यक हैं; तथा-

(१) देवताओं का स्वरूप जैसा शास्त्रों में वर्णन किया गया है ठीक उसी के अनुसार प्रतिमा का होना;

(२) शास्त्रीय विधानों द्वारा प्रतिमा की प्रतिष्ठा का किया जाना;

(३) प्रतिष्ठा होने के पश्चात् यथाविधि जप, पाठ पूजन, हवन आदि द्वारा देव-मूर्ति की पूजा होना; और

(४) देव-स्थान में शास्त्र-विरुद्ध व्यवहार और निर्माता की इच्छा के विरुद्ध कार्यों का न होना ।

इन चारों बातों का जितनी उत्तम रीति से पालन होता है उतनी ही अधिक देव-प्रतिमायें दैवी-शक्ति-सम्पन्न होंगी और उपासकों का उतना ही अधिक कल्याण होगा, इन बातों की जितनी उपेक्षा होती है उतनी ही मूर्तियाँ दैवी कलाहीन हो जाती हैं ।

Apparently, drinking the milk from the udder is the cause of the fondness for the attraction the whole body of the cow, this kind of feeling of devotion is widespread for those that are attracted to gaining the energy centred in the idol of Paramatma. For bringing the divinity (divine power) of the image of the *deva* (deity) and thereof the way for the worshipper's happiness, four points are necessary;

(1) The image of the gods are to be exactly according to the description in the *Shastras*.

(2) Installation of the idol of a deity is to be done by the arrangements in the *Shastra*.

(3) According to rule, after the installation, by way of *japa*, reading, *havana* (oblation fire) etc there is to be *puja* of the god's *murti* (idol).

And

(4) In the place of the god, there is to be no business contrary to the *Shastra* nor actions contrary to the wishes of the creator. From as much as the rule of these four points is cherished one will be possessed of the god's divine energy, and the worshipper will be that much more happy. As much as these points are disregarded divine *murtis* are going to be quarrelsome [subjects].

पूजक अपनी तप-शक्ति, भावना और पूजन की विशेषताओं द्वारा देव-प्रतिमाओं में अधिकाधिक दैवी-शक्ति की बुद्धि कर सकता है और उसी के द्वारा अभीष्ट सिद्धि प्राप्त कर सकता है ।

The worshipper's own energy, of penance, feeling and reverence, are the different ways one can increasingly sense the divine energy in the images of a god and one can gain the desired success this way.

जहाँ देव-मूर्तियों में विधिवत् अर्चन, पूजन, वन्दन आदि होता है वहाँ सदा ही मंगल रहता है, सुख-सम्पदा की वृद्धि होती है और सब प्रकार से अभ्युदय प्राप्त होता है ।

Wherever idols of god are regularly reverenced, with *puja*, *vandana* etc, there auspiciousness always remains. There is happiness and advancement of wealth, and all kinds of progress is gained.

जिन देवालयों में मूर्तियों की प्रतिष्ठा द्विज जातियों द्वारा की गई है उनमें अन्त्यजों के मन्दिर-प्रवेश से स्पर्श-दोष के कारण मूर्ति और

मन्दिर दूषित हो जाते है। शास्त्र में प्रमाण मिलते हैं इस प्रकार प्रतिमाओं के दूषित होने से उनमें देवी शक्ति का ह्रास हो जाता है और इन देवत्व-विहीन प्रतिमाओं में भूत, प्रेत आदि का वास हो जाता है तथा इन भूत-प्रेत-निवसित प्रतिमाओं के पूजन से देश में भूकम्प-अग्नि-प्रकोप, रोग, दुर्भिक्ष, राजा प्रजा का क्षय आदि अनिष्ट होते हैं।

The installation of images in temples of a god is done through the lineage of twice-born. Contaminating contact with persons of low caste admitted to the *mandir* (temple) causes the *murti* (idol) and *mandir* to be defiled. Contained in the *Shastra* is the testimony that these sort of images are defiled, in them the divine energy decays. And in these images abandoned by divinity, the *bhuta* (ghost) and spirits of the dead go to be resident and in the place these ghosts of the dead live in and are worshopped in idols. From earthquake-fire-wrath, disease, famine, destruction etc, the *raja's* subjects are to be harmed.

आस्तिक समाज को चाहिये कि अपने और सब के कल्याण के लिए अभी तक दूषित हुए मन्दिरों की शास्त्र-विधानों से पुनः प्रतिष्ठा कर विधिवत् पूजन आदि की व्यवस्था करे। दूषित प्रतिमाओं के पूजन से लाभ के बदले हानि ही होती है। किन्तु, यह निश्चय है कि अपने सामने देव-मन्दिरों की मर्यादा भंग होते देख कर भी यदि आस्तिक-समाज चुप रहता है तो उसे इस घोर पाप का फल भोगना पड़ेगा।

द्विज जातियों द्वारा प्रतिष्ठित मूर्त्तियों के पूजनादि का अधिकार अन्त्यज आदि को नहीं है। इसका यह अर्थ नहीं कि शास्त्र में अन्त्यज और शूद्रों के कल्याण की अवहेलना की गई है। केवल भगवन्नाम-स्मरण और कीर्तन मात्र से ही कितनों को परमगति प्राप्त

होने के प्रमाण पुराणों में पाये जाते हैं। और, धर्मशास्त्र का यह निदान है कि द्विज जातियों को स्नान, संध्या आदि करके पवित्रतापूर्वक जप, तप करते हुए शास्त्रोक्त और पूजन-सामग्री आदि से सम्पन्न होकर देव-पूजन करने से जिस पुण्य की प्राप्ति होती है वही पुण्य अन्त्यज आदिकों को मन्दिर के कलश, स्तूप और ध्वज को सभक्ति प्रणाम करने मात्र से सहज में ही प्राप्त होता है। इस प्रकार धर्म-शास्त्र में सभी के कल्याण के लिए उपाय बताये गये हैं। अधिकारी भेद से किसी के उपाय सरल हैं और किसी के कठिन।

You should want a devout congregation, and for the happiness of one and all arrangements should be made for the performance of re-consecration of images in occordance with the *Shastra* in the temples that have been defiled. From the worship of idols of deities that have been defiled, is disadvantage and loss. But this certainly appears to defeat the rules of one's own deity's temples. Also, if the devout congregation remains silent then it will suffer the effects of this horrible wickedness.

By means of the lineage of the twice-born is established the right to do *puja* etc to the idols. To a person of low caste etc is not. This is not meant as any disrespect in the *Shastra* to the happiness of a person of a low caste and *shudras*. Simply recollecting the name of the Lord and from a little *kirtan* (devotional music), how many have gained final beatitude as verified in the Purananas? Besides, the conclusion of the *Dharma Shastra* is that the lineage of twice-born, prior to evening bathing, do *japa*, *tapa* (penance) that is ordained by the *Shastras*, and with the paraphenalia of *puja* do worship of the deity. This very same holiness is easily gained by a person of a low caste etc who merely does *pranaam* (salutation) to the dome, spire and flag of the temple. This the means for all happiness is told in the *Dharma-Shastra*. The scheme of the shepherd is straight and arduous.

शास्त्र की आज्ञा मान कर अपने अधिकार के अनुसार आचरण

करने से ही कल्याण हो सकता है । मनमाना दुराग्रह करके वेद-शास्त्र
की अवहेलना करने से किसी का कल्याण नहीं होगा; इसलिए अपने
कल्याण की कामना करने वाले को सतर्क होकर करने योग्य कार्य
करना चाहिये ।

To value the command of the *Shastra* one can be happy by
behaving in accordance with the rights of one's entitlement.

Doing just that which is agreeable, behaving willfully, by
neglecting *Veda-Shastra* one will not be happy; therefore for
one's own happiness one should be careful to do suitable work.

मृत्यु से डरा मत; क्योंकि एक दिन अवश्य ही मरना है । जितने
क्षण जी रहे हो सतर्क होकर कार्य करो । कहीं कोई ऐसा कार्य न हो
जाय कि मरते समय उसके लिए पश्चाताप हो ।

Do not fear death; because for certain one is to die one day. Be
careful, however many moments a soul is living. Don't do
anything that will cause remorse at the time of dying.

सच्चा मरना वही है कि फिर जन्म न हो । स्वधर्माचरण रत
भगवद्-भक्तों का मरण ऐसा ही होता है ।

To die righteous is not the same as being born again. Absorbed in
one's own religious practice the death of God's devotees is to be
like this.

गो-रक्षा का प्रश्न हिन्दू-धर्म, जीवन और समाज-रक्षा का प्रश्न है ।
इसकी अवहेलना अधिक समय तक होना देश के कल्याण में घातक
है । प्रत्येक गृहस्थ का कर्तव्य है कि गो-पालन और गो-रक्षण के
लिए तत्पर रहे और भारतीय शासन-सत्ता का भी महान कर्तव्य है
कि गो-वंश की उन्नति लिए अधिकाधिक प्रयत्न करे ।

The question of cow protection is the existence of Hindu *dharma*

and the question of the protection of society. As long as more time
is spent in neglect, it is a destroyer of happiness. It is necessary
that each householder defends cows and is engaging in protecting
cows and the Indian government has a great obligation to make an
effort for the betterment of the posterity of the cow.

Maharishi Recounts Guru Dev's Lifestory

"Guru Dev, life of Guru Dev was very, very grand and very great, we are all proud of it.

And... All that was necessary for all the people in the world to go through, the hardships and all the difficulties to realise the Supreme, he went through for all of us.

It's surprising how a child of nine years leaves his home for the Himalayas in search of God. Born and brought up in a good family, a respectable family, disappears from home one evening and then, just along the Ganges bank, 'Where going? What going? Not much in the mind. What is the intelligence of the child of nine years? Walking all along the Ganges, reaching, it took four years to reach Uttarkashi and the one objective in the mind was, to find a good *guru*. That was it. And the criterion that was set by the child of nine years, about the *guru* was, there was three things. That he should be realised. Now how the realisation will be experienced? He decided that he should not be an angry man at least. Loss of anger was one criterion. He should be a life-celibate, shouldn't be a married man. And the third criterion was that he will attract me. I would feel to surrender myself at his feet, that inner feeling. With these three criterions for a *guru*, Guru Dev set out from his house at the age of nine. And where he was to go? Not much known, but, go to the Himalayas!

This is, at about the age of thirteen he went to Uttarkashi, and there, surrendered to the .. Now there are so many very interesting incidents that took on the way, that happened on the way, but we'll not go much in details about it.

There was heard a very good, a famous saint. And in India when they, those saints who wear the orange robes, they are called *sannyasi's. Sannyasi's* are such that they are not expected to touch fire, not expected to behave with fire. Like that they don't cook for themselves. It is others who feed them or they go for alms in the villages and come back.

He went, he was heard to be a famous saint, then he went to him and made some disturbance on the door and when he came he asked him, 'Can I have some fire?'

And then this saint blew into anger, he said 'Fire, I am a *sannyasi* and you don't know this. Small children leave home and come about and disturb us. How can a *sannyasi* have fire? You want fire from me?' And he blew into fire of anger.

He quietly whispered a word, he said, 'If it was not there, from where this came?' And retreated from there. He just let the saint know that he had quite a lot of fire in him.

See the tricky boy, going to test his *guru*, because he thought the *guru* should be tested. And if he is an angry man, and if you say something his order, or something, and if he doesn't blow up, then...

And then certainly he came down, immediately the fire extinguised and then he said, 'Oh doesn't matter, these are the symptoms. These are not the symptoms, these are the characteristics of the mind, and the soul is ever the same. You don't bother, the mind is sometimes like this and sometimes like this.' He said, 'Yes, yes, sometimes its burning and sometimes quiet..

The saint was very much moved by the intelligence of the boy, but, but he didn't appeal to him, he had his way ahead.

Like that, many, many instances went on.

At the age of about thirteen his been to Uttarkashi, and then surrendered to the feet of the master, Swami Krishnanand Saraswati, a saint.

There were quite a good many disciples there, people doing practises of *yoga*, and *hatha yoga*, and *raja yoga*, and *mantra yoga*, so many people, disciples, engaged in their own practices, and he happened to be the youngest.

Now that looks to be very odd, that the master gets, gets a sort of attached to the youngest boy, of about thirteen or fourteen years. Whereas there were people of thirty, forty, fifty, sixty years of age, living in the *ashram* for many, many years past. One night he said, the master said that, 'Alright, tomorrow, tomorrow morning I will just find some fault with you in the prescence of all the people, and we'll ask you to get out of our *ashram*, our ask someone to take you two miles away in that cave. So you will not mind my sending you out of the *ashram*. That I have to do because you are the youngest and I can't put you on these practices, whereas other people are, don't deserve such these practices of *yoga*. So I'll do that like that.'

Next morning he came out and he said, 'Oh you boys, making mischief in the *ashram*. Get out from here! Oh you, come on, take him and put him there two miles in little cave there, Send him off!'

He was expected to come back once a week on Thursdays. And spend the night there and go on the Friday again.

In these *ashrams*, what happens, after all, it's human, habitation. Always because the masters are like the oceans, full, fully, the full, pond full of water. Now the water has no tendency to go out or in, and they are just full like the ocean. Anyone who wants to take the water to their field make the connection and take the water, ready to go. Not making the connection the water is unable to flow, and having made the connection it doesn't resist going, it goes. So those who communicate to the mind of the master, naturally keep on deriving from all that is there, in that cosmic mind. And those who are not able to make the connection with the master, naturally they are left behind in their effeciency of attainment.

So, after about two or three years. One day the master said, said to that man, Yogananda was his name, quite an old disciople of his, 'Yogananda, I want to go in that area and spend some days in silence. You go to that brahmachari and ask him if there is some place for me to come. And you will have to ask him, the youngest brahmachari, to ask him and find out from him,' because that territory belonged to him at this time.

He went and asked him, 'Oh, Gurudev wants to come here and what place will be best for him. He has asked to find out from him.'

He said, 'I am sorry, there is no place here for Gurudev. No more place is there for him.'

And he couldn't bear these words from the brahmachari. And he said, 'This is what you have become here, living so far, and you have become so obstinate as to refuse this place to the master?'

And he said, 'Now, Yogananda Ji, you are my elder and I worship you and I have all admiration for you. You are a messenger at this time, brought a message from the master to me. Please give him in the turn what I am delivering to you, just as a messenger.'

Look to the great significance in it, and it later on it comes to be disclosed, but the sharpness of the mind of the youngest, that baffled the mind of the oldest, Yogananda.

He came back and he said, 'He seems to be, the brahmachari seems to be very obstinate, and he has gone off his mind and he said to me something to me that I can't repeat in front of you.'

Everybody became curious what happened, what happened, 'He said, he said "There is no place there." And I have seen with my eyes there are that cave, and that cave, and there is that cave, that cave.'

Everybody in the *ashram* was simply against the brahmachari, and they said 'No, no, he must be properly dealt with. We can't bear such an insult to our master.'

Next Thursday night he came, and people were sitting around the master and when he came he was thought to be a great culprit having insulted the master. And he came and sat down as he used to sit, in a very humble way, all apart from, at a distance from the master.

Then someone asked the master, 'If some disciple insults the *guru*, what is the punishment for him? How can he be relieved of that sin?' Because the punishment is always to relieve the man from his sin that he has committed.

And there was great silence in the room.

The master looked at the brahmachari and said, 'What have you to say? Probably these people have not understood the message you sent through Yogananda. Err, tell them what did you did mean by it, and by that.'

He said the.. 'If I knew that I was sending the message to these people in the *ashram* I would have sent the message in other way. I thought I was sending the message to the master. And if they want clarification it is a simple thing. The day I entered this *ashram* I had surrendered the whole of my being to the feet of my master and every fibre, every atom of my body is now filled with the being of the master. No more there is any place which I could offer anymore. Had I known that the place would be demanded sometime to come then I would have reserved some corner of my being...' And there was that flash of enlightenment in the whole assembly of there. Such a great fullness of surrender to the master. And this it was that made him so great in his achievements that now the whole world is going to enjoy that glory. And this was the technique that was adopted, complete surrender to the feet of the master. And to such a great fullness that whatever be the question, whatever be the thought, but that state of surrender prevails.

He said, 'The *guru* dwells not in the caves of the earth or stone, not in the houses of bricks and mortar, he dwells in the heart of the people, and there he is already dwelling in my heart. No more is any corner left vacant to be provided now at this demand.'

Such was the fullness.

He remained with his master for about twelve or thirteen years, and then went **deep** into the Himalayas, came out into the deep forests of Central India. Always away from the population. Always away from the population in such deep forests Guru Dev spent many, many years of his life, where even the sunrays wouldn't touch the ground, so thick foliage. And he was unknown to the people but he was well marked in the destiny of India and the inner vision of the good saints of India. This was the condition till the age of seventy-one. From the age of nine to the age of seventy-one this was the life of a recluse, complete seclusion out of every contact of human beings, and so many stories are told, that in the Central India in those days there were lots of small, small states. So, mostly he used to live in the deep dense forest dividing the boundary of the states, this side and that side. So when some foreigner or some cowherd man would inform the people in the village, 'Oh that saint is there, and a very good saint, and so bright and...' Because the whole being, in and out of samadhi all the time, the whole being was simply shining with great light, and that couldn't be seen.'

One who sees it tells to hundreds of others and they go to see, and by the time he is not found the next day there. Gets deeper on the other side. Like that, the princes used to almost chase him just to have a glimpse of his darshan, just to have a look of him. In India its a great conception that if you happen to see a good saint, the sight of a good enlightened soul purifies him, the seer. Like that he was living all the time.

Now, there are the seats of Shankaracharya, there are four seats of Shankaracharya in India. Shankaracharya is the head of Hindu religion, as the pope is of Catholicism, Shankaracharya is the head of Hindu religion. In Shankaracharya dissolve all the differences and distinctions of different sects, creeds of Hindu religion. That is a platform common to all. His philosophy is that of Vedanta,

"About 2500 years ago, the first Shankaracharya established these four principal seats, one in the north in Jyotirmath in the Himalayas, one in the south in Shringerimath near Mysore, one in the east near Puri near Calcutta, and one in the west near, that's the most extreme end of India near Dwarka, Sharada Peeth. These are the four principal seats of Shankaracharya. The seat of the Shankaracharya of North, of the Himalayas, was vacant for a hundred and sixty-five years. That was a time when Mohammedan reign was, rule was falling apart and Britishers were coming in and there was a chaos all the time, from a hundred and sixty... from now about a hundred and eighty years ago. Like that, somehow the seat of Shankaracharya remained vacant, there was no occupant of that great throne of Shankaracharya. All the conscientious leaders of public life, and good saints, were concerned with this seat of Shankaracharya remaining vacant. They held national conferences to select some Shankaracharya, and on the highest circle of the saints, Guru Dev was known. So they decided to approach him wherever he was. The story goes that it took him twenty years of persuasion to accept this seat of Shankaracharya. Because the life was so drawn out of the field of activity. Complete, An ideal, most ideal life of a recluse, of a *sannyasi.* Eventually, after twenty years of persuasion, at the age of seventy-one years, in 1941, he was installed as a Shankaracharya.

Now, Shankaracharya means; a great institution in himself. Hundreds of people surround him and all this great commotion. His life had been complete silence. Whatever it was, that was the time when he came to, when Shankaracharyas used to come, they take him out on great processions with great, all paraphenalia. In one of the processions I happened to see him, and when I saw him first time I said now this is it. That was a flash to me, and then I surrendered myself. It took me about two years for a proper kind which could be said to be surrender and then thereafter the life was a real blissful life.

As a Shankaracharya he was found to have the great intellect of the first Shankaracharya and the heart of Buddha. The loveable soft heart of Buddha and the great intellect of Shankara, and that was his personality. He wouldn't go much in details of the philosophical discussion but what he spoke was simple truths of life, but very simple, so piercing they went straight home to heart. People have been telling us, I think there were, that those were the meetings in open air, all the time in open air except in the rains. Open air meetings. We used to have sixteen, twenty, twelve, eight, big, big, twelve mikes [loudspeakers] to cover the range of about fifty thousand people, a hundred thousand people, like that. Just for his evening discourses. And he would hardly speak thirty minutes, forty, forty minutes was the maximum he went sometime. But every word that he spoke was so powerful, was so piercing, was so convincing. People would see him and be transformed to all good life. Whatever remained there, buried in the subconscious would come out when they hear his words. Very great thief has just been transformed, not by the logic or not by the exposition of anything great which they not know before, but the truth exposed in so simple words and in such great force of life force, that they couldn't but only be transformed. The motor would pass from there, and he would be speaking, and if the car is not very fast, if the driver happens to hear to hear some words he will immediately put up the brake and stop and listen. Can't pass on, he has to stop and hear it. Such charm was there in his words, and such great simplicity and depth of thought and he charmed the child and the old alike. It was a pindrop silence of fifty thousand, a hundred thousand people." [2]

Maharishi Recollects First Meeting With Guru Dev

Apparently Mahesh first met the *guru* in the city of Jabalpur in central India (this being Mahesh's hometown where it is said he worked sometime as a clerk at the Gun Carriage Factory). He recalls:-

'I was fond of visiting saints, and when I heard there was a saint - this was in some Summer vacation - "Some saint has come but it's very difficult to approach him and he is far away," and all that, all that. Then I made more enquiries; "Where is he? And what?", then I found one can only see him about midnight or something, because no one is allowed to go there, and you have to go in all darkness without making noise and all kinds of things. I met some friends here and there and just we went there and, on a small house somewhere far into the, in the forest somewhere. There was a terrace, small terrace, and there, it was all dark, absolutely dark. About ten or eleven we arrived there. I and someone or two more.

And there was a *brahmachari* on the ground floor. He said, "How you are here?" and "Who told you?" and, "You are not **expected** to come!"

And said, "So maybe we forgot our way and we are here then, *darshan* coming;. And tell us about the saint, and we want to hear.." I said.

And he said, "Don't talk, don't talk, just sit quietly." And he disappeared and he went up and after about half an hour he came back. He said, "Follow me very quietly." I said, "Alright, alright." We quietly went up, there was nothing to see, it's all dark and somehow we felt someone was sitting on a sort of chair or something, reclining, comfortable. We sat down quietly, we found two or three other men were also sitting. No one was talking, whispering, it was all dark, everything. It so happened, about maybe fifteen, twenty minutes passed and it happened that far distance a car was coming and it showed the light on the terrace, and that was the first sight of Guru Dev. Just on the flash of the car, maybe a mile away from the car, but it just turned, it just turned for a moment and I was.. it was just enough to have a glimpse of him. And then I thought, "Yes, it seems the time has come." That one glimpse of a flashy light and that was enough to take decisions.

Then I came, and I came, and I came, and I said, "Could I not be at your service?"

He said, "What you are doing?"

"Studying."

"Oh better finish your studies."

"And then, where will you be?"

"Oh you will find me somewhere."'

So, perhaps this was a test set by the *guru,* to evaluate the young man's enthusiasm to become a monk?

'And I was asked to complete my studies. And then I did not argue with him because once I saw him, I know he knows best and whatever he said was my action.'

'Then Guru Dev was gone back to the lonely forests. It was hard to locate from where he had come and where he had gone, because those who knew him were strictly prohibited to tell others his whereabouts. There was no way to keep contact with him.'

'About three years later, I saw him in the market of a big city of north India, being carried in a big procession. And this was when he visited the city as Shankaracharya of north India.'

'He had become the Shankaracharya of Jyotirmath. To become a Shankaracharya is a very, is a democratic thing. All the *pandits* and saints and all that, they join together and they elect the

Shankaracharya. The head of.. the custodian of Hindu religion.'

Mahesh joined the *guru's* busy *ashram* at Varanasi (Benares) and discovered dozens of learned people there:-

"Right in the beginning, I joined the *ashram*, I came, and then I was amongst thirty or forty *brahmacharis,* and *pandits* and all that, all that. And they were very wise people, *pandits* of all the six systems of philosophy, and *pandits* of all the *smrittis, shrutis,* and all that. The whole learning round about Shankaracharya was vast retinue of learned people and I was absolutely insignificant. I had some knowledge of Hindi, and some of English, and a little bit of Sanskrit, but in that big huge learned assembly, this was absolutely insignificant, and English, of course, it was not necessary at all.

And then it was about a week and as everyone in the morning would go and do the prostrations and come out and then there was nothing to do. And one week passed and then I thought. "It's ridiculous to waste all this time." Was just once in the morning and once in the evening, go and prostrate and come out. So I made friends with a man who was cleaning his room, something like that, like that. Adjusting his table, this, this, this.

I said, "Oh, could you not take rest? You must be feeling very tired," and something, something.

And I said. "I could..."

But he said, "You can't. You can't come in this room," and this and this.

But I said, "Maybe when Guru Dev is not here, when he is taking his bath, and I could clean or something."

And he said, "Yes, that time you can come but get out quickly, and don't disturb things." Like that. So I started on that, some cleaning of the floor, something, something, adjusting something.'

During a temporary absence of the *pandit* who dealt with the clerical work of the *ashram*, Mahesh saw an opportunity to assume the role of clerk to the *guru*. He checked through the incoming mail and offered to read certain of the letters out loud to Guru Dev.

'One letter was there. It came for his blessing from some state in India asking that they are going to perform a big *yagya* and they want the blessings of Shankaracharya. And that letter was there and that date was approaching, about a week was left. And that I thought was a letter very responsible for the organisation to answer.

And I asked Guru Dev, "Oh, oh, the answer of this letter?"

And he would just not mind it, because in his eyes just one organisation doesn't mean anything, or something.

But, I thought it's a very great responsibility of the organisation, it's if someone wants Shankaracharya's blessing then it's for the organisation to reply, and reply his blessings and create goodwill and inspire that organisation.'

Over the following days Mahesh repeatedly attempted to elicit a response from the *guru* but without result, and then went so far as to suggest that he write something himself. He recalls:-

'One day I said, "It's only about four, five days left. Shall I make a draft and read to Guru Dev, or anything?"

And he said, "What you will write?" And that was the end he said.'

Mahesh returned to his own room to gather his thoughts:-

'I said, "Now come on, I have to write an answer to this. What? What? How to write? What to do? Now supposing if I was a Shankaracharya? What I'll say in that letter?" And I just imposed Shankaracharyaship on myself. And I said. "Yes, all the religious organisations look to Shankaracharya, head of the religion. The main thing is, that they should get inspiration from the blessing of

Shankaracharya. As an organisation doing this great *yagya*, inspiring the people in the locality for religious life, so they should have the approval of Shankaracharya for this good act of religious value." I somehow wrote. And in the evening - it was just a very short thing, because nothing very long has to go from Shankaracharya, who is a **great** authority on religion, so very short inspiration. I made some few lines.

In the evening when I opened the door and entered and I read out that thing, in one simple breath quickly. And it sounded **so** apt, **so** appropriate.

And then he said, "Will these people get it if you write? Then send it."

I said; "Yes, they can get it, it's yet four days."

That's all he said.

Then I quickly wrote and put on a seal of Shankaracharya and did the whole paraphernalia, and sent it. From that day probably I gave an impression that I could write something useful. That was the first thing. And from there, the letters came to me for replying and I was replying and sometimes reading to him.'

Wishing to get even closer to the *guru* he attempted to attune himself to the master's thinking:-

'And it took about two and a half years, and I thought two and a half years were wasted, but it came out to be quite early to adjust myself to his feelings. And the method that I adopted was just to sense what he wants at what time - what he wants. I picked up activity as a means to adjust to his thought, to his feelings.'

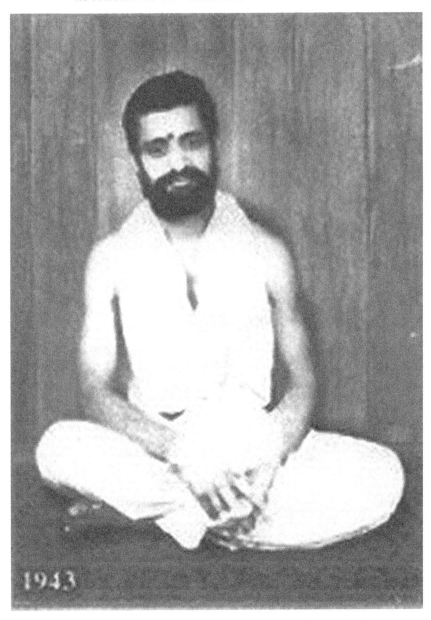

'And from there on for me the whole thing was very light and beautiful, no obstacles, clear, everything. Then I was living around him without even feeling that I was living. It's a very genuine feeling of complete oneness with Guru Dev, just like that. People who have seen me moving with Guru Dev know that I was not as if in this isolated, single body or something.'

'Even ignorant people like me were blessed, and this was his great, extreme value of adaptability, He could adopt [sic] himself to even such sheer ignorance, and raise the value. This adaptability is what I found most useful for me, as far as Guru Dev is concerned. Very great fortune to have found him..' [3]

Brahmachari Mahesh at Lucknow, March/April 1952

Shankaracarya Day in Mussoorie

In 1952 Guru Dev visited the hill station of Mussoorie where on Tuesday 23rd September 1952 Shankaracharya Day was celebrated. There are five known photographs taken of Guru Dev in Mussoorie, all apparently taken on Tuesday 23rd September 1952. The images show Guru Dev seated in the lion throne set upon a open-chassis vehicle.

The disciples surrounding Guru Dev in this photograph are not easy to identify, but the moustached face of the handsome man to the left of the photo, standing in the background, appears to be that of Dandi Swami Narayanand Saraswati. The attendant standing to the far left of the photo closely resembles Swami Swaroopanand Saraswati. To the right of the picture the attendant could well be a young Swami Shantanand Saraswati whilst unmistakeably, at the front is Brahmachari Mahesh (aka. Maharishi Mahesh Yogi), with his arm outstretched. To the lower left of photo one can just make out the shape of the steering wheel of this unusual vehicle.

Apparently several photographs were taken, at the suggestion of a businessman who visited a local studio, a branch of Delhi Photo Studio. The company still exists and is run as a family business by Ajay Shankar (grandson of founder Bhagwati Prasad Shankar). Hand-tinted photographs of Guru Dev and high-resolution black-and-white prints of Guru Dev are available from Delhi Photo Company, 78, Janpath, New Delhi – 110001, India.

Whilst in Mussoorie Brahmachari Mahesh wrote an introduction to the *'Amrit Kana'* book, a compilation of quotations of Guru Dev.

Shankaracharya's Press Officer

A visit to Delhi was arranged and on Wednesday 15th October 1952 (several weeks before the *guru's* arrival there) the *brahmachari* convened a press conference:-

The Great Saint of the Himalayas is Coming to Shower His Blessings on the Metropolis.

The Statement issued by: BAL BRAHMACHARI SHRI MAHESH JI.

Press conference convened by Shri Shankaracharya Reception Committee, Delhi on the 15th Oct., 1952 at 5 p.m. in the Young Man's Tennis Club Queen's Gardens, in connection with the visit of HIS HOLINESS SHRI JAGATGURU SHANKARACHARYA MAHARAJ OF JYOTIRMATH.

My own self in different forms.

It gives me a great pleasure to welcome you all and have your company here this afternoon. It gives me enough encouragement and support to acquaint you with the details of the mission for whose fulfilment His Holiness Shri Jagatguru Shankaracharya Swami BRAHMANAND SARASWATI MAHARAJ will be visiting your city about the 12th of November 1952 and stay here for about a month for Dharmopdesh.

Swami Brahmand Saraswati Maharaj, the present Shankaracharya of Jyotirmath Badarikashram (in the Himalayas) is a magnetic personality with a sweet amalgam of

High Wisdom and Love of humanity. He combines in himself the Knowledge of the self with the mysterious powers -- the siddhis arising out of yogic perfection and hard penances, which he has undergone throughout his life. He is a great living yogi and scholar and is revered by millions of Hindus as their Supreme Religious head.

This great Saint of the modern age was born in U.P. in a well to do and renowned Brahman family in 1871 and was enthroned to the seat of His Holiness Jagatguru Shankaracharya in 1941 at Benares, during the ninth session of the All India Sanatan Dharma Maha Sammelan convened by the Bharat Dharma Mahamandal in conjunction with a countrywide support of almost all the ruling princes and different socio-religious institutions all over the country. It may be recalled that it was a long persuasion of about twenty years which could convince Param Virakt Swami Brahmanand Saraswati to accept the great responsibility of the Shankaracharya at the age of seventy.

From the tender age of nine when he came out of his home in Search of God, till this time, his life was mostly spent in the lonely hidden regions of the Himalayas, Vindya Giris and the Amarkantakas which are rarely frequented by men and are chiefly inhabited by wild animals. For years together he has lived in hidden caves and thick forests where even the midday sun frets and fumes in vain to dispel the darkness that may be said to have made a permanent abode there in those solitary and distant regions.

But today he is easily accessible as he is
now the presiding head of Shri Jyotirmath
which is the greatest religious institution
of the Hindus of Northern India, covering
all different creeds and sampradayas and
branches lying under the fold of Hindu
Religions.

One unique principle of the great Sage
that distinguishes him completely from other
living saints of today is that he does not
accept money as gift from his visitors or
disciples.

This brief description attempts to mirror
a few hurried and short glimpses of the life
journey of this great living sage who has
actually transformed into a living fact the
inner latent potentiality of the soul. He
has known the great universal Truth, whose
realisation is the aim of the entire scheme
of life. For him the mists of ignorance have
completely disappeared and having known the
Divine Reality he has verily become an
embodiment of the great Divinity.

His aim of life, if the life of a realised
soul can be said to possess any such aim, is
to broadcast the message of the Great Divine
light that he has himself realised, the
Light that is the Soul of all human beings.
Having himself attained the pinnacle of Self
development, he aims at transforming the
worldly minded people into the Godly minded,
and through his inner Divine touch to change
the materialistic hearts of iron into
spiritual hearts of gold.

His entire personality emanates the sweet

perfume of spirituality. His race radiates
that rare light which comprises love,
authority, serenity and self assuredness
that comes only by righteous living and
Divine Realisation -- one feels as if some
ancient Maharishi mentioned in the pages of
the Upanishads has assumed human form and
feels that it is worth while leading a pious
life and to strive for the realisation of
the Divine.

His Spiritual teachings are simple and
clear and go straight home to heart. He
strictly adheres to the course of inner
development laid down by the Systems of
Indian Philosophy and ethics and he raises
his voice never in opposition but always in
firm support of the Truths and principles
contained in the Hindu Scriptures.

According to the tradition from the
worldly point of view, the dignity of the
Shankaracharyas throne has got to be
maintained by the rich paraphernalia around
his Holiness, but those who have come in his
contact know the fact that the private life
of the Sage is quite simple and
renunciation.

I believe that he is a living embodiment
of titanic spiritual force. If I were asked
on the basis of my personal experience,
about the living saints of today, as to who
is the greatest amongst them, I would
unhesitatingly name Shri Jagatguru
Shankaracharya Swami Brahmanand Saraswati
Maharaj of Jyotirmath the Beacon Light of
the holy sanctuaries of the Himalayas.

Shri Shankaracharya Maharaj has clear
insight into the mind and the thoughts of
the modern age. His teaching and
commandments are based on sound reasonings
which are quite agreeable to any reasonable
thinker. He is a great critic of prejudices
and narrowmindedness arising out of
irrational love of caste, creed, nationality
or any "ism". His life is a living proof of
the Truth of the vedas and shaastras. He has
opened a new era of renaissance of True
Religion. He extends his recognition to
anything that is good in any religion. He is
accessible to all. Everyone can enjoy and
derive benefit from his holy Darshan and
elevating discourses.

He is coming shortly to shower his
blessings on the busy and restless souls of
the metropolis. I beseech you, my friends,
to extend your hearty co-operation for the
great cause in the interest of each
individual of our society, in the interest
of our nation and in the interest of the
world at large. The great Saint of the
Himalayas is coming in your midst and in the
fitness of the great occasion, I appeal to
your good sense to extend your valuable
support so that his elevating discourses may
reach the masses in every nook and corner of
our country and abroad.

Thanking you for giving me a pertinent
hearing, I would like to say something, in
short, about the shrine of Jyotirmath, the
prime spiritual centre of Northern India and
the headquarter of Shri Shankaracharya
Maharaj. Jyotirmath is one of four seats
established by Adi Shankaracharya in this

continent -- two thousand and five hundred
years ago. It is situated in the heart of
the Himalayas 173 miles up from Hardwar and
only 18 miles south of Shri Badrinath and
may be said to be the queen of the Himalayas
for natural beauty and spiritual values.
Jyotirmath it was that the first
Shankaracharya selected for his stay in
Himalayas where he taught the highest
philosophy of existence -- the Vedanta - to
his disciples, wrote his immortal
commentaries on the eleven principle
Upanishads, the Bhagavad Gita and Brahma
Sutras and established a seat of Spiritual
light to function as sansorium, a supreme
centre of the Eternal Religion of India to
keep the Light of Pure civilisation and
culture burning for all the millennium to
come. It is an ancient culture centre of
yoga, the Light House which has preserved
and disseminated the Light of the Sanatan
Dharma all the way down the ages.

1952-1955

Some days after Brahmachari Mahesh's public relations announcement, Guru Dev arrived in Delhi. and on 4th December 1952 received a visit President of India Dr Rajendra Prasad, Delhi. During the lengthy meeting he told the President:-

"जब से महार्षियों का सम्पर्क राजां ने छोड़ा तभी से रसातल को चले गये।"

' Jab se mahaarshiyon kaa samparka raajaaon ne chodaa tabhii se rasaatala ko chale gaye.'

'Things have gone to hell since *raajas* neglected to keep the company of *maharishis*.' [4]

A couple of snaps survive of the occasion, one of Guru Dev seated with the President, and a group photo outside with Brahmachari Mahesh to centre of shot. Two other images have surfaced, seemingly based on one of the photos taken that day.

The *guru* was by now in his eighties and because of concerns about his health he returned to his *ashram* in Varanasi and stopped touring. However, after some months a decision was made to travel to Calcutta for a speaking engagement. Whilst staying in Calcutta it was necessary for doctors to attend the *guru* and apparently he breathed his last on Wednesday 20th May 1953 (*vaisakh shukla saptami* 2009), barely a fortnight after his arrival in the city. It has been suggested that the cause of death was Jalodara (dropsy or *oedema*).

The *guru's* body sitting upright and cross-legged was then transported back by train from Calcutta to Varanasi for the funeral rites of *jal samaadhi* (immersion in water). The lifeless body was taken to Brahmanivas Ashram in Varanasi from where it was then taken by boat to Kedar Ghat and then to Kedareshwar Mahadeva Mandir, from where the seated corpse, sealed in a stone casket alongwith some personal effects, was ceremoniously lowered into the River Ganga.

*

It is told that when Guru Dev had initially been offered the post of Shankaracharya he was very reluctant to accept the honour and capitulated only after considerable persuasion. It is said that Swami Karpatri (1905-1980), his long-time disciple since 1927, managed to persuade him and that Guru Dev then declared:-

> 'You want to put a lion to chains who moves about in the jungle freely. But if you so like, I honour your words and am ready to shoulder the responsibilities of the *piiTh* (monastery) management. By shouldering this responsibility, I would be serving the cause for which Adi Shankaracharya stood. I fully dedicate myself for the mission.' [5]

He went on to give more than thirteen years of conscientious service but at no time did he name a successor, so, when some weeks after his death a shortlist of disciples who might succeed him was produced, questions were naturally raised about its provenance. On the basis of the document, purported to be the will of Guru Dev, a disciple named Swami Shantanand Saraswati was promptly enthroned as Shankaracharya of Jyotir Math, on 12th June 1953.

Amongst Guru Dev's senior students, the one known as Karpatri (more properly addressed as Swami Hariharananda), who originally nominated Guru Dev for the office of Shankaracharya, had refused the post himself.

According to Diana L. Eck; "In addition to the darsan of temple images and sacred places, Hindus also value the *darsan* of holy persons, such as *sants* ('saints'), *sadhus* ('holy men'), and *sannyasins* ('renouncers'). When Mahatma Gandhi traveled through India, tens of thousands of people would gather wherever he stopped in order to 'take his *darsan*.' Even if he did not stop, they would throng the train stations for a passing glimpse of the Mahatma in his compartment. Similarly, when Swami Karpatri, a well-known *sannyasin* who is also a writer and political leader, would come to Varanasi to spend the rainy season 'retreat' period, people would flock to his daily lectures not only to hear him, but to see him." [6]

Because of doubts over the legitimacy of the *guru's* will and concerns about the credentials of Swami Shantanand Saraswati, Karpatri now proposed that another candidate be considered and on 25th June 1953 Swami Krishna Bodhashram was installed as Shankaracharya of Jyotir Math (he laid a condition that he would not involve himself in any legal disputes, and this condition was accepted).

According to Shankara tradition only a *brahmana (brahmin)* can become a *sannyasi (swami),* and only a *sannyasi* can be a *guru* and take disciples. In the scarce Hindi book of quotations of Guru Dev entitled *'Shri Shankaracharya Upadeshamrita'*, Guru Dev is quoted upholding this view:-

"परन्तु गुरु सब नहीं बन सकते । गुरुत्व केवल ब्राह्मण ही को है ।"

"parantu guru sab nahin bana sakate. gurutva keval braahmana

hi ko hai."
'But not everyone can be a *guru*. Actually, only *brahmanas* are in
the position to be a *guru*.'[7]

On account of his Kayastha *varna* (caste), Brahmachari
Mahesh could never have hoped to succeed his master nor could
he ever become a *guru* himself.

In fact, having participated in the installation of his *gurubhaiee*
(brother disciple) Swami Shantanand, he withdrew from *ashram*
life to spend time alone at a remote location in north India. Later,
when asked about the conditions there, about whether there were
any wild animals in the caves, he replied:-

'Some wandering monks and sannyasi sit in caves like that,
but where I stay in a small Ashram in Uttar Kashi, the cave is
like a small basement under a room. The entrance is through an
opening only big enough for one person to enter. Down there is
quiet. No sound. Cool in summer. Warm in winter.'

'Food is not always needed, but when I am eating, a man
comes from the village and cooks vegetables. I do not break
silence by seeing or talking to anyone.'[8]

Apparently he sometimes met with an elderly *sannyasi* to
whom he confided his desire to visit the city of Rameshwaram in
southern India. He recalls that at first the old man discouraged
him from going there, but after six months or more, when the
brahmachari still talked about the idea, the *sannyasi* suggested
that it might be better for him to go, just to get rid of the desire.

Meanwhile, back at Guru Dev's *ashram,* things were not going
well for Mahesh's *gurubhaiee* as rivalry over the title of
Shankaracharya was now turning into a legal battle. In January
1954 those who supported Swami Krishnabodhashram's claim to
the title filed a suit in the Munsif Court at Lucknow, while Swami
Shantanand Saraswati applied for a certificate of succession.

*

Some believe that Brahmachari Mahesh spent years in
seclusion, but it is likely that he actually stayed in Uttarkashi for
no more than a matter of months before leaving to accompany an
ailing aunt from Calcutta to a medical facility near Bangalore in
southern India. It is recorded that during his sojourn in
Madanapalle, sometime in June or July of 1954 he began teaching
local people to meditate, furthermore, it has even been suggested
that Mahesh drew attention to himself by putting up a sign saying
'WHO WANTS INSTANT ENLIGHTENMENT', allegedly
conferred by a blow on the forehead! [9]

Several months later, in 1955, he travelled further south to
Rameshwaram and to Kanyakumari.

> 'I went to Kanyakumari - I had a divine revelation. I left and
> went to Trivandrum, to the biggest temple. I was followed by a
> man and he asked me to speak about the Himalayas - he
> arranged a 7 day lecture program and he supplied the topics. In
> 6 months I was lecturing in Delhi. At this stage I had never
> initiated anyone. When I got to Hardwar the philosophy had
> become clear - to turn the mind inward was easy!' [10]

During his time in the south, he spent several months in Kerala
moving from town to town advocating a method of meditation.

The technique he taught necessitated repetition of a *mantra*, a
practice he claimed was easy and very effective at bestowing
happiness. Responding to an advertisement in a local paper, Mrs
Thankamma N Menon and her husband attended a three and a
half-hour talk at Ernakulam and afterwards met with the speaker.

> 'Maharshi asked us about our Ishta-Devata and advised us
> to go to him the next morning for Pada Pooja of Guru Deva,
> Maha Yogi Raj Ananta Sri Vibhushith Sree Sankaracharya
> Brahmananda Saraswathi Maharaj of Jyothir Math who was
> going to be our Guru.' [11]

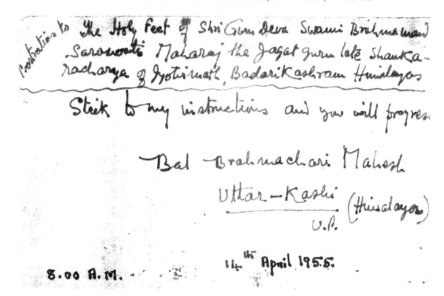

Prostrations to The Holy Feet of Shri Guru Deva Swami Brahmanand Saraswati Maharaj the Jagat guru late Shankaracharya of Jyotirmath, Badarikashram Himalayas

Stick to my instructions and you will progress.

Bal Brahmachari Mahesh
Uttar-Kashi (Himalayas)
U.P.

8.00 A.M.   14th April 1955.

Many others were interested in learning this easy method of meditation, amongst them Sri C R Vaidyanathan.

'Somebody said that Swamiji was giving initiations and if one followed his directions he would get Bliss quickly. I was really sceptic about this "Ananda" business.'

'I presented myself with the necessary puja materials on Thursday. Swamiji made me offer puja to Guru Deva and under closed doors gave me Mantra of the Ishta Devata I chose and asked me to repeat the same and also gave the necessary instructions in the new method for meditation.' [12]

Professor P S Atchuthan Pillai observed:-

'His talk, behaviour and everything about him are as though he is in constant contact with his Gurudev. That is a feature which has surprised many of us closely moving with him. Maharshi Bala Brahmachari always acts as the messiah between his "Gurudev" and his own disciples. He modestly claims to be only the conduit pipe conveying the Gurudeva's blessing on to his devotees in Kerala, or to use his own expression, he is only the "bulb through which the spiritual electrical current from Gurudev shines in radiating light on all".' [13]

Teaching in the name of his *guru,* the *brahmachari* was promoting an apparently novel philosophy, offering assurance that the quest for spiritual fulfillment does not require one to forgo any material comforts. The theory behind his teaching was that only a *sannyasi* can benefit from abandoning desires whereas the householder only finds happiness in the fulfillment of desires.

Five or six months after the library talks in Trivandrum, a *yajna* religious ceremony was celebrated at Cochin, Kerala in late October 1955 during which the *brahmachari* made several speeches.

Day 1 Discourse

"It gives me great pleasure this afternoon to be in the company of you all here assembled in the close vicinity of the Maha Yagna Mandapam. From the early morning the atmosphere here is being surcharged with the Divine Vibrations of Rig Veda and Yajur Veda Parayanam and the chanting of the Maha Yagna Mantras. From the morning till noon today when the Shiva - Laksha - Archana was being performed by the learned Vedic Pandits, everybody must have felt the thrilling and Divine presence of the Vedic Gods here. In such a pure, Serene and Godly atmosphere, your Kerala Maha Sammelan has commenced.

It is a matter of good fortune and pride for every one of us that we have assembled here to discuss and decide, as far as it is possible intellectually, about the easy and practical ideologies of mind-control and spiritual development. This auspicious occasion, I find is graciously sanctified by the presence of the great Lord Shiva and his retinue, and the divine radiance of Shri Guru Dev who is famous for his benevolence and generosity in showering His blessings on all.

In this atmosphere of all-embracing Divinity the inauguration of this Maha Sammelan by the speech from a saintly and princely personality has added grandeur to the occasion. His Highness's inaugural address is the most appropriate speech for the occasion. When I came to Kerala I heard that His Highness the Maharajah of Cochin is a very learned and religiously cultured soul. Now after listening to his inaugural address I am convinced that he is fully worthy of the great name and fame he has earned. In his speech he has successfully laid down the essentials of Adhyatmic Vikas of Spiritual Development. He has very clearly explained the distinction between the theoretical and the practical aspects of Adhyatma Vidya. All this shows his clear understanding and unflickering approach to the subject.

The clarification of "Pravrithi Marga" and "Nivrithi Marga" by His Highness is the most remarkable feature of his speech. It leads me to conclude that His Highness is in full possession of the golden treasures of the rich and old traditions of learning. That is why he could clearly claim Jeevan Mukti for the "Pravrithi Margi" also. This is a very important lesson because in the present Atmosphere of too much talk about Vedanta, it is often argued that Peace in day to day life, experience of Atmananda, and realisation of God are not possible without Vairagya or Renunciation. This ideology is basically wrong and I am glad His Highness has spoken what is right.

For such a noble, intelligent and befitting inaugural address I can only congratulate His Highness and pray to Guru Deva to shower his choicest blessings upon him for a healthy, prosperous and long life.

Another thing which encourages me to speak at this stage is the Asirvatham sent by Shri Shankaracharya Maharaj of Sringeri Math. You have heard his Asirvatham. Therein you would have noted the sentence that this Kerala Maha Sammelan of the Adhyatmic Vikas Mandal is the need of the Nation. In this one sentence His Holiness has spoken volumes. If time would permit, hours could be spent in elucidating the glorious principles compressed in this one small sentence. Obviously enough His Holiness means that after the advent of the political freedom of the country, a Spiritual Renaissance throughout the vast continent of India is the need, and now is the time to accelerate the spiritual development, because spiritual development alone will ensure abiding peace and lasting happiness in the country. This spiritual development of India can alone erect a permanent light house of peace and joy, to guide the destiny of the storm-tossed ship of the suffering humanity of the whole world and save it from wreck.

Shankaracharya Maharaj has also meant and wished in that one sentence that the Mandal should rise up on a national basis. It is a clarion call of peace and happiness for the people and therefore His Holiness has called it the need of the Nation.

Adhyatmic Vikas or spiritual development is the process which brings to light and to our direct experience, the hitherto unknown and unexperienced glories of the subtler aspects of our being. Adhyatmic Vikas or spiritual development is the process of unfolding the essential nature of the soul and bringing it out to light from the hidden chambers of ignorance - ignorance that stands as a covering and hides the subtle and glorified aspect of our inner personality. Adhyatmic vikas or spiritual development is the process of revelation of the ultimate truth of our life, the Sat-Chit-Anandam, which is the greatest heritage of one and all.

The most treasured heritage is really the fountain head of all joy in life, material and divine. Adhyatmic vikas is the process to unfold the glories of the soul and to enjoy all aspects of life, material and divine. Adhyatmic vikas is the process of bringing out the great fountain-head of peace and joy hidden with us. Adhyatmic Vikas or spiritual development is the process of sharpening the mind to enable it to enter into the kingdom of the soul which is the subtlest aspect of our life, the "Anoraniyan" and directly experience its essential nature which is Sat-Chit-Anandam.

Everybody can have, should have and must have, the great privilege of enjoying the glories of the soul, the glories of the glorified aspect of everybody's life. Caste, creed or nationality is no hurdle in the realm of the soul or on the royal road to it. Soul is the individual property of everybody. It is the natural and inseparable possession, nay, the very existence of every man. Everybody has a right to enjoy his own possession. Everybody has a right to enjoy the Sat-Chit-Anandam nature of his own soul. In the most natural manner everybody has every right to enjoy permanent peace, Bliss Eternal, which is the nature of his own soul. Everybody has a birth-right to enjoy abiding peace and unbounded joy which is the essential nature of his own soul. And I hold **Everybody already possesses the capacity** of enjoying it, because it is already there in the innermost recess of everybody's heart. Nothing from outside can stop a man from experiencing the nature of his own soul. Nothing from outside can stop a man from enjoying lasting peace and permanent joy in life, for, it is the essential nature of his own soul.

The doors of Sat-Chit-Anandam are wide open alike for one and all. The path is straight and entry is free. Then why waste time in helplessness and suffer any agony in life? Why suffer when you can enjoy? Why be miserable when you can be happy? Now, let the days of misery and peacelessness be over and let their operation become tales of the past. Allow not the past history of agony to be continued in the present. Be happy and gay. Come on straight and enjoy the enjoyable. Come on and enjoy the fountain-head of all joys in life, enjoy the overbright chambers of your own inner personality. All suffering will cease, all agony will go, and all peacelessness and misery of life will simply disappear. Today you are under the divine radiance of Shri Guru Deva. Time is at hand. Under the universal benevolence of Guru Deva enjoy all glories of life, material and divine. Let not the caravan of life be tossed about and wander aimlessly in the darkness of ignorance; under the dark clouds of agony and peacelessness. Let it enjoy the royal entry into the gates of protection, peace and happiness; let it enter into the Kingdom of bliss and be blissful for ever.

Under the high flying banner of spiritual development alone can the suffering humanity find solace and peace. Spiritual development of the members of the family of nations, alone can ensure abiding peace in the world. Let the standard of everybody's mind be raised to the heights of his own inner glory and then man will feel for himself the greatness of the higher values of life and would be tempted to bring them down into practical life, and live them. Unless the steps of spiritual development are ascended and the pinnacle is reached, the hope of peace and happiness in life will ever remain unrealised. It was on the basis of this spiritual development that India was once so great and it is the glory of the same spiritual development that can make India great once again, to shine as a rising sun of peace and happiness on the horizon of the world.

I believe in something practical. Mere talks of peace and fussing over it have no practical value in any field of life. If one peaceless and miserable man of the world could be made peaceful and happy, it would mean something of value, positive and concrete for the suffering humanity. If a formula could be brought out to light a formula for transforming peacelessness and miseries of life into peace and joy of a permanent nature, that would be a boon to society and for the whole of mankind. Here we find that great boon, in the dust of the Lotus feet of Shri Guru Deva. Any number, millions and crores of the suffering souls can come and take refuge in the universal benevolence of Guru Deva and can, within a few days of Sadhana, transform their peacelessness and sufferings into real peace and permanent joy. You have already heard the experiences of many on this platform.

What else can be a greater boon in life? What else can be a better sift in lose of humanity? Guru Deva is now out to shower His Grace on one and all. Like a flood has come His Grace here in Kerala. Thousands are enjoying peace and joy in their daily life. Anybody who came, was blessed, and allowed to take the path of peace and happiness. Time is favourable, opportunity is yours. Enjoy, enjoy to the maximum the overflowing grace of Shri Guru Deva.

Mysterious are the ways of destiny. I cannot say, for how long in the atmosphere of the present age, we will succeed in holding on to this great and overflowing generosity of Shri Guru Deva. I can only speak in terms of the present. I can only offer to you the dishes ready in hand today; for tomorrow I cannot promise, for, I have nothing of my own. The bulb is shining here, but the current is coming from the power house. Any time the main switch may be put off and then the bulb will cease to spread the light. Therefore under the light of the shining bulb at hand, lay out your own lines to the powerhouse and be independent and free from the fear of darkness when the light that is, chooses to switch off.

Here is the Divine call for you. Adhyatmic Vikas Mandal of Kerala is the clarion call to awaken the world from deep slumber of ignorance, suffering and peacelessness. Here is the invitation from the universal benevolence of Shri Guru Deva; the invitation, the universal invitation for everyone suffering the agony of peacelessness and miseries, to come out of the dark night of life into the brilliant light of Divine Grace and enjoy all glories of life, material and divine.

Remember, it is nothing new that the Adhyatmic Vikas Mandal of Kerala is saying today. It is not any new message of life that the Kerala Maha Sammelan is broadcasting today. It is the same age-old voice of eternal peace and happiness for which India stands out from times immemorial. It is the same age-old voice of eternal peace and happiness which the child of Kerala, the pride of India, Shri Shankara gave out to the world more than two thousand years ago. Kerala Maha Sammelan is giving out today, on the basis of personal experience, the same age-old lesson of Shri Shankara which declared the unimpeachable universality of Anandam as the Ultimate and Absolute Reality of existence; it is the same principle of Anandam that the Eternal Vedas and Upanishads have been singing down the ages-

aanandaaddhayeva khalvimaani bhuutaani jaayante.
aanandena jaataani jiivanti.
aanandam prayantyaabhisamvishantiiti.

(Taittariya Upanishad)

[*Taittiriya Upanishad* 3:6]

"From Anandam is the whole creation born. In Anandam do the creatures live and in Anandam shall all this ultimately merge! Anandam is the one reality of the universe, ultimate and absolute. Anandam is the one reality of life eternal and absolute. Anandam is the life of every body. Anandam is the very existence of every being". This is the Anandam which the Adhyatmic Vikas Mandal of Kerala is enjoying and this is the natural and universal Anandam for whose enjoyment Kerala Maha Sammelan is raising a voice and inviting the people. This is the Anandam, which was considered to be so difficult of experience, and which now has become so easily attainable under the grace of Shri Guru Deva. It is this great miracle of Guru Deva that is tempting the Kerala Maha Sammelan to feel for the suffering humanity. Although nothing is new in the realm of the soul, the experience of it which was thought to be very difficult has now become very easy under the grace of Guru Deva. It is the joy of this easy way of approach which is encouraging Kerala Maha Sammelan to raise a voice unique and unheard of elsewhere in contemporary times. Kerala Maha Sammelan is raising a voice, that under the universal benevolence of Shri Guru Deva, MIND CONTROL IS EASY, PEACE IN DAILY LIFE IS EASY AND EXPERIENCE OF ATMANANDAM IS EASY.

The voice of Kerala Maha Sammelan is not a voice of catch-words and charming sentiments, it is a voice coming out of the acid test of personal experience.

Kerala Maha Sammelan stands only to flash out the age old light of Eternal Peace and happiness, the light Celestial blazoned by the Maharshis of yore and kept alive in the heart of the holy tradition of the Maharshis of the country; the Light serene whose one ray is sufficient to enlighten the dark nights of ignorance misery and peacelessness of the whole world. And you have seen it for yourself, how under the amazing influence of that light, hundreds of miserable and peaceless souls of Kerala have put an end to their suffering and peacelessness and have begun to enjoy peace and happiness in life. Whatever the material circumstances and surroundings of the man, his life has been raised to a high pitch of real peace and joy. Under the flash of this unfailing light of Guru Deva's Blessing, Kerala Maha Sammelan stands to proclaim sure cure for all the miseries and peacelessness of everybody everywhere in the world. This is the one treasure of Adhyatmic Vikas Mandal, on the basis of which it stands "to bring peace and happiness everywhere in everybody's every-day life".

"Today we have considered the nature of Adhyatmic Vikas, the

Omnipresence of Anandam, and the aim of the Adhyatmic Vikas Mandal. Tomorrow we shall deal with the theory of Adhyatmic Vikas, the principle of attaining peace and happiness in life.

Jai Shri Guru De...va. [14]

Day 2 Discourse

"JAI GURU DEVA"

What a happy time we have this evening. Yesterday's Shiva - Laksha - Archana Maha Yagna, it seems, has really pleased Lord Shiva much. It was the pleasure of Lord Shiva, that doubled this morning, the programme of Vishnu - Laksha - Archana. Instead of one, two Vishnu - Laksha - Archanas were performed today. This shows the delight of the Almighty Gods, Lord Shiva and Lord Vishnu, in the celebration of this Kerala Maha Sammelan of Shri Shankaracharya Brahmanand Saraswati Adhyatmic Vikas Mandal. In the midst of this great delight of Gods and under the divine radiance of Shri Guru Deva, in this holiest of the holy atmosphere of all embracing divinity, what encourages me most is the Ashirvadam of the great successor of Shri Guru Deva, Swami Shantanand Saraswati Maharaj, the present Shankaracharya Swamigal of Jyotirmath, Badarikashram. I take it to be the Ashirvadam of Lord Shiva appearing on the Lap of Lord Vishnu. Yesterday we performed Shiva - Laksha - Archana and today we received the Ashirvadam and the best of it was that today it was received in the midst of the two Vishnu - Laksha - Archanas. This is not an ordinary coincidence. I find very great meaning in it. 'SHANKARAM SHANKARACHARYAM' Shankaracharya is said to be the Avatara of Lord Shiva. And Lord Vishnu has himself said - 'ACHARYAM MAM VIJANEEYAT', i.e. know the 'Acharya' to be 'My-self'. And therefore according to Lord Vishnu, the Dharmacharya Shankaracharya is Lord Vishnu Himself. So this Ashirvadam of Bhagawan Shankaracharya is the

Ashirvadam of Lord Shiva and Lord Vishnu, both. Happy I feel to say that your Kerala Maha Sammelan has really been blessed by the All Powerful Divine influence of both Lords Shiva and Vishnu.

You have heard and received the great Ashirvadam. In that Divine Message you have heard that "Spiritualism is the backbone of India". In this one sentence His Holiness has spoken volumes and has expressed great truths of Indian Philosophy and culture. Spirituality deals with the realm of the soul, and this is the subtlest field of our existence. It is also the very basis of all the gross aspects of life.

The spirit or soul is the basic motive force of our existence and spirituality is the science of that motive force. The material science of today speaks highly of atomic power. Today the political power of a nation depends upon its resources of atomic energy. But we know in India know that the atomic energy is not the basic motive power of existence. It can only be called the basic motive force of material existence, because it is found to be very gross when compared with the powers of our mental and spiritual existence. That is the reason why India laid more importance on the field of the soul which is the ultimate motive power behind our life in all its aspects; spiritual, mental and physical. That is the reason why India always regarded the science of the soul as the best and most useful of all sciences. This is the reason why His Holiness has called spirituality as the backbone of India. Under the high-flown banner of spiritualism alone can India regain its past glory, and cultured in the spirit alone, can the children of India be great masters of Nature and Universe. This is what His Holiness has meant, when he said "Spiritualism is the back-bone of India". It is the keystone of the arch of all developments. Spirituality trains the mind to rise from the experience of the subtlest field of objectivity and enables it to transcend the field of objectivity for entering the realm of the soul, the field of Eternal Bliss. Spirituality trains the mind to enter into the realm of the soul and becomes all powerful for enjoyment of all the glories of life, mental and material.

By a perfect system of spiritual development, the great sages of yore have given to us the keys to lay open the treasures of great energy and power hidden within us. The Mundaka Upanishad declares that anybody who establishes himself on the highest attitude of spiritualism becomes capable of developing his will-power and mental force to such a great extent that he can attain any object or get into any strata of the universe by a mere "SANKALPA" or a thought. This is the glory of spirituality which can make a man worthy of attainment of everything by the agency of thought alone. This all powerful spirituality is valued and cherished most in India. That is why His Holiness has said it to be the backbone of our country. But this spirituality tends to be ignored today in the heat of the modern currents and Western ideologies. If India is to become strong and great let her not sleep over spirituality, the science of the very motive force of existence.

If Society is to become great, every man has to become great spiritually. Be he a beggar or a millionaire, if only he turns spiritual can he have peace and happiness, and enjoy all the glories of life spiritual, mental and material. This is the great strength of our ancient wisdom, the great efficacy of spiritual development for bringing peace and happiness to every body irrespective of his material standard of life or status in society. This is the reason why His Holiness has said that "Spiritualism is the backbone of India".

We feel the flash of the spirituality of our Guru Deva in the Ashirvadam of His great successor. We in Kerala today are immensely blessed by this great Ashirvadam and in reverence we offer our devotional pranams to the Lotus feet of His Holiness.

Yesterday, we considered the Omnipresence of Anandam. Anandam, which is present everywhere and pervading. As a matter of fact everything is but Anandam in its essential nature. Just as a mountain of snow is nothing but water, so also the whole Universe is nothing but Anandam. Just as the different shapes and forms of pots are made of the same clay, so also the different objects in the Universe are made of the same formless Anandam. Anandam is the ultimate reality of the Universe.

The world of concrete forms and objects is made from the formless. This truth of Indian Philosophy has been supported by the findings of the modern science also. According to the electronic theory of modern science, electrons and protons are the ultimate reality of matter. All these different forms of matter are nothing but involved energy. This solid concrete wall is nothing but abstract formless energy. This concrete mike, all its components and the whole mechanism of it, is nothing but abstract formless energy. All these multifarious material objects in phenomenon are nothing but formless abstract energy. No sensible man can refuse to accept this finding of the modern material science. Now if we are able to conceive that the whole material universe is nothing but formless energy, then it is easy to conceive, on similar lines, that all this concrete universe is nothing but Abstract Formless Brahman "Sarava Khalu Idam Brahma". All this is Brahman and 'Anandam Brahmano Vijnan' i.e. Brahman is Anandam. All this is Anandam. Sat-Chit-Anandam.

To be more clear - Electrons and protons of the modern science, seen through the Indian system of analysis of the universe are manifestations of Agni-Tatwa and Vayu-Tatwa combined. The energy of the electrons and protons is due to the Agni-Tatwa and motion in them is due to Vayu-Tatwa. Thus we find, the present day science has reached up to Vayu-Tatwa in the field of analysis of the universe. But our Indian analysis of the universe has found out much more of the subtler phases of existence. According to our system of analysis - finer than the Agni-Tatwa and the very cause of it is the Vayu-Tatwa; finer than the Vayu-Tatwa and the very cause of it is the Akash-Tatwa; finer than the Akash-Tatwa and the very cause of it is the Aham-Tatwa; finer than the Aham-Tatwa and the very cause of it is the Mahat-Tatwa; finer than the Mahat-Tatwa and the very cause of it is the Prakriti-Tatwa; and finer than the Prakriti-Tatwa and the very cause of it is the Brahma-Tatwa which is the Ultimate Reality, the subtlest "Anoraniyan", Sat-Chit-Anandam. This is the analysis of the universe according to our Indian thought which speaks of universality of Anandam and establishes that Anandam is the ultimate and absolute Reality of existence. This universality of

Anandam we have already considered yesterday.

Today we shall try to find out why this Omnipresent Anandam evades common experience. And having found out the cause, we shall try to find out the means to eradicate it. A thing which is present everywhere has gone out of our experience! Obviously it seems to be a great paradox. But this is experience in life which cannot be denied. Omnipresence of Anandam we accept intellectually, but Omnipresence of 'Dukham' is our day to day experience in life. Which of the two is correct? What is the truth of life? Is it to remain a paradox or an unsolved problem of existence? If Anandam is the reality of life then all our experience of the world which are, in one way or the other, allied with 'Dukham' are the experiences of a non-reality. The Reality of life which is Anandam of unbounded nature is not at all being experienced. A real life of all Anandam, the most cherishable aspect of our being is out of our consciousness. What is the reason? Something seems to have gone wrong with our machinery of experience. Our machinery of experience is able to experience only one aspect, the gross aspect of the ultimate reality and fails to experience the subtler aspect of its essential nature.

There are two states of the ultimate Reality Brahman - the unmanifested state, and the manifested state. In the unmanifested state the Brahman is 'Anoraniyan' the atom of the atoms, the minute of the minutae; and in this unmanifested minute state, its essential nature is Anandam Sat-Chit-Anandam; but in its manifested state the Anandam becomes latent to give rise to other properties which come on the scene of the manifested objects, just as the fluid property of water becomes latent i.e. when water becomes ice. Water in its essential nature is Fluid and transparent, but when it becomes ice it is translucent or opaque, and solid. The solidity and opacity of ice are quite contrary to the fluidity and transparency of water. When water becomes ice the transparency of water becomes latent giving rise to its opposite characteristic of solidity. Thus we see, when a thing transforms its original and essential characteristics it becomes latent and gives rise to different characteristics which may even be contrary to the original. These changed characteristics deviate from the original characteristics according to intensity of the change Vapour, cloud, mist, snow and ice are the various manifestations of water; Water itself is liquid, but of its manifestations some are gaseous and others are solids.

This analogy helps explanation of the experience of misery (or Dukham) in the midst of the Omnipresence of Anandam. When the unmanifested Brahman becomes manifested, the Sat-Chit-Anandam characteristics of it become latent to give rise to other characteristics which may even be Asat, Achit and Anandam. The never changing (Sat), absolute existence (Chit) and absolute bliss (Anandam) which are the characteristics of the Unmanifested 'Anoraniyan' become latent giving rise to their opposite characteristics, viz. the ever changing, relative existence, and relative joy characteristics of the manifested objects and universe.

I think it is clear now, why the quality of Omnipresent Anandam is not exhibited on the forms and objects of the Universe. Although Anandam is the essential nature of the ultimate reality of the material objects, it has become latent in them and only the qualities of the gross objectivity are being experienced at the outset.

Hail to the perfect system of Indian philosophy which offers the theory and practice of directly experiencing the Sat-Chit-Anandam; and hail to the Maharshis of India who have opened the gates of spiritual glory in material life and who have laid out practical paths for experiencing the nature of the 'Anoraniyan' in the midst of all this manifested gross universe, and have floated the ideology of Jeevan-Mukti, the most exalted state of human existence, the state of constant experience of Sat-Chit-Anandam.

Today we have to look into this ideology of Jeevan-Mukti, and consider the theory and practice for experiencing Sat-Chit-Anandam.

Our instrument for experience viz. the mind, is constantly engaged in apprehending objects through the senses which can only perceive the gross objectivity. Our physical eyes can see only the gross form. When the form is minute or subtle our eyes fail to perceive it and we need a microscope to see it. Similarly ears can hear only gross sounds. When the sound becomes subtle, our ears fail to catch it. Similar is the case with the other senses of perception. Because these senses can experience only gross objects, the mind, which is always experiencing things through the senses, is able to experience only the gross field of manifested objectivity. Due to the long-standing experience of gross objectivity, the mind itself has become gross and blunt. In its gross condition the mind naturally fails to enter into the realm of the subtlest "Anoraniyan", and that is how it misses the Anandam which is Omnipresent.

If the mind could be trained to apprehend the experience in the subtler fields in objectivity itself, it will definitely become sharp and in its increasing sharpness can definitely enter into the realm of "Anoraniyan", the Sat-Chit-Anandam, and have the direct experience of it. The path of spiritual Sadhana lies therefore in training the mind to march through the field of subtler objectivity, in spiritual development.

For practice we can select the field of objectivity pertaining to any of the senses of perception - sense of sight, hearing, smell or touch. In any of the fields we are required to reduce the objectivity to its increasingly subtler stages and help the mind to go on experiencing them till it reaches the subtlest stage of objectivity, and its experiences.

At this stage when the mind is able to experience the subtlest in objectivity, it becomes sharp enough to enter into the realm of "Anoraniyan" which transcends the field of subtlest objectivity, it becomes sharp enough to enter into the realm of "Anoraniyan" which transcends the field of subtlest objectivity and in this state it tastes the essential nature of that realm, which is Sat-Chit-Anandam.

If the mind is proceeding through sound, the field of Anoraniyan is the field which transcends the field of subtlest sound, which is the field of "no sound", i.e. "Ni Shabdam"; and the Upanishads call it "Paramam Padam", "Ni-Shabdam Paramam Padam". This Paramam Padam is Sat-Chit-Anandam in its essential nature. The man experiencing it, rises to Eternal life of Eternal life - a life of Eternal life - a life of Eternal Bliss and Absolute Consciousness.

For training the mind through sound we can take any word. Even the word "mike" can be taken. By reducing the sound of the word "mike" to its subtler and still subtler stages and allowing the mind to go on experiencing all the stages one by one, the mind can be trained to be so sharp as to enter into the subtlest stage of the sound 'mike', transcending which it will automatically get into the realm of Sat-Chit-Anandam and experience it. Thus we find that any sound can serve our purpose of training the mind to become sharp. But we do not select any sound like 'mike', flower, table, pen, wall etc. because such ordinary sounds can do nothing more than merely sharpening the mind; whereas there are some special sounds which have the additional efficacy of producing vibrations whose effects are found to be congenial to our way of life. This is the scientific reason why we do not select any word at random. For our practice we select only the suitable mantras of personal Gods. Such mantras fetch to us the grace of personal Gods and make us happier in every walk of life.

While making a reference to the mantras in this manner. I feel like touching a very vital aspect of Sadhana, which things are blurred in the present atmosphere of too much talk of Vedanta.

Obviously enough there are two ways of life, the way of the Sanyasi and the way of life of a householder. One is quite opposed to the other. A Sanyasi renounces everything of the world, whereas a householder needs and accumulates everything. Shastras declare both ways of life to be the paths of emancipation. Both are said to be the "Moksha Marga" Nivarthi Marga and 'Privrithi Marga'. The one realises, through renunciation and detachment, while the other goes through all attachments and accumulation of all that is needed for physical life. We have two different sets of Mantras to suit the two ways of life. Mantras for the Sanyasis have the effect of increasing the sense of detachment and renunciation and also have the power of destroying the objects of worldly affections, if there should survive any such objects for him. Quite contrary to this are the Mantras suitable for the householder which have the efficacy of harmonising and enriching the material aspect of life also.

The Mantras of the Sanyasi have a destructive effect in the material field of life, whereas the Mantras suited to the householder envisage constructive values also.

"Om" is the Mantra for the Sanyasi. The Sanyasi repeats "Om" "Om" "Om". It is given to him at the time of 'Sanyas - Diksha', at the time when he has completely renounced attachment to the world. Renunciation and detachment increase with the repetition of 'Om'. 'Om' is chanted aloud by a Sanyasi to put on end to his desires. Desires are destroyed by loudly chanting the mantra 'Om'. And if there is any desire deeply rooted in the mind of a Sanyasi, the chanting of 'Om' will result in the destruction of the object of such desire in order to make the Sanyasi, wholly desireless. The Sanyasi thus attains Peace through the renunciation and destruction of desires, whereas the peace comes to the householder when his needs are satisfied, when his desires are fulfilled. The mantras for the householders have the effect of fulfilling the desires.

If unfortunately, the householder begins to repeat the pranava Mantra viz. 'Om', 'Om' 'Om' he experiences destructive effects in his material life. The effect starts with monetary loss and then goes on to destroy objects of affection, one by one. Such a man, when he finds loss of money and separation from the dear ones, he is reduced to utter peacelessness and frustration. Where is the chance of spiritual development or experience of Peace and happiness for such a dejected soul? The path of peacelessness and misery in the world, cannot lead to Eternal happiness. If the man is proceeding towards Eternal happiness every day he should feel the increase of peace and happiness, and this alone will assure him that he is proceeding towards abiding peace and eternal happiness. If you walk towards the light you should be able to feel the increase of light at every step. If you are spending some time in devotion to God, you should feel peace and happiness in life. If you are not feeling peace and happiness you should be wise enough to doubt the correctness of your devotion, you should be wise enough to think that your method of devotion is wrong, that the Mantras that you are repeating do not suit you. The mantras that suit the Sanyasis can never suit the householders. Hundreds of God-loving and God-fearing families, have been ruined due to the destructive effects of Sanyasa Mantra viz. "Om". "Om" destroys desires and also destroys the objects of desires and therefore it produces calmness of mind and renunciation and detachment from material life only to Sanyasis when they repeat Om; to them it brings the experience of peace of mind and from this experience they generally recommend the chanting of 'Om' to their followers. But when a householder repeats 'Om', he experiences that as long as he is repeating 'Om' he feels peace of mind, but when he comes out to indulge in business or household work, he finds he finds that the air is against his desire and schemes. The silencing effect on the mind and destructive effects in material life, both are lived side by side. Some people say that we should ignore material life in regard to the devotional practices and Mantras. But this is a fool's ideology. Can you possibly ignore the considerations of material life, when the Mantras do affect it? Select a path which will make you happier in your material life also. Do not live in a fool's paradise. Do not think that your sufferings and miseries of today will work as reservations in the galleries of heaven for tomorrow. Be peaceful and happy in the present and try to make this state permanent. This is the path of Deliverance in Life Jeevan-Mukti, the most exalted state in human existence, the state of abiding Peace and Eternal Bliss. And this you are entitled to have through correct and suitable Sadhana. And because the Mantras play an important role in the field of Sadhana, you must be very very careful in the selection of the Mantra. The theory of Mantras is the theory of sound. It is most scientific and natural. Ladies should never repeat any Mantra beginning with Om. The pronunciation of Om is like fire to the ladies. This is the practical experience of many devoted ladies who repeated 'Om Namah Shivaya' or 'Om Namonarayanaya' or

'Om Namo Bhagawate Vasudevaya' or any such mantra beginning with Om. It cannot be God's wish that you should suffer in your devotion to him. Do not cling to the unhelpful Mantras. The moment you find you have got into the wrong train, it is wise to get down from it as soon as possible. It is foolish to stick on to the wrong train and go wherever it takes you.

I hold that the devotees of the Almighty God should not suffer at all. That is the fundamental condition of the path to Eternal Bliss. I hold that bliss or happiness should increase at every step till we get into the realm of eternal happiness. I hold that the devotees of the god should enjoy peace and happiness at every stage, because he is the fountain head of all peace and happiness. It cannot be that our march towards the light should at any stage increase the darkness before us. The march towards the Anant Anandam must give the experience of increase of Anandam at every step and in every walk of life.

The devotee of the Almighty cannot suffer. If he is found to suffer, he cannot be said to be a devotee of God. It pains me when I find people suffering in the name of God and devotion. I offer an open invitation to such aspirants and seekers of God. I invite them to come out of their miserable devotion, and step into the peaceful blissful chambers of Sadhana, blessed and illuminated by the divine radiance of Shri Guru Deva. I invite them to put an end to their sufferings and peacelessness and crown their day to day life with success peace and joy. Do not waste time and life. Life is to enjoy. So come on to the field of all joy. The gates of all glories of life are open for you. "Make hay when the sun shines". Avail the opportunity in hand and enjoy life to the fullest. [15]

––––––––––

Day 3 Discourse

Today is Nava-Ratri, the most auspicious and holy-day of the
Divine Mother. From the very early morning today we had been
feeling the thrills of the divine vibrations of Lalita - Laksha -
Archana. We had been feeling the joy and great delight of the
universal mother just as a child feels on the lap of his dear mother,
when mother is happy. How much the Mother Divine is pleased
with the Kerala Maha Sammelan. There was the programme of
only two Laksha Archana today but Laksha Archanas were
simultaneously performed this morning. This is nothing but the
sure and positive indication of the great pleasure and satisfaction
of the Divine Mother who so kindly and profusely blessed her
children of Kerala. (Clappings) Blessed you are my dear good
souls. Fortunate you are. You have been blessed by Vishnu, Shiva
and Shakti in the Divine presence of Guru Deva. (Clappings and
rings of Jai Shri Guru Deva from delegates).

Today, as if on the happy lap of the Divine Mother we have
assembled here to discuss and finalise the scheme of peace and
happiness in life. We have been discussing this matter for the last
two days and I think today we shall be able to complete it.

Yesterday I had remarked that according to my methods of
Sadhana even a busy house-holder can enjoy all the benefits of
mind control and peace in daily life and can very well experience
Atmananandam and that renunciation is not at all necessary for it.
Today one learned man wanted me to clarify how my statement
reconciles with the teachings of the Upanishads which declare that
Atmananda can not be had unless everything has been renounced.

"Yawat Sarwam Na
Santyaktam Tawat-Atma Na Labhyate"

and "Tyage Naike Amritatwam Anshuh"

I hold that the teachings of the Upanishads are the bare truths
of Existence and the Eternal Laws of Nature. Every Shruti is

perfectly all right, in its correct sense. It is bare fact that
Atmananda cannot be experienced unless every thing has been
renounced, i.e. unless the mind is free from everything of the
objective field. This teaching of the Upanishads is one truth of
life, and another truth of life is that the householder can enjoy
Atmananda remaining in his family affairs and without
renouncing the world. Now we have to see how both of these
apparently opposed truths are not really conflicting. We have to
see in other words, how they are the same.

The emphasis of the Shruti on the necessity of Tyaga for
Realisation has got to be scrutinised to see how this requirement is
fulfilled in the life of a householder whose life apparently is full
of Raga as opposed to Tyaga.

For a clear understanding we shall analyse the state of mind of
a Tyagi. If some monetary or golden offerings are made to a man
who professes to be a Tyagi, he says "remove this from here."
Now analyse the condition of the mind of this Tyagi. When gold
is brought before him, he sees it as gold and the impression of its
value is carried on to his mind. When the mind recognises the
value of gold, obviously the gold has occupied a seat in the mind.
Once the gold finds a place in the mind, clearly enough, it
becomes the abode of gold and this is nothing but acceptance of
gold and not its renunciation or Tyaga. All of us know that a
wealthy man never carries wealth on his head. All the wealth
remains in the bank, and only the impression of its value is carried
in the mind. Thus possession of wealth is nothing but an idea of
wealth in the mind, and therefore, when the idea of wealth of gold
has come to the mind, i.e. when the gold has occupied a seat in the
mind, then it can only be "possession" of gold and not"
renunciation (Tyaga) of it, irrespective of whether the gold
remains near or far.

Thus we find Tyaga, in its true sense, has little to do with the
objects remaining near or far. Tyaga therefore, has to be defined
as giving up or foregoing the mental impressions of objects
perceived. In other words, Tyaga is keeping the mind free from
the impressions of values and natures of the objects perceived by

the senses: or Tyaga is, not allowing the objects of senses to leave the impressions of their qualities in the mind.

This is the essential meaning of Tyaga mentioned in the Shruti referred above. This ideology of perfect Tyaga has to be lived by all those who want to realise the Atman or Brahman. Since realisation is the ultimate aim of both the ways of life, it goes without saying that both the house-holder and Sanyasi have to attain this ideology of Tyaga, and then alone will it be possible for them to realise the Truth. We shall analyse and see in what manner it is possible for a 'Pravrithi Margi Grihastha' (House-holder) to fulfil this requirement of Shruti through his own way or life which is obviously full of "Raga" (attachment).

By nature, a house holder is a "Ragi". Raga as opposed to Tyaga, is embedded deep down in the nature of a house-holder. Wife, children, friends, relatives, money, name and fame, for example, are seven points of attachment (Raga) for a house-holder. He is always devoted to these points of attachment. To these seven points of Raga, he adds one more point and begins to devote himself to this eighth point of Raga also, as he has been devoting to the seven others. This eighth point of Raga is his "ISHTAM" - his personal God - his beloved Deity - Almighty. "SAT-CHIT-ANANDAM". Gradually, he experiences that the eighth point of Raga is capable of giving him more Peace and Happiness in life than the others. When he devotes himself and meditates on the name and form (NAMA AND RUPA) of the LORD, he begins to experience some ANANDAM and also the Grace of the Lord in every walk of life. This experience of Peace and Anandam is Sadhana. And Sadhana naturally increases his devotion to God and makes him more and more attached to Him. Thus he develops intensity of Raga for the ISHTAM. Gradually, this final Raga goes on increasing and this increase of Raga and Love for the ISHTAM enables the Grihastha to feel the presence of his 'ISHTAM' always with him, in all his ways of life, in all his thought, speech and action. The man, although acting on the world as before, experiences that throughout all his actions the idea of his personal deity predominates in his mind and the actions and experiences of the senses fail to engage his mind with that great intensity with which they used to do before. Thus the objects of the senses fail to leave any enduring impression of their values in his mind, and this is the state of mind of a real Tyagi as explained above. This is how through the virtue of Raga, a householder - a full-fledged Ragi finds his way to place himself on the plane where he is essentially a Tyagi also. And this is how a householder is able to establish himself in a position to meet the requirement of the said Shruti for Realisation. And this is how, through his own quality of "Raga" a householder can very well establish himself on the plane of human perfection, the plane of Jeevan-Mukti, the most exalted state of existence, the state of Perpetual Peace and Bliss Eternal.

Thus we have seen that it is not at all necessary for the householder to go for a direct practice of "Tyaga" or "Vairagya" (Renunciation) for realisation. That practice is unnatural for him, antagonistic to his nature and opposed to his way of life. If a householder begins to practice detachment in his life, he finds himself in a plane where he is not able to reconcile the mental attitude of detachment with his physical tendencies in life viz. one of all-attachment. He need march only through the quality of Raga which is rooted deep down in his nature and is the essential quality of his heart and mind. He needs only to increase his Raga (Attachment) for his Ishtam or God. And to increase Raga for Ishtam (attachment for God) it is not at all necessary to practice Vairagya (detachment from or renunciation of the world). To love one child more than others, it is not necessary that all others should be ignored or kept away. If you have seven children you maintain your love for all but if you come to know of some brilliant qualities of a particular child, you begin to pay more attention to him without ignoring the others. Maintaining your love for all, you begin to love him more than others. Decrease of love for others is not all necessary for increase of love for one. The motivation is the knowledge of his superior or better qualities. In the same way, it is not at all necessary to renounce the world for the sake of increasing the Love of God. What is necessary is that the Sat-Chit-Anandam - quality of God should come to the limelight of personal knowledge or experience. Once you begin to experience Anandam through the Nama-Japa or Rupa-Dhyanam of the Lord. He is bound to attract you more than any other object of attraction in the world, because that joy is much greater than the joy received through any worldly means of joy. And this is the reason why I say that renunciation is not at all an essential requisite for God Realisation. According to my methods of Sadhana, a householder can very well experience that great joy, unbounded, and can very well realise God without any direct practice of Renunciation whatsoever. Methods of Sadhana, which I am advocating these days, are simple and easy to practice. Everybody can easily practice in the most comfortable posture for half an hour or one hour in the morning and evening daily and soon experience the great advantages of it. Normally it does not take more than one or two weeks for a man to experience the great unbounded joy - called Samadhi or Atmanandam and it does not take more than about seven days to experience calmness of mind or peace in day-to-day life. However peaceless or worried a man may be feeling, if he but starts the Sadhana, he is sure to feel some calmness and lightness in the mind from the very first or second day of Sadhana and he is sure to feel completely peaceful and happy within about seven days. This looks to be a miracle, but it is so. And the truth of this statement has been supported by the personal experiences of those who have seriously taken to the practice and have narrated their experiences before you on this platform.

All these attainments are only due to the blessings of Shri Guru Deva. I am glad that hundreds of respectable families and thousands of people in Kerala have taken good advantage of my stay in these parts and they are enjoying 'Heavenly Bliss' as some of them have called it, in their own earthly homes; the 'Peace of the Himalayas' in the midst of all business and their householder affairs. Gates of Heavens are now open for them in their life on earth. this is the greatness of Shri Guru Deva's Blessings. Here is the positive experience of 'Heavenly Bliss' during life time. Come on who desires for it, is all the word of value that I can give out to you now towards the end of your Kerala Maha Sammelan.

JAI SHRI GURU DEVA

(Rings of Jai Guru Deva from the audience numbering not less
than ten thousand). [16]

'Ready to start for Avabrithasnanam GURU DEVA'S portrait placed on the
Simhasanam with Chathram, Chamaram and all other paraphenalia mounted on
an improvised chariot.'
[*'Beacon Light of the Himalayas'*, page 52]

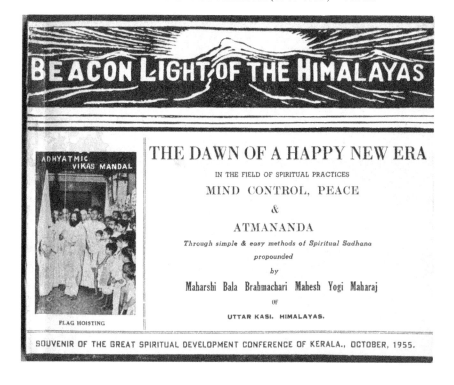

BEACON LIGHT OF THE HIMALAYAS

THE DAWN OF A HAPPY NEW ERA
IN THE FIELD OF SPIRITUAL PRACTICES
MIND CONTROL, PEACE
&
ATMANANDA
Through simple & easy methods of Spiritual Sadhana
propounded
by
Maharshi Bala Brahmachari Mahesh Yogi Maharaj
OF
UTTAR KASI, HIMALAYAS.

SOUVENIR OF THE GREAT SPIRITUAL DEVELOPMENT
CONFERENCE OF KERALA., OCTOBER, 1955.

BEACON LIGHT OF THE HIMALAYAS
THE DAWN OF A HAPPY NEW ERA
IN THE FIELD OF SPIRITUAL PRACTICES
MIND CONTROL, PEACE
&
ATMANANDA
Through simple & easy methods of Spiritual Sadhana
propounded
by
Maharshi Bala Brahmachari Mahesh Yogi Maharaj
OF
UTTAR KASI, HIMALAYAS

**SOUVENIR OF THE GREAT SPIRITUAL DEVELOPMENT
CONFERENCE OF KERALA., OCTOBER, 1955**

Adhyatmic Vikas Mandal – Spiritual Development Circle

'Our Spiritual Guide'
'His Holiness Maharshi Bala Brahmachari Mahesh Yogi Maharaj.
Uttarkasi, Himalayas.'

Maharshi's Message to

Oh ye of the peaceless and
suffering humanity !
        My happiness desires to
root out your suffering. Will
you extend your arm and allow
me to lift you up from the mire
of misery and peacelessness ?
        Come on, here is the call
of peace and joy for you. Here is
an invitation, a cordial invitation
for you all to come and enjoy the
Blissful Grace and All Powerful
Blessings of my Lord the Great
Swami Brahmanand Saraswati,
the Great among the greats of the
Himalayas. I have found a treasure
in the Dust of His Lotus Feet and
now I invite you to share it with
me and make yourself happy.
        Come on; I invite you to get
into the Blissful Realm of His
Universal Benevolence. See, the
path is straight and entry is free.
Come on with faith and you will find

Peaceless and Sufferings

that the very cause of your peacelessness and misery will be eradi-
cated and you will be adorned with
lasting peace and real happiness
in your day to day life.

"Feel not disappointment in
life and shirk not from your responsibilities in despair. Whatever are
your circumstances, rich or poor, if
you are not in peace and if you
want peace and happiness, come
on with faith and you will have it.
Here is the message of hope for you.
Here is the Divine Call of rescue for
you. Peace and joy of living await
you. Do not reject it. Come on
and have it.

The sun of Guru Deva's Blessings
is now up on the horizon. Wake up
from the deep slumber of apathy and
agony and enjoy all glories of life
material and divine.

Bal Brahmachari Mahesh.

28.11.55

'His Divinity Jagadguru Bhagwan Sankaracharya
Anant Shri Vibhushit Maha Yogi Raj "Brahma Leen"
Swami Brahmananda Saraswathi Maharaj, Jyotir Math,
Badarikashram, Himalayas.'

OUR GUIDING LIGHT

By

His Holiness Maharshi Bala Brahmachari Mahesh Yogi Maharaj.

Our guiding light is the ever-shining, never-setting sun of the Divine Grace. Ever the same constant as the northern star and bright as the mid-day sun, our Guiding Light is the Divine Grace of Shri Guru Deva Maha Yogiraj Swami Brahmananda Saraswati Maharaj, the most illustrious in the galaxy of the Jagad Guru Shankaracharyas.

Our Guiding Light is the celestial Light of "The Supreme"[1], the heatless, smokeless light of the Divine Effulgence, of "Vedanta Incarnate"[2] the pure, serene, ever-guiding light of "the embodiment of Sanathana Dharma"[3]. Our Guiding Light is the light of perfection which emanated from the "Personified Divinity" and permeated the atmosphere of earth and heaven, to keep the path lighted for all times, to guide man to the Gods in heaven and the Gods to men on earth to elevate them. Our Guiding Light is the Universal loving benevolence of "Manifested Godhood" whose 'darshan' was the one solution to the miseries in life, and now whose rememberance is the one cure for all ills and sufferings in life[4].

[1] Justice Paul of international fame described Shri Guru Deva as **'The Supreme'** in his presidential address at the conference of the eminent philosophers of the world during the Silver Jubilee Celebrations of the Institute of Indian Philosophers held at Calcutta in December 1950.

[2] In the same conference Dr. S. Radhakrishnan addressed Shri Guru Deva as "Vedanta Incarnate"

[3] Describing the personality of Guru Deva, the great Sanskrit Poet of the Aryavartha Santhana Dharma Maha Mandal, Kanpur, wrote in his poem मूर्तिष्मान् एष धर्मः "Murtiman eish dharmah" i.e. He is **<u>Dharma Embodiment.</u>**

[4] Another famous Sanskrit Poet of Benares, 'Ashu Kavi' Pt. Veni Madava Sastri 'Shashtrartha Maharathi' wrote in his prayer to Guru Deva - ब्रह्मानन्द सरस्वतिं गुरुवरं प्रत्यक्ष देवं भजे। ["Brahmaananda Sarasvatim guruvaram <u>pratyaksha devam</u> bhaje."]

i.e. I bow down to Swami Brahmanand Saraswathi who is the Great Guru and 'Present God' or 'God in Person' or "Personified Divinity."

He was the one novelty, who was divine grandeur "par excellence". His sitting posture, His standing pose, His style of lying down, His royal pace. His movements and His silence in samadhi; everything was an inspiration and joy to one and all who had the eye to see and good fortune to enjoy. When He sat; His sitting pose attracted and inspired the eyes that fell on Him and inspired the minds and hearts that came under the divine aura of His gracious presence. His sitting posture was the ememplary sitting pose of a perfect Yogi, and when He walked, oh! it was a sight which Royalties have enjoyed and Gods have cherished on earth. Such was the perfection of His Personality, every aspect of which was an inspiration for one and all.

Words that fell from His lips surcharged the atmosphere with vibrations holy and divine. Every word that He spoke charmed the ear and captivated the heart. The charm of His voice surpassed the melody of music. Well disciplined music of the best musician of the world would not charm as much as His simple words charmed the child and the old alike. Whatever He spoke was heard and enjoyed with undivided attention by one and all. His moving lips were the one point of focus for a million eyes gathered to listen to His evening discourses. Spell bound sat the audience with captivated mind and heart in His presence. It was an atmosphere of all joy around him. It was Anandam vibrating around Brahmanandam - (The "Conditioned Brahmanandam" was as it were conditioned transcendental Brahmanandam). When His words thrilled the air with joy, the whole atmosphere was surcharged with delight as if waves were set up in the silent ocean of Omnipresent Anandam - The Immoveable was moved by "the

Expression of the Inexpressible".

It was the grandeur of the perfection of inner and outer personalities of Guru Deva that attracted the eyes and hearts of the elevated and learned pandits of Bharata and that tempted them to adorn their learning by finding a suitable expression for the inexpressible Divinity. An expression was found in the words "Ananta Shri Vibhushit" which means "beautified with ever-the-same immeasurable grandeur". This is an expression in Sanskrit Language which was used for the first time in the history of India, to synthesise his Greatness.

In the English Language, his devotees felt that the expression "His Holiness" didnot adequately describe this personified Divine Effulgence; and so the new expression of "His Divinity" was used. With such unique adoration of newer and fuller grandeur, transcending the glories of the expressions of antiquity, was worshipped the holy name of Guru Deva, the living expression of Upanishadic Reality, the embodiment of the transcendental Divinity.

He was Maha Yogiraj in the family of the Yogis of Indias and was held by the "Gnanies" as personified Brahmanandam, the living expression of - "Poornamadah Poornamidam"*. The divine radiance blooming forth from His shining personality revealed the truth of "Poornamidam" (this manifested Brahman is poorna) and His Sahaja-Samadhi brought home the truth of both - "Poornamadah" and "Poornamidam". It was the perfection of this great spiritual Master which innovated a religious and spiritual renaisance in northern India and where ever He travelled.

* That unmanifested Brahman is perfect and This Manifested Brahman is (also) perfect.

This Great Pride of India was "Rajaram" in his early days when he was the love of his great family and was cherished as the "rising sun" in the community of Mishra Brahmans of village Gana, near Ayodhya in Uttarpradesh. He was born on Margashirsh Shukla 10 Samvat 1928 (equivalent to December

1871) with a silver spoon in his mouth, but his hour of nativity claimed him for the recluse order and not for that of the secular.

At the tender age of nine, when the other children of the world were mostly busy in playgrounds, he had matured in the idea of renunciation; and by continuous and deep thinking was convinced of the futility and evanescence of worldly pleasures. He realised so early that real and lasting happiness cannot be had without the realisation of the Divine. The joys and pleasures that are obtained from the phenomenal world are mere shadows and smudged images of the ideal happiness and bliss, that is not far from man but exists in his own heart, enveloped by the dark clouds of ignorance and illusion. When he was barely nine years old he left home, and went to the Himalayas in search of God, the Light that dispels the great darkness in the human mind, the darkness that stands between man and the inner Enlightenment.

During the search for a perfect spiritual guide, he came across many masters and good beginners but none of them came up to the ideal that he had set for himself. He desired his spiritual master to be not only well-versed in philosophic learning but also to be a person of realisation; and over and above these dual achievements he also wished his Master to be a life-celibate - perhaps the natural and legitimate desire of an aspirant who himself had decided to maintain that high ideal for life.

In the world as it is constituted to-day, to find a personality combining these three conditions and attributes is difficult, if not altogether impossible, and so the young truth-seeker had to wander far and long before he arrived at the goal of his search. After about five years of wandering on the Himalayas, he reached the township of Uttar-Kashi. In that "valley of the saints", at that small and distant Himalayan hermitage there resided in those days a great spiritual master, Swami Krishnanand Saraswati Maharaj, a sage deeply versed in philosophical lore, representing a rare and perfect blend of theory and practice, of learning and realisation.

To that realised soul, the young ascetic surrendered himself for being initiated into the mysterious realms of the spirit, whose real key-practices are attainable not from books and treatises, but only from perfect spiritual masters, who pass these top-secret practices from heart to heart.

After sometime with the permission and order of his master he entered a cave at Uttar-Kashi with a resolve not to come out before he had realised the Light Supreme. His desire to attain the Highest knowledge was not merely an ideal wish or intention; it was a mighty, overpowering determination that burned like fire in his heart. It permeated every particle of his being and bade him not to rest or stop before the complete realisation of the Bliss Eternal.

Soon he arrived at the Heatless, Smokeless Effulgent of the Self and realised the Divine Truth, the Ultimate Supreme Reality, Satchitanandam.

The greatest attainment of a saint is his life itself, the high edifice of a realised Upanishadic living that developes under the stress of rigorous discipline and sincere truth-seeking. To understand that inner personality one must approach such realised souls with an open and receptive mind, and try to visualise the great internal life that is the basis of their actual and real form of living.

At the age of 34 he was initiated into the order of Sanyas by his Master and then he again proceeded to Blessed Solitude, the only Blessedness. This time he did not go to the Himalayas but went to the Amarkantakas, the source of the holy river Narbada.

For the greater part of his life he has lived in quiet lonely places, the habitats of lions and leopards, in hidden caves and thick forests where even the mid-day sun frets and fumes in vain to dispel the darkness that may be said to have a permanent abode in those solitary and distant regions of Vindhyagiris and Amarkanthas.

He was out of sight of man but was well marked in the eyes of the destiny of the country. For more than one and a half centuries the light of Jyotirmath was extinct, and North India had no Dharmacharya to guide the religious and spiritual destiny of the people. Here was a bright light of spiritual glory well adorned by the perfect discipline of Sanatana Dharma; but it was hidden in the caves and valleys, in the thick forests and mountains of central India, as though the blessed solitude was giving a proper shape and polish to the personality which was to enlighten the religious and spiritual darkness that had overtaken the country, by the Flash of His mere presence.

It took a long time, twenty years, to persuade him to come out of His loneliness and accept the holy throne of Shankaracharya of Jyotirmath in Badarkashramam. At the age of 72, in the year 1941, a well marked time in the political and religious history of India, He was installed as Shankaracharya of Jyotirmath, and that was a turning point in the destiny of the nation. The political freedom of the country dawned under His Divine Grace and He was worshipped by Dr. Rajendra Prasad, the first President of the Indian Union.

His Policy of Dharma-prachar was all embracing. He inspired all alike and gave a lift to every body in his religious, virtuous, moral and spiritual life. He was never a leader of any one party. All parties found a common leader-head in Him. All the differences and dissensions of various castes, creeds and sampradayas dissolved in His presence and every party felt to be a thread in the warp and woof of society, and that all the threads make the cloth and that no thread can be taken out with advantage from it. Such was His Universality and all embracing nature.

One unique principle of the Great sage that distinguished him completely from other living, saints, was that he did not accept money as a gift from his visitors or disciples. He was running the greatest religious institution of Northern India at his own expense, the sources of which were known only to himself.

His entire personality exhaled always the serene perfume of spirituality. His face radiated that rare light which comprises love, authority serenity and self-assuredness; the state that comes only by righteous living and Divine realisation. His Darshan made the people feel as if some ancient Maharshi of Upanishadic fame had human form again and that is worth-while leading a good life and to strive for the realisation of the Divine.

His spiritual teachings are simple and clear and go straight home to your heart. He strictly adhered to the course of inner development laid down by the systems of Indian Philosophy and ethics and he raised his voice never in opposition but always in firm suport of the truths and principles contained in the Hindu Dharma.

He stood at the pinnacle of human development and moved as only Jeeven-Muktas can move under the strong hold of "prarabdha". He for himself would allow things to go on as they are ordained by the hand of destiny, but His devotees have many a time changed the course of fate of themselves and of the people. Innunerable instances can be counted when by virtue of His Dhyanam, His devotees have wrought miracles worked in the innerman and transformed the materialistic hearts of iron into spiritual hearts of gold.

As time would have it, after 12 years that flashed by, the Manifested merged with its original, the unmanifested, and "Brahma Leena Brahmanandam" is now appearing in the hearts of His devotees as waves of Brahmanandam. He cast off His mortal coil, but left behind a few others in mortal coil to keep burning the light of His grace and pass the torch of His teachings from hand to hand for all the millennium to come. [16]

1957, Madras - Maharishi speaks about vegetarianism, & launches Spiritual Regeneration Movement

Vegetarianism and All Isms Through Spiritual 'Ism'

Address of His Holiness Maharishi Bal Brahmachari Mahesh Yogi delivered at the 15th Session of the World Vegetarian Congress held at Madras on 30 -11-1957

My own Self as Representative of East and West:

We are here today to find a solution for a complicated problem of existence, confronting the whole humanity on the civilised world - the problem of safety of life, of love, protection, peace and happiness: not only of individuals but of the whole creation and of nature too. All the creatures are sprung from God. Man is probably the polished son of God. And so unto him the great responsibility. Man must be sensible enough to look to the protection of life on earth, the precious property of the Great Father.

Vegetarianism is a direct means to this, is the claim of this World Vegetarian Congress. True it is. Accepted that Vegetarianism leads man for all Good. Accepting all values of Vegetarianism, the question arises how we are going to establish it. How are we going to change the 'killing world' of today into a non-killing world of tomorrow? How are we going to change the spirit of killing, the spirit of aggression, the spirit of violence into the spirit of *kindness and love* - overflowing love for the whole creation? How are we going to change hardness and cruelty of heart to softness and overflowing love for everybody?

Through platform speaking? No, it is not possible. Through outer suggestions? No, it is not possible. Through singing the values and glories of Vegetarianism into the ears of the non-vegetarians? No, because their ears may receive the message but the hardness of their heart will repel it. How then are we going to establish Vegetarianism? Suggestive knowledge - suggestions from outside do not much change the man. You have heard on this platform the experience of the President of the World Vegetarian Congress. They have experienced, speaking does not go a long way to change a man. All the great religions of the world have been speaking for it from the time immemorial - Eternal Vedas have been speaking of it, Holy Bible has been speaking of it, Holy Koran has been speaking of it, yet the killer kills. The killer knows that he is killing and in return he will be killed. The sinner knows that he is committing a sin and that he will be punished for it. Not that he does not know. He knows it. But, with this information, the cruel is not afraid - his cruelty is hardened still. The killer declares his action is the role of a saviour, he kills in the name of life, he kills in the name of saving life, he kills in the name of maintaining life. He kills and murders ruthlessly in the name of protections and peace. In the name of world peace and protection have been waged the deadliest of wars. In the name of peace and protection are preparations being made for the murder of man and creation. Shame to the greatness of the human intelligence which fails to recognise the Judge Supreme!

Our task of the day is to find a cure for this major ill of humanity. The heart of man is be changed. The inner man has to be transformed. If we want to establish real and good vegetarianism in the world we have to rise with a practical formula to transform the inner man.

My experience says the inner man is *instantaneously transformed by a flash of Divine Experience*. A direct experience of the Blissful nature of Soul, the inner man is completely transformed. The mind experiencing the Great Bliss feels satisfaction and this satisfaction of the mind results in right understanding and virtuous action, kindness, love and compassion for all. And here in this great assemblage of the eminent people of the world I declare that the experience of the Blissful Nature of the soul is not at all difficult. It is easy of attainment by one and all irrespective of caste, creed, or nationality. Without much elaborating the glories of Divine experience I invite you all to my Spiritual Development Camp at Mylapore to have direct experience of the Divine through simple, easy and effective methods of meditation which directly lead the mind to the glorious realm of the Divine. And with this experience the life of every man is transformed for all good. Not only will virtues dawn in us, but also the increase of vigour, energy, courage and confidence in life will be experienced. You will begin to enjoy innumerable advantages of concentrations and control of mind and efficiency in the field of action which will go to glorify all aspects of life - material, mental and spiritual. And then your world will be a better world. And then vegetarianism, rationalism, materialism, and even socialism or any other 'isms' of life will prove to be a useful 'ism' will be useful and successful 'ism' of life. Therefore my message is that -

If we want to establish real and good vegetarianism and if we want to live successfully any 'ism' of life - individual, social or national or international - it is first necessary to rise to Spiritualism and through Spiritualism we can successfully rise to an 'ism' according to our taste. All the 'isms' of life are good. But they become bad with the the bad minds. Spiritualism trains the mind for all good. And so through Spiritualism can be lived any ism for all success in life. May be that you have been hearing till now that there are many pre-requisites for a spiritual life but I convey to you the message of the holy tradition of the Great Maharishi of India, I convey to you in the name of the spiritual master of India, His Divinity Swami Brahmananda Saraswathi Maharaj, the Illustrious in the galaxy of the Jagad Guru Sankaracharyas of India that it is easy to live spiritual life in the midst of all the material glories of the world. It is really easy to experience the Blissful Nature of the Divine through simple techniques of 'taking a dive within.' Just half an hour sitting in the morning and evening daily is quite sufficient to raise you up to the high pedestal of spiritual glories and at the same time increase your capacity of action in daily life. So there is key to lay open the gateway of all glory of life. You have come to India from far off countries with the message of vegetarianism. Now Mother India wants you to go with the joy of the Divine and the glorious message of Spiritualism, and that through spiritualism will be established real, good and lasting vegetarianism - which is the action of this World Congress.' [18]

To celebrate the birthday of Guru Dev, an event entitled the 'Seminar of Spiritual Luminaries' was convened between the 29th December 1957 and 1st January 1958. On the last day Brahmachari Mahesh (Maharishi) gave a long address, extracts of which were later republished:-

'Spiritual Regeneration Movement is the natural consequence of the growing worries and miseries in the daily life of man everywhere in every part of the world and in every walk of human life – individual, national, and international.

'The main cause of the spiritual degeneration of society is the wrong approach to spirituality preached in plenitude by the pioneers and pleaders of spiritual glory. Needless stress has been laid on detachment and renunciation for the realization of the Divine.

The path of spiritual development through renunciation does not reconcile itself with the natural life of the majority. Renunciation is foreign to the way of life of the majority of people, who are householders, men of action in the world, whose life is naturally a life of attachment – not detachment or renunciation. Spiritual development through renunciation and detachment is an ideology of the order of the recluse, and its application should be restricted to that order alone. He feels that he is not in a position to detach himself from the responsibilities of an active life; and if renunciation is essential for realization, then unfortunately he is not meant for it. Such an attitude of the majority of the people has created a gulf between materialism and spirituality, breaking the natural harmony of the inner and outer life and leading consequently to the spiritual degeneration of man, depriving the majority of the great gains that spiritual development lays open to them.

'We owe all reverence and devotion to all those who renounced the world, experienced bliss and, out of kindness, came back to the world to awaken us from the deep slumber of ignorance to rise to the glories of God and glorify our life. Their message of the "great treasure hidden within" was right, and for that we owe all gratitude to them; but the path of renunciation they advocated was not suited for the busy man of the world.

'It is clear to the Divine Will working out the plan for spiritual regeneration of the world that the mode of spirituality which has amply propagated either the sense of detachment and renunciation or the gross form of ritualism for the blessings of the Almighty has failed to serve man in his quest for peace and happiness. The Divine Nature has therefore now planned to bring about regeneration through regenerated spirituality, which has the capacity to synthesize the two vital aspects of life – material and spiritual, practically harmonizing the material and spiritual "isms" of life – the regenerated spirituality coming on to us through the universal benevolence of the great spiritual Master, the Supreme, the Sage, the Seer, Vedanta Incarnate, His Divinity Shri Swami Brahmananda Saraswati Maharaj, the Illustrious in the Galaxy of Jagadguru Shankaracharyas of India. We are only tools in the hands of His Will; we are only to act as He dictates – as the Lord said in *Gita*:

"निमित्तमात्रं भव सव्यसाचिन"

"nimittamaatram bhava savyasaachin"
[*Bhagavad Gita* 11:33]

'Oh Savyasaachin (Ambidextrous One), merely be an instrument.' [19]

And as Maharishi Mahesh Yogi, Brahmachari Mahesh embarked on his first World Tour in April 1958, travelling to Rangoon, Penang, Kuala Lumpur, Singapore and Hong Kong, before arriving in Hawaii and then San Franscisco in the USA. His travels monitored with descriptions being published in the 'Torch Divine', the newsletter of the Spiritual Regeneration Movement.

TORCH DIVINE

Organ of the Spiritual Regeneration Movement

launched by

His Holiness Maharshi Bala Brahmachari Mahesh Yogi. Himalayas

'Vedanta Incarnate' His Divinity Swami Brahmananda Saraswathi

Maharaj, the illustrious Jagadguru Sankaracharya,

Jyothir Mutt, Bhadrikashramam. — *Our Guiding Light.*

VOL. I, NO. 3   JANUARY 1959

Quotes of Guru Dev Appear in Spiritual Regeneration Movement Literature

In January 1959 the *'Torch Divine'*, the 'Organ of the Spiritual Regeneration Movement' published a series of quotes from 'Shree Guru Deva':-

Drops of Nectar

(Sayings of Shree Guru Deva, "Vedanta Incarnate", His Divinity Swami Brahmananda Saraswathi Maharaj, the illustrious Jagadguru Shankaracharya, Jyotir Mutt, Badrikashramam.)

Having become a devotee of God one can never remain unhappy anywhere. This is our experience.

* * * *

People are unhappy because they do not have "ISHTA" (chosen Deity). Without 'Ishta' people are turning out to be orphans.

* * * *

It is only the 'ISHTA' that saves one from 'ANISHTA' (Untoward happenings).

* * * *

See your 'ISHTA' as all-pervading. That is 'ANANYATHA' (one pointed devotion).

* * * *

Among Vishnu, Shankara, Devi, Surya and Ganesha, none is greater or smaller. All of them are quite capable of bestowing on their devotees all that is good in its entirety.

* * * *

By repetition of the "Manthra" given to you by your Guru as per your qualifications, your sins shall be destroyed.

* * * *

Develop fully one 'ISHTA'; then no 'ANISHTA' can ever befall you.

* * * *

By doing Japa your sins shall be destroyed, JAPATO NASTI PATHAKAM.

* * * *

Of the five Deities Shankara, Vishnu, (Rama, Krishna), Surya, Ganesha and Devi, whosoever is more adorable to you the Manthra of that Deity should be repeated by you everyday.

* * * *

You must get to know the Manthra of your 'ISHTA' and the method of 'Dhyana' thereof, through an experienced 'SATGURU' and somehow or other devote some time every day for Japa of the 'Ishta Manthra' and Dhyana.

* * * *

Through Japa "SIDDHI" (Realisation) shall result. There is no doubt about this. "JAPAT SIDDHIR JAPAT SIDDHIR JAPAT SIDDHIR NASAMSAYAM".

* * * *

See your 'ISHTA' everywhere. There should be no place where your 'ISHTA' is not seen.

* * * *

It is absolutely difficult to get the vision of your 'ISHTA' until and unless you get one pointedness on your ISHTA. To cure a disease both "OUSHADA" (medicine) and "PATHYA" (Dietic Restriction) are necessary. To cure the disease of restlessness of the mind "ABHYASA" (Practice) is "OUSHADA" and 'VAIRAGYA' (Detachment) is PATHYA.

* * * *

To apply your mind to your ISHTA is ABHYASA.

To constantly think of ISHTA, meditate on it, talk always about It and think always about It is ABHYASA.

When the mind is engrossed in the ISHTA, detachment automatically comes in. Therefore, we say you need become a "RAGI" (a person having attachment). That is to say there is need for the mind to develop attachment to the ISHTA.

* * * *

Let constant thinking of God be the main work for the mind and carrying on "VYAVAHARA" (worldly activities) only secondary. In that case you will have "LADDOOS", (sweets) in both hands.

* * * *

There is no need to apply your mind entirely in order to carry on "VYAVAHARA."

It is possible to carry on "VYAVAHARA" with only a little co-operation of the mind.

* * * *

Just like the Miser whose mind, even while attending to VYAVAHARA, mainly and constantly thinks of the money, you should be attending to VYAVAHARA while your mind mainly and constantly think of God.

*

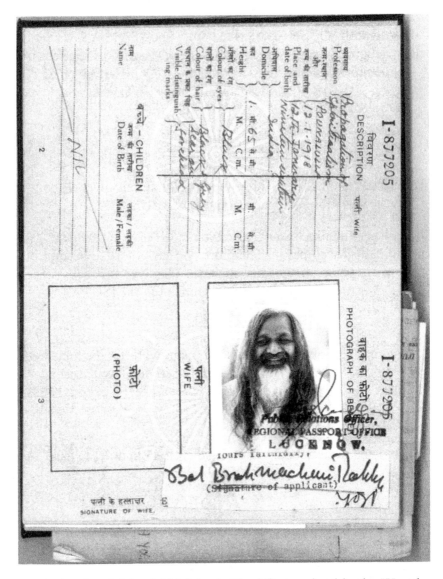

In 1959, when Maharishi Mahesh Yogi first arrived in the West he proclaimed:-

'My life truly began 19 years ago at the feet of my master when I learned the secret of swift and deep meditation, a secret I now impart to the world.' [20]

'108 Names of Guru Dev'

Maharishi extolled the greatness of his master, and each year, on the full moon day of July he would celebrate Guru Purnima. On Monday 20th July 1959 in Los Angeles, USA he conducted a *puja* and recited the '108 Names of Guru Dev':-

Jai Guru Dev.

First, I'll invoke the great masters of the holy tradition of Shankaracharya through chanting prayers of invoking, and then, having invoked their prescence, in order to get their grace, we shall offer flower offerings. And that will be through offering the flower petals along with the names of the great master, His Divinity Swami Brahmananda Saraswati Maharaj. Having offered the flower petals at his holy feet we shall collectively offer the light. [21]:-

अनन्त श्री अनन्त श्री अनन्त श्री विभूषिताये नमः

Ananta Shri Ananta Shri Ananta Shri Vibhushita-ye namah
To the one who is adorned with limitless wealth, limitless wealth, limitless wealth, I bow down

श्री ब्रह्मानन्दाय नमः

Shri Brahmanandaya namah
To the one who is blessed absolute-bliss, I bow down

पूर्णेन्दुकला धराय नमः

Purnendukala Dharaya namah
To the one who wears the phases of the moon [on his brow], I bow down.

परम सौभाग्य दायकाय नमः

Param Saubhagya Dayakaya namah
To the one who provides supreme prosperity, I bow down

परमानन्दाय नमः

Paramanandaya namah
To the one who is supreme bliss, I bow down

पीताम्बर धराय नमः

Peetambara Dharaya namah
To the one who wears the yellow garments, I bow down

दिव्य भालचन्दन् चर्चिताय नमः

Divya Bhalachandan Charchitaya namah
To the one whose divine forehead is smeared with sandalwood
paste, I bow down

रुद्रक्षमाला धराय नमः

Rudrakshamala Dharaya namah
To the one who wears the *rudraksha* necklace, I bow down

ऋद्धि सिद्धि संसेविताय नमः

Riddhi Siddhi Sansevitaya namah
To the one who has the good fortune to be served by *siddhis*,
I bow down

स्वर्णसिंहासनाधीश्वराय नमः

Swarnasinhasanadhishwaraya namah
To the one who is master of the golden lion-throne, I bow down

दैवी प्रभा प्रसारकाय नमः

Daivi Prabha Prasarakaya namah
To the one who emanates celestial light, I bow down

सर्व जन मनमोहनाय नमः

Sarva Jana Manamohanaya namah
To the one who captivates the minds and hearts of everybody,
I bow down

सर्वानन्दकरय नमः

Sarvanandakaraya namah
To the one who gives bliss to all, I bow down

सर्व लोक जन वन्दभाय नमः

Sarva Loka Jana Vandabhaya namah
To the one who is praised by people throughout the world,
I bow down

साधु जनाराध्याय नमः

Sadhu Janaradhyaya namah
To the one who is worshipped by saints, I bow down

सौभाग्य संप्रदायकाय नमः

Saubhagya Sampradayakaya namah
To the one who brings welfare to the religious sects, I bow down

श्री लोकनाथाय नमः

Shri Lokanathaya namah
To the blessed master of the world, I bow down

पूर्णगिरि पीठागताय नमः

Purnagiri Peethagataya namah
To the one who came to the Purnagiri Peeth, I bow down

परमेश्वराय नमः

Parameshwaraya namah

To the one who is the Supreme Being, I bow down

पूर्णागिरि प्रतिष्ठापताय नमः

Purnagiri Pratishthapataya namah

The one who installed Purnagiri [in the temple at Jyotirmath], I bow down

परम शिवाय नमः

Param Shivaya namah

To the supreme Shiva, I bow down

श्री ज्योतिर्मठागताय नमः

Shri Jyotirmathagataya namah

To the one who went to Jyotrimath, I bow down

ज्योति स्वरूपाय नमः

Jyoti Swarupaya namah

To the one who is personified enlightenment, I bow down

ज्योतिष्पीठोद्धारकाय नमः

Jyotishpeethoddharakaya namah

To the one who restored Jyotir Math, I bow down

श्री ज्योतिष्पीठाधीश्वराय नमः

Shri Jyotishpeethadhishwaraya namah

To the one who is master of Jyotir Math, I bow down

चन्द्र मौलीश्वर प्रतिष्ठापताय नमः

Chandra Maulishwara Pratishthapataya namah
The one who installed the image of Chandramaulishwar (Lord
Shiva, with the moon in his matted hair), I bow down

श्री विद्य धराय नमः

Shri Vidya Dharaya namah
To the one who applies [knowledge of] Shri Vidya, I bow down

बदरीकाश्रमागताय नमः

Badarikashramagataya namah
To the one who went to Badrika Ashram [near Badrinath,
Himalayas], I bow down

तपश्चर्या चरणाय नमः

Tapashcharya Charanaya namah
To the feet of the *tapasi* (one who has done penance), I bow down

बदरीयात्रा संवर्धकाय नमः

Badariyatra Samwardhakaya namah
To him who protects and nourishes those on pilgrimage to
Badrinath, I bow down

श्री बदरी विशालाय नमः

Shri Badari Vishalaya namah
To the vast Shri Badri, I bow down

शंकर पीठोद्धारकाय नमः

Shankara Peethoddharakaya namah
The one who restored the Shankara Peeth, I bow down

श्री शंकराचार्य नमः

Shri Shankaracharya namah

Shri Shankaracharya, I bow down

अष्टवर्षे गृहस्यागी वियोत्तमाय नमः

Ashtawars-he Grihasyaagi Viyottamaya namah

To the one who at eight years old left home to become a hermit,
I bow down

राजारामाय नमः

Rajaramaya namah

To he who is Raja Ram, I bow down.

सरयूपारीण कुलोत्भवाय नमः

Sarayuparina Kulotbhawaya namah

To he who was born of the Sarayupeen tribe (of the upper Saraya
river), I bow down

गानामिश्राय नमः

Ganamishraya namah

To he who was of Gana (village) of the Mishra family,
I bow down

उत्तरकाशी समागताय नमः

Uttarakashi Samagataya namah

To the one who arrived in Uttarkashi, I bow down

नैष्ठिकाय नमः

Naishthikaya namah

To the one with religious faith, I bow down

बालब्रह्मचारिणे नमः

Balabrahmachari-ne namah
To the one who from childhood was *brahmachari*, I bow down

कल्मषाद्मये नमः

Kalmashadma-ye namah
To he who is free from impuritites, I bow down

ऊर्ध्वरतसे नमः

Urdhwarata-se namah
To he who has been living in chastity, I bow down

महातेजसे नमः

Mahateja-se namah
To the one of great splendour, I bow down

महासिद्धये नमः

Mahasiddha-ye namah
To the one of great *siddhis*, I bow down

महाबुद्धये नमः

Mahabuddha-ye namah
To the one with the great mind, I bow down

सत्गुरवे नमः

Satgura-ve namah
To the one who is *satguru*, I bow down

जगत्गुरवे नमः

Jagatgura-ve namah
To the one who is a universal *guru*, I bow down

चतुर्वर्ण शिक्षकाय नमः

Chaturvarna Shikshakaya namah
To the one who gives instruction to the four castes, I bow down

सदाचार प्रवर्तकाय नमः

Sadachara Pravartakaya namah
To the one who proceeds virtuously, I bow down

कल्याण गुण गण सेविताय नमः

Kalyana Guna Gana Sevitaya namah
To the one who visits the quality of prosperity on the community,
I bow down

कल्याण स्वरूपाय नमः

Kalyana Swarupaya namah
To the one who in reality is happiness, I bow down

शिष्यकोटि समर्चिताय नमः

Shishyakoti Samarchitaya namah
To the one who is adored by ten million disciples, I bow down

भक्त वत्सलाय नमः

Bhakta Vatsalaya namah
To the one who is kind to devotees, I bow down

सुरासुरादि संसेविताय नमः

Surasuradi Samsevitaya namah
To the one who is served by the gods and the *asuras* etc,
I bow down

सच्चिदानंद स्वरूपाय नमः

Sachchidananda Swarupaya namah
To the one who in reality is Absolute Bliss Consciousness,
I bow down

स्वतम् वेद्याय नमः

Swatam Vedyaya namah
To the one who demonstrates Vedic knowledge, I bow down

स्वयम् प्रकाशाय नमः

Swayam Prakashaya namah
To the one who is spontaneously shining, I bow down

वेद् वेदान्त सिद्धान्त रूपाय नमः

Veda Vedanta Siddhanta Rupaya namah
To the one who is the established truth of *Veda* and *Vedanta*,
I bow down

परमात्मने नमः

Paramatma-ne namah
To the one who is the Supreme Being, I bow down

परात्पराय नमः

Paratparaya namah
To the one who is senior to the highest, I bow down

लोक कल्याण निरताय नमः

Loka Kalyana Nirataya namah
To the one who is occupied with the welfare of the world,
I bow down

लोक रञ्जनाय नमः

Loka Ranjanaya namah
To the one who charms the world, I bow down

ध्यान मार्ग प्रतिष्ठापताय नमः

Dhyaana Marg Pratishthapataya namah
To the one who shows the way of meditation, I bow down

ध्यान योगीश्वराय नमः

Dhyaana Yogishwaraya namah
To the one who is Lord of Yoga meditation, I bow down

भुक्ति मुक्ति प्रदायकाय नमः

Bhukti Mukti Pradayakaya namah
To the one who bestows the enjoyment of liberation, I bow down

परम सिद्धाय नमः

Param Siddhaya namah
To the one who is the greatest *siddha*, I bow down

भक्तिज्ञान योग समन्वय मार्ग प्रकाशकय नमः

Bhaktigyaana Yoga Samanwaya Marg Prakashakaya namah
To the one who illuminates the connection of the ways of
devotion and knowledge, I bow down

सर्वध्याय नमः

Sarvadhyaya namah
To the one on whom all meditate, I bow down

अध्यात्म युक्ति प्रदायकाय नमः

Adhyatma Yukti Pradayakaya namah
To the one who bestows a connection to the Supreme Spirit,
I bow down

सहज मार्ग प्रदर्शकाय नमः

Sahaja Marg Pradarshakaya namah
To the one who demonstrates the natural way, I bow down

सर्वाशान्ति निवारकाय नमः

Sarvashaanti Nivarakaya namah
To the one who prevents all lack of peace, I bow down

चिर शान्ति प्रदायकाय नमः

Chira Shaanti Pradayakaya namah
To the one who bestows peace for a long time, I bow down

अध्यात्म विकाशान्दोलन् प्रवर्तकाय नमः

Adhyatma Vikashandolan Pravartakaya namah
To the one who causes ripples of spiritual knowledge to appear,
I bow down

विश्व शान्ति लक्षकराय नमः

Vishwa Shaanti Lakshakaraya namah
To the one who aims at world peace, I bow down

श्री शान्तानन्द प्रकाशकाय नमः

Shri Shantananda Prakashakaya namah
To the one who illustrates the bliss of blessed peace, I bow down

दिव्य देवता प्रमोहनाय नमः

Daivi Samprita Pradayakaya namah
To the one who bestows divine complete satisfaction, I bow down

दिव्य देवता प्रमोहनाय नमः

Divya Devata Pramohanaya namah
To the one who infatuates the celestial deities, I bow down

दिव्यतेय प्रकाशाकाय नमः

Divyateya Prakashakaya namah
To the one who illustrates godliness, I bow down

कल्मष नाशनाय नमः

Kalmasha Nashanaya namah
To the one who removes impurities, I bow down

दिव्य दृष्टि प्रदायकाय नमः

Divya Drishti Pradayakaya namah
To the one who bestows vision of the Celestial, I bow down

दिव्यतेय मनोहराय नमः

Divyateya Manoharaya namah
To the one who is beautifully divinely brilliant, I bow down

दिव्याय नमः

Divyaya namah
To the one who is Celestial, I bow down

दिव्याकाय नमः

Divyakaya namah
To the one who does divine work, I bow down

शुद्धाय नमः

Shuddhaya namah
To he who is pure, I bow down

शुद्धकाय नमः

Shuddhakaya namah
To he who purifies, I bow down

विमलाय नमः

Vimalaya namah
To he who is without blemish, I bow down

विमलकाय नमः

Vimalakaya namah
To he who clarifies, I bow down

निर्मलाय नमः

Nirmalaya namah
To the one who is virtuous, I bow down

निरञ्जनाय नमः

Niranjanaya namah
To the one without embellishments, I bow down

आनन्दकन्दाय नमः

Anandakandaya namah
To the one who is the root of joy, I bow down

ब्रह्मानन्दाय नमः

Brahmanandaya namah
To the one who is absolute bliss, I bow down

परम गुरवे नमः

Parama Gura-ve namah
To the greatest *guru*, I bow down

श्री ब्रह्मानन्द सरस्वत्यै नमः

Shri Brahmananda Saraswatyai namah
To Shri Brahmananda Saraswati, I bow down

जगत गुरवे नमः

Jagat Gura-ve namah
To the universal *guru*, I bow down

श्री शंकराचार्य पूज्य पादाय नमः

Shri Shankaracharya Pujya Padaya namah
To Shri Shankaracharya whose feet are worthy of worship,
I bow down

श्री ज्योतिर्मठ बदरिकाश्रमाधीश्वराय नमः

Shri Jyotirmath Badarikashramadhishwaraya namah
To the one who is Supreme Lord of Shri Jyotirmath,
Badarikashram, I bow down

सच्चितानन्दाय नमः

Satchitanandaya namah
To the one who is Absolute Bliss Consciousness, I bow down

श्री ब्रह्मानन्दाय नमः

Shri Brahmanandaya namah
To the one who is blessed Absolute-Bliss, I bow down

Later Reflections

Jai Guru Dev

Mahesh the former *ashram* secretary, who eulogised his master as *maharishi* (*maha* = great, *rishi* = sage) and perfect *yogi*, now made a name for himself as 'Maharishi Mahesh Yogi', publicly extolling the benefits of *mantra* meditation and establishing a worldwide organisation to promote his own views. It appears that Guru Dev had not prepared this *brahmachari* for such a mission:-

Maharishi Mahesh Yogi - 'Oh, he must have known. He never said to me, otherwise quite a long time would have been wasted in planning. He saved us that waste, waste of planning. It just blossomed and blossomed and blossomed and blossomed.' [22]

'But the great impact of Guru Dev, in his lifetime, in bringing out so clearly and in such simple words this technique of TM. And his blessing for this movement, which came out much after he left his body, because there was no occasion during his lifetime for any of his intimate blessed disciples to go out of his presence and that's why this any such movement to bless the world couldn't have started during his time.' [23]

'And he never, he, he never, trained me or anything, just it was living in the *ashram*.' [24]

Millions have paid to be taught the simple practice of Transcendental Meditation (TM). TM has dual objectives in that one is instructed to repeat a *mantra* in order to bring about a pleasanter frame of mind, but also it is hoped that the mind will transcend thought altogether and bring about increased peace and serenity for the meditator, a state known as Pure Consciousness. Further, it is also taught that the repeated experience of the transcendental leads to a permanent state of higher awareness known as Cosmic Consciousness. Anyhow, all initiates are required to attend a short puja ceremony celebrated in front of a portrait of Guru Dev, so everyone is led to assume that the TM technique comes directly from the *guru*. However, meditators are told nothing about the actual teachings of Guru Dev.

Journalist Dinesh Khare recalls:-

'The initiation took place in front of a picture of Guru Dev and I was told that I should consider neither my initiator nor Maharishi Mahesh Yogi as my spiritual teacher but the Guru Dev himself. It was a thrilling experience and the very first day my turbulent mind experienced such a serene calm that when I got up after practising TM for the first time, I bowed my head to the lotus feet of Guru Dev and since that day have regarded him as my spiritual teacher and guide.' [25]

Asked by one of his students if Transcendental Meditation is exactly the same meditation technique as that taught by Guru Dev, the Maharishi answered:-

M M Y - 'Must be using **better** techniques than I am using.'

Questioner - 'Was he still using the long *mantras* and all of that?'

M M Y - 'It's very difficult for me to find out what he was using, because initiation is all in private.....

And I was never interested who was given what *mantra*; I was interested in myself.....

Full of divine radiance. People don't have to do the *mantra* and meditation in his presence. Just, the transformation was in his air, so full of life.' [26]

With regards to how *mantras* are selected Maharishi was clear that in certain circumstances it could be simplicity itself:-

Q. 'Maharishi, how may a person find, you know, which of the, of the, the five materials [elements?] are predominant in them?

MMY. They, they have their method of, uh, oh, from the tendencies they know, from the, from the cut of the face they know. From the tendency. From the tendency.

Q. Do you take that into consideration when you give the person a *mantra*?

MMY. I don't go into all these vibrations, botherations. I ask him "Which god you like?" He says "Shiva" - Okay, Shiva! [Maharishi laughs, very loudly]

Where is the time to go into complications and all that? Ask him directly "What he likes?" and that is it. [more laughter].

And somebody comes, "Oh my, I don't have any liking for anybody", then I trace behind, And then, "When you were young?" and "Which temple you were going more?" and "What your father was worshipping?" and then he comes round. [Maharishi resumes the laughter]

Q. How would you apply this to the westerners?

MMY. Oh here we don't go into these minute details. [more laughter]

We get the *mantra* direct and that does all good for him. [yet more laughter]

Into, not into so much details.

Q. [question unclear]

MMY. Tendencies are, different and according to that the *mantra* comes, uh it naturally comes. And so far it has found to be working. [more laughter]

Q. Not everybody gets the same *mantra*?

MMY. Uh?

Q. Not everybody gets the same *mantra*? Do you give the same *mantra* to everyone?

MMY. No, not the same, but for some it may tally also, for some, because we don't have as many *mantras* as we have men. [more laughter]

For some it may tally also, uh but that is no, that is no

guarantee.[27]

He told journalist Lewis Lapham:-

M M Y - 'Mention my love for my master, I consider myself only the loudspeaker.' [28]

However, in practice the Maharishi seldom speaks about the *guru*, but students of TM still press for more information:-

M M Y - 'From the age of nine until the age of seventy-one, when he became Shankaracharya, life was mostly in deep silence, seclusion.

It's very, it's very interesting.

If I was not caught up in this whirlpool I would have been writing life account of Guru Dev and would have been exposing the whole wisdom of the *Vedas* in that one narration of his life.' [29]

Questioner - '"What it was that Guru Dev did that makes him important as the source of the revival of this knowledge?"

M M Y - "In his *ashram* he manufactured **me**" [29]

*

Maharishi Mahesh Yogi described what it was like to be in Guru Dev's presence:-

'When His words thrilled the air with joy, the whole atmosphere was surcharged with delight as if waves were set up in the silent ocean of Omnipresent Anandam - The Immoveable was moved by "the Expression of the Inexpressible".' [30]

आचर्य वंदन
Acharya Vandana

Puja to Guru Dev

आत्म शुद्धि - *aatma shuddhi* - PURIFICATION

अपवित्रः पवित्रो व सर्वावस्थां गतोऽपि वा ।
यः स्मरेत्पुंडरीकाक्षं सबाह्याभ्यंतरः शुचिः ॥

apavitrah pavitro va sarvaavasthaan gatoapi vaa.
yah smaretpundariikaakdham sabaahyaabhyantarah shuchih..

Whether all places are permeated with purity or with impurity,
whosoever remembers the lotus-eyed Lord (Vishnu, Rama,
Krishna) gains inner and outer purity.

आवाहनं - *aavaahanam* – INVOCATION

नारायणं पद्मभवं वसिष्ठं शक्तिं च तत्पुत्रपराशरं च ।
व्यासं शुकं गौडपदं महान्तं गोविन्दयोगीन्द्रमथास्य शिष्यम् ॥

naaraayanam padmabhavam vasishtham shaktim cha
tatputraparaasharam cha.
vyaasam shukam gaudapadam mahaantam
govindayogiindramathaasya shishyam..

To Narayana, to lotus-born Brahma, to Vashistha, to Shakti and
his son, Parashara,
to Vyasa, to Shukadeva, to the great Gaudapada, to Govinda, to
Yogindra his disciple.

श्री शंकराचार्यमथास्य पद्मपादं च हस्तामलकं च शिष्यम् ।
तं त्रोटकं वार्त्तिककारमन्यान् अस्मतगुरून् सन्ततमानतोस्मि ॥

shrii shankaraachaaryamathaasya padmapaadam cha
hastaamalakam cha shishyam.
tam trotakam vaarttikakaaramanyaan asmataguruun
santatamaanatosmi..

To his disciple Shri Shankaracharya, to his disciples Padmapada,
Hastamalaka,
to him Trotakacharya, to the writer of famous *vaarttika's*
(Sureshwara), to others, to our tradition of *gurus*, I bow down.

श्रुतिस्मृतिपुराणानां आलयं करुणालयं ।
नमामि भगवत्पादं शङ्करं लोकशङ्करम् ॥

shrutismritipuraanaanaam aalayam karunaalayam.
namaami bhagavatpaadam shankaram lokashankaram..

To the *shruti* ('that which is heard'), *smriti* ('that which is
remembered) and *puraanaanam* (ancient stories) - the abode of
kindness,
I bow down to the feet of the Lord Shankar, emancipator of the
world.

शङ्करं शङ्कराचार्यं केशवं बादरायणम् ।
सूत्रभाष्यकृतौ वन्दे भगवन्तौ पुनः पुनः ॥

shankaram shankaraachaarya keshavam baadaraayanam.
suutrabhaashyakritau vande bhagavantau punah punah..

To Shankar Shankaracharya (Shiva), Keshava (Vishnu, Krishna),
Badarayana (Veda Vyasa),
to the commentator of the *Suutrabhaashya* (Brahma Sutras), at the
feet of the lord I bow down again and again.

यद्द्वारे निखिला निलिम्पपरिषत्सिद्धिं विधत्तेऽनिशं श्रीमच्छ्रीलसितं

जगद्गुरुपदं नत्वात्मतृप्तिं गताः ।

लोकाज्ञानपयोदपाटनधुरं श्रीशंकरं शर्मदं ब्रह्मानन्दसरस्वतीं गुरुवरं

ध्यायामि ज्योतिर्मयं ॥

yaddvaare nikhilaa nilimpaparishatsiddhim vidhatte.anisham,
shriimachchriilasitam jagadgurupadam natvaatmatriptim gataah.
lokaagyaanapayodapaatanadhuram shriishankaram sharmadam,
brahmaanandasarasvatiim guruvaram dhyaayaami jyotirmayam..

At whose door the whole galaxy of gods pray for perfection day
and night.
Adorned by immeasurable glory, preceptor of the whole world,
having bowed down at His feet, we gain fulfilment.
Skilled in dispelling the cloud of ignorance of the people, the
gentle emancipator,
Brahmananda Saraswati, the supreme teacher, full of brilliance, on
Him we meditate.

षोडशोपचार पूजन - *shodashopachaara puujana*
PUJA of 16 OFFERINGS

आवाहनं समर्पयामि श्रीगुरु चरण कमलेभ्यो नमः

aavaahanam samarpayaami shriiguru charana kamalebhyo namah

Offering invocation to the lotus feet of the blessed *guru*,
I bow down.

आसनं समर्पयामि श्रीगुरु चरण कमलेभ्यो नमः

aasanam samarpayaami shriiguru charana kamalebhyo namah
Offering a seat to the lotus feet of the blessed *guru*, I bow down.

स्नानं समर्पयामि श्रीगुरु चरण कमलेभ्यो नमः

snaanam samarpayaami shriiguru charana kamalebhyo namah
Offering a bath to the lotus feet of the blessed *guru*, I bow down.

वस्त्रं समर्पयामि श्रीगुरु चरण कमलेभ्यो नमः

vastram samarpayaami shriiguru charana kamalebhyo namah
Offering a cloth to the lotus feet of the blessed *guru*, I bow down.

चंदनं समर्पयामि श्रीगुरु चरण कमलेभ्यो नमः

cha.ndanam samarpayaami shriiguru charana kamalebhyo namah
Offering sandal paste to the lotus feet of the blessed *guru*,
I bow down.

अक्षतान् समर्पयामि श्रीगुरु चरण कमलेभ्यो नमः

akshataan samarpayaami shriiguru charana kamalebhyo namah
Offering full unbroken rice to the lotus feet of the blessed *guru*,
I bow down.

पुष्पं समर्पयामि श्रीगुरु चरण कमलेभ्यो नमः

pushpam samarpayaami shriiguru charana kamalebhyo namah

Offering flower to the lotus feet of the blessed *guru*, I bow down.

धूपं समर्पयामि श्रीगुरु चरण कमलेभ्यो नमः

dhuupam samarpayaami shriiguru charana kamalebhyo namah
Offering incense to the lotus feet of the blessed *guru*, I bow down.

दीपं समर्पयामि श्रीगुरु चरण कमलेभ्यो नमः

diipam samarpayaami shriiguru charana kamalebhyo namah
Offering light to the lotus feet of the blessed *guru*, I bow down.

अच्मनियम् समर्पयामि श्रीगुरु चरण कमलेभ्यो नमः

achmaniyam samarpayaami shriiguru charana kamalebhyo namah
Offering water to the lotus feet of the blessed *guru*, I bow down.

नैवेद्यं समर्पयामि श्रीगुरु चरण कमलेभ्यो नमः

naivedyam samarpayaami shriiguru charana kamalebhyo namah
Offering fruit to the lotus feet of the blessed *guru*, I bow down.

आच्मनीयं समर्पयामि श्रीगुरु चरण कमलेभ्यो नमः

aachmaniiyam samarpayaami shriiguru charana kamalebhyo namah
Offering water to the lotus feet of the blessed *guru*, I bow down.

ताम्बूलं समर्पयामि श्रीगुरु चरण कमलेभ्यो नमः

taambuulam samarpayaami shriiguru charana kamalebhyo namah
Offering betel leaf to the lotus feet of the blessed *guru*,
I bow down.

श्री फलं समर्पयामि श्रीगुरु चरण कमलेभ्यो नमः

shrii phalam samarpayaami shriiguru charana kamalebhyo namah
Offering coconut to the lotus feet of the blessed *guru*,
I bow down.

आरात्रिक्य - *aaraatrikyam* - ARATI -
OFFERING CAMPHOR FLAME

कर्पूरगौरम् करुणावतारम् संसारसारं भुजगेन्द्रहारम् ।
सदावसन्तं हृदयारविन्दे भवं भवानी सहितं नमामि ॥

karpuuragauram karunaavataaram samsaarasaaram
bhujagendrahaaram.
sadaavasantam hridayaaravinde bhavam bhavaanii sahitam
namaami..

White as camphor, the incarnation of kindness, the essence of the
world, the one who is garlanded by the Serpent King,
ever dwelling in the lotus of my heart, Bhavam (Shiva) together
with Bhavaanii (Parvati), I bow down.

आरात्रिक्यं समर्पयामि श्रीगुरु चरण कमलेभ्यो नमः

aaraatrikyam samarpayaami shriiguru charana kamalebhyo
namah
Offering light to the lotus feet of the blessed *guru*, I bow down.

आच्मनीयं समर्पयामि श्रीगुरु चरण कमलेभ्यो नमः

aachmaniiyam samarpayaami shriiguru charana kamalebhyo
namah

Offering water to the lotus feet of the blessed *guru*, I bow down.

पुष्पाञ्जलिं - *pushpaanjalim* -

OFFERING FLOWERS WITH FOLDED HANDS

गुरुर्ब्रह्मा गुरुर्विष्णुर् गुरुर्देवो महेश्वरः ।
गुरुःसाक्षात् परम्ब्रह्म तस्मै श्री गुरवे नमः ॥

gururbrahmaa gururvishnur gururdevo maheshvarah.
guruhsaakshaat parambrahma tasmai shrii gurave namah..

Guru is Brahma. *Guru* is Vishnu.
Guru is the god Maheshwara (Shiva).
In the presence of the *guru*, the infinite Brahma, to him the
blessed *guru*, I bow down.

अखन्दमन्दलकरम् व्याप्तम् येन चरचरम् ।
तत्पदम् दर्शितम् येन तस्मै श्री गुरवे नमः ॥

akhandamandalakaram vyaaptam yena characharam.
tatpadam darshitam yena tasmai shrii gurave namah..

The one who has made it possible to realise Him who pervades
this entire infinite
universe of animate and inanimate existence,
I bow to the blessed *guru*.

श्री ब्रह्मनन्दम् परम सुखदम् केवलम् ज्ञान्मुर्तिम् ।
विश्वातीतं गगन सद्रिशम् तत्त्वमस्यादि लक्ष्यम् ॥

shrii brahmanandam parama sukhadam kevalam gyaanmurtim.
vishvaatiitam gagana sadrisham tattvamasyaadi lakshyam..

Blessed *brahmanandam* (Absolute Bliss), the giver of greatest
happiness, who is only knowledge personified,
beyond the universe [of opposites], one who is like the sky, the
goal of 'That Thou art' etc.

एकम् नित्यम् विमलम् अचलम् सर्वधीसाक्षिभुतम्।
भावातीतम् त्रिगुनसहितम् सद्गुरुम् त्वम् नमामि ॥

ekam nityam vimalam achalam sarvadhiisaakshibhutam.
bhaavaatiitam trigunasahitam sadgurum tvam namaami..

The one, the eternal, steady without impurity, the one who exists
as the witness of all intellect,
the transcendent without the three *gunas*, the true *guru*,
to him I bow down.

आज्ञान तिमिरान्धस्य ज्ञानाजन शलकया।
चक्षुरून्मीलितम् येन तस्मै श्री गुरवे नमः ॥

aagyaana timiraandhasya gyaanaajana shalakayaa.
chakshuruunmiilitam yena tasmai shrii gurave namah..

With the application of the ointment of knowledge,
by whom the eyes are opened,
to him I bow down to the blessed *guru*.

पुष्पाञ्जलिं समर्पयामि श्री गुरु चरण कमलेभ्यो नमः

pushpaanjalim samarpayaami shrii guru charana kamalebhyo
namah

Offering a handful of flowers to the lotus feet of the blessed *guru*,
I bow down.

The Poet and the Puja

Many of the verses of this puja will already be familiar to those with knowledge of Indian culture, however one of the verses is specific to the worship of Guru Dev, being written for that purpose.

There is a poem attributed to a Sanskrit Poet of Benares, an "Ashu Kavi" (spontaneous poet), Pt. Veni Madava Sastri 'Shashtrartha Maharathi' who in about 1952 wrote a prayer to Guru Deva.

In 1955 on page (i) of the preface to *'Beacon Light of the Himalayas'*, Brahmachari Mahesh mentioned the 2nd verse, quoting a phrase from it - *'brahmaananda sarasvatim guruvaran pratyaksha devam bhaje*. i.e. I bow down to Swami Brahmanand Saraswati who is the Great Guru and 'Present God' or 'God in Person' or "Personified Divinity.".

The 1st verse can also be found at the beginning of the Hindi booklet *'Shrii Jyotishpeethaddharaka'*, the lifestory of Guru Dev in Hindi.

Five versese of the poem are given in the back of the 2nd edition of *"Amrit Kana"*, a book of Guru Dev's quotations. In another publication, *"Shriishankaraachaaryo Vijayatetaraam"*, - a booklet of prayer to Guru Dev, all five verses are included alongwith a Hindi summary of each verse. And in a leaflet of the similar name - *Shriishankaraachaaryo Vijayatetaraam – Shri Sadgurudeva ki Aarti* - the five verses appear again.

*

Maharishi Mahesh Yogi spoke about the 5th verse of this prayer, mentioning that it is included in the TM puja:-

"This was done by us, I didn't compose those lines, because I am not a Sanskrit scholar, but this was done by a, very, very eminent Sanskrit poet of Banares, and he was, such a mysterious man, the poet. [Ashu Kavi Pandit Veni Madhava Sastri] He used to live us, just like us, and a good *pandit*, and when some, some *pandits*, learned people used to come to pay their respects to Guru Dev, and he would sit like that. And generally it is traditional, that in the presence of Shankaracharya, *pandits* gather. *Pandits* mean the learned people, highly great intellectuals of the country. They sit together, and they, try to bring home to Shankaracharya, each one of them, that he is the greater *pandit* than the others. And these dialogues are so highly intellectual and so very interesting, because they, everyone wants to, to win the grace of Shankaracharya, apart from his spiritual development for their material glorification, because a certificate from the Shankaracharya, of the great learning of the *pandits* will make him flourish in his area. So, they, very beautiful, and this *pandit* he used to defeat everyone, because he was a born poet, poet. He would versify anything that he wants to say. In poetry he would speak. And when in poetry, and so fluent and so high-class, so, high-class fluent Sanskrit poetry, and others would just sit and listen to him, what he says.

He was very dear, sweet *pandit*. He wrote lots of stanzas of Guru Dev, absolutely and, and this was one of them. What happened was... this is very interesting.... this great *pandit* in his flight of, of the poet, he wrote Guru Dev's life, and he, he didn't know Guru Dev's life. Because all the time was spent in loneliness in the jungles, and, nobody would know. And he said to me, "I am going to write."

And I said "Yes, you write", and this was our agreement that I'll get it printed, and he wrote, and I enjoyed it so much, but someday it was to come to Guru Dev for sanction. So, Guru Dev, he enjoyed hearing the whole thing. It was highly scholarly and very great, and everything that, that a good poet could put in that, he put it.

And then, when it was finished Guru Dev said, "It's very good, yes." And when the *pandit* went out of the room he asked him to take it to the Ganges, tie it down with a big stone, heavy, put it in the Ganges.

And I, it was a shock to me, I said "But, but there are beautiful passages in it".

He said, "Don't talk!'

He said, "Nobody should read it, tell him to take it", it is because he didn't know his life and he said "If you don't put it in the Ganges I'll ask someone else to do it."

I said, "I'll do it".

We would have used all those beautiful, sen... poetry. These days you would have enjoyed all. But he wouldn't allow it to remain.

He was absolutely divine, simple and great, very great, he was very great." [31]

'One day a man who was considered to be very wealthy came to Guru Dev. He said to him:

"I have been so happy whenever I have come to you. Would you allow me to donate something for your *ashram*?"

"No", said Guru Dev, "I do not want your money but I want from you what is dearest to you!"

"Do you want my estates?"

"No, your estates do not belong to you, you have so many debts."

Now the man was deeply frightened! Guru Dev continued quietly:

"You have a little box in your pocket, what is in it, that is what I want, for that is dearest to you! For that cocaine you have been spending all your money and have made your family unhappy. If you have to make an offering, offer not your money but your defects, so that you are redeemed and made whole."

Trembling the man took out of his pocket a little box and handed it to Guru Dev. He prostrated before the master for a long time and then thanked him from the deepest bottom of his heart for having been cured of his addiction.

Guru Dev said: "Now go and work and make your family happy!" [32]

Connecting with Guru Dev through seeing an image of him

Maharishi is recorded as having said:-

"...It's a very beautiful question and very sweet, the question was and still is, Guru Dev must have been fully enlightened. Now after leaving the body nothing remains in the Relative, just Absolute. Then how do we invoke and to whom? And if nobody is to be invoked, then what is the use?

Some such similar question I asked Guru Dev once, what happened was naturally people come to the *ashram* from all over India to pay respects to Guru Dev, once or twice a year according to their own convenience.

And when they would come they would narrate all sorts of stories, the child was sick or they had a law suit, all sorts of difficulties and then thinking of Guru Dev, that thing disappeared.

And hearing all these things for a long time, one night I asked Guru Dev 'What is this?' These people don't even write to Guru Dev, Guru Dev doesn't know they are in difficulty on the surface of life and then how do they report they had a vision or some thought of Guru Dev and then from that time everything started to be smooth?

If they wrote a letter and the difficulties came to the notice of Guru Dev and then they got out of their difficulty, I could understand it, but they don't write letters. they just have the devotion to Guru Dev and they have some thought of Guru Dev,

And Guru Dev reply was 'It's the Department of the Almighty and he does it'

And it took me about two years to understand because I quite remember the time what is meant by it's 'The department of the Almighty'. And now I understand it is this.

We have the picture of Guru Dev as when we do *puja* and that form, that photo, that picture is the physical expression of the form which had a mind that was fully enlightened and Omnipresent. So once we see the form our eyes associate with the form very naturally because the physical and mental run parallel.

And once the form is in our vision, in our awareness, then naturally our mind gets in tune with the mind which occupied that form once upon a time. The form was occupied by a mind, that mind is an all time reality, eternal, the barriers of time are no barriers to it, continuum.

The body is no more but the form is there and once we tune our eyes our vision, perception, cognition to that, because that was held up by a mind that was enlightened, naturally our mind gets in tune and because that mind was and is and will forever be Omnipresent, immediately our mind gets in tune with the Omnipresent and right away the help comes from where we are.

The help comes from Absolute Being which is the nature of our own mind, but that image, that picture becomes a positive and concrete medium to have that mechanics performed for our mind. So help comes from our own Being because it comes through that form naturally our devotion to that. It's the department of the Almighty which does it, not the individual, its the department and it's only one way, it's not two ways, its one way. The help is not given, it's received, it's received by our ability to attune with that, and that ability develops with devotion, surrender and service. These three things.

Automatically one is elevated to that level and help doesn't come from outside, it comes from right where we are, from our own Being. But those unaware of ones own Being have those mechanics to help them.

This is true of all the saints of the times throughout the world."[33]

Notes

Foreword

1. Author's transcription of recording made of Maharishi Mahesh Yogi in Rishikesh, India, February 1968.

Maharishi Recounts Guru Dev's Lifestory

2. Author's transcription of tape recording (recorded 27th July 1961, California USA) in which Maharishi offers this sketch of Guru Dev's life up to the time he became Shankaracharya.

Maharishi Recollects First Meeting with Guru Dev

3. Author's transcription from video of Maharishi Mahesh Yogi speaking, entitled:- *'Invincibility to Every Nation Maharishi's Supreme Offer to the World Courses for all areas of society to structure invincibility for the nation - Core courses on invincibility -Theme Fifteen - Global unfoldment of the age of enlightenment: Improving the quality of world consciousness - Tape 1 - Maharishi Speaks on Guru Dev and the History of the Movement: Enlivening Supreme Silence to Raise World Consciousness'.*

1952-1955

4. Translation of a Hindi quotation - included in Hindi biography, translation contained in *'The Biography of Guru Dev: The Life and Teachings of Swami Brahmananda Saraswati, Shankaracharya of Jyotirmath (1941-53) - Volume II'*, Paul Mason, Premanand, 2009, page 297.

5. *'Sadhus of India: The Sociological View'* - B.D. Tripathi, Pilgrims Publishing, 2004, p221.

6. *'Darsan: Seeing the Divine Image in India'*, Diana L. Eck, Chambersburg: Anima, 1981. pp4-5.

7. *'108 Discourses of Guru Dev: The Life and Teachings of Swami Brahmananda Saraswati, Shankaracharya of Jyotirmath (1941-53) - Volume I'*, Paul Mason, Premanand, 2009, 74 page 199.

8. Quotation of Maharishi Mahesh Yogi from page 67 of *'Hermit In The House'* by Helena Olson, Los Angeles, 1967.

9. Account passed on through Maharishi's secretary, Tom Anderson.

10. Maharishi Mahesh Yogi in Rishikesh, India 9th February 1970 - lecture notes.

11. Quote from speech of Mrs Thankamma N Menon, October 1955, from *'Beacon Light of the Himalayas'*, page 50, published 1956.

12. Quote from speech of Sri C R Vaidyanathan, October 1955, from *'Beacon Light of the Himalayas'*, pages 36-7, published 1956.

13. Quote from speech of Professor P S Atchuthan Pillai, October 1955, from *'Beacon Light of the Himalayas'*, page 79, published 1956.

14. Quotation from Brahmachari Mahesh, October 1955, from *'Beacon Light of the Himalayas'*, published 1956, pages 43-58.

15. Quotation from Brahmachari Mahesh, October 1955, from *'Beacon Light of the Himalayas'*, published 1956, pages 59-68.

16. Quotation from Brahmachari Mahesh, October 1955, from *'Beacon Light of the Himalayas'*, published 1956, pages 73-77.

"Beacon Light of the Himalayas"

17. Quotation from Brahmachari Mahesh, October 1955, from *'Beacon Light of the Himalayas'*, published 1956. pp i-v.

1957, Madras - Maharishi speaks about vegetarianism and launches the Spiritual Regeneration Movement

18. Quoted later in *'Torch Divine'* Vol 1 No. 1 July 1958 pp 8-9.

19. To celebrate the birthday of Guru Dev, an event entitled the 'Seminar of Spiritual Luminaries' was convened between the 29th December 1957 and 1st January 1958. Brahmachari Mahesh (Maharishi) gave a long address, extracts of which were later republished in *'Maharishi Mahesh Yogi, Thirty Years Around the World'*, vol. 1, MVU, 1986, pp 204-208.

20. Quoted from:- *'Maharishi Mahesh Yogi, Thirty Years Around the World'*, vol. 1, Maharishi Vedic University, 1986, p. 244.

'108 Names of Guru Dev'

21. Author's transcription of tape recording of Maharishi Mahesh Yogi speaking in 1959 and loosely translated into English by author.

Maharishi Reflects on Guru Dev

22. Author's transcription of recording of Maharishi Mahesh Yogi made in Rishikesh, India, c.March 1969.

23. Author's transcription from recording, of Maharishi Mahesh Yogi on 8th July 1971 in Amherst, U.S.A.

24. Author's transcription of recorded talk by Maharishi Mahesh Yogi at Poland Springs, USA, 10th July.

25. From 'Strange Facts About A Great Saint' by Raj R P Varma, 1980, pages ii-iii.

26. Author's transcription from recording of Maharishi Mahesh Yogi, made in Rishikesh, India, c.March 1969.

27. Transcription of recording of Maharishi Mahesh Yogi speaking in the USA in 1959.

28. Quotation from p135 'With The Beatles' by Lewis Lapham, Melville House Publishing, 2005.

29. Transcription of talk by Maharishi Mahesh Yogi at Poland Springs, USA, 10th July 1970.

30. Extract from 'Our Guiding Light' by Bala Brahmachari Mahesh (later known as Maharishi Mahesh Yogi), Kerala, 1955/6.

The Poet and the Puja

31. Author's transcription of recording of Maharishi Mahesh Yogi speaking at his ashram in Rishikesh in February / March 1969.

32. A tale allegedly told by Maharishi Mahesh Yogi, the transcipt being circulated about.

Connecting with Guru Dev

33. Related by Raja Steven Rubin as part of the 12th January 2009 celebration at Vlodrop, Holland.

Glossary

aachaarya, acharya teacher
aadhyaatma, spiritual contemplation
aananda, joy, bliss
aastika, religious
aatmaa, soul
abhyaasa, practice
adharma, vice, sin
agni, fire
agyaana, ignorance
ahamkaara, egotism, arrogance, conceit, empty pride, vanity
ahimsaa, non-violence, inoffensiveness, benevolence
akshara, permanent
amrita, nectar
anishta, mishchief, evil
antahkarana, conscience, inner self
artha, wealth
arya, noble
ashaanti, unrest
ashram, hermitage
ashrama, stage of life
ashubha, unfortunate, inauspicious
asura, demon
atma, atman, Soul
avataar, incarnation
aviveka, absence of discrimination
bhaagya, destiny
Bhaarata, India
Bhagwan, Bhagwan, *bhagavaana,* Supreme Being, God
Bhagavat, God
bhagavattatva, essence of the divine
bhajan, hymn

bhakti, devotion
Bharat, *bhaarata* India
bhavaroga, birth-sickness
bhavasaagara, sea of experience
bhavateet, transcendental
bhoga, the experience of pleasure or a pain
bhuta-preta, ghosts
biij, seed
brahmana, brahmin, Hindu caste
Brahma, Absolute Divine Truth, Hindu god of creation
brahmachari, celibate student
brahmacharya, celibacy
Brahmanand, *brahmananda* Absolute bliss
brahma-nirguna brahma, without qualities),
brahmavidyaa, theology taught in the Upanishads
brahmin, learned or priestly caste
brhmanishtham, possessing knowledge of immortal self
chaitanya, consciousness
charan, ray of sun or moon
chela, disciple
chimtaa, the funeral pyre
chit, consciousness
chitaa, worry
chitta, faculty of reasoning
daana, charitable gift
daitya, demons
darshan, darshana Holy look, vision
deepak, light, lamp
Devaloka, the world of the gods, paradise
devataa, god
devataaon, gods/goddesses
dhaarmik, (virtuous, devout, religious, godly, upright, etc.)
dharma, righteous duty
dharmashaala, a dwelling house for pilgrims
dhoop, sticky incense, fragrant lamp
dhoti, sheet
dhyaana, dhyan, meditation

diksha, initiation
duhkha, pain, suffering
dushkarma, wicked action
Gangajal, the sacred waters of the River Ganga
Ganapati, Ganesha Hindu god with elephant trunk
Gandharvas, celestial musicians
Gandharva-Ved, Indian classical music
ganja, marijuana
gita, song
grihastha, householder
grhasthon, householders
guna, quality
gupha, cave
guru, teacher, master
gurudwara, Sikh temple
gyaanii, learned
gyan, gyaan, gnan, jyaan knowledge
hansa, swan
hare, lord
hawaii, pertaining to the air
Ishwar, Isvara, God
ishta, deity
jaati, caste
jagadguru, world teacher, universal teacher
jai, jay, jaya, jaaya hail, glory
japa, repetition of *mantra*
ji, term of respect
jiiva, the individual soul
jiivanmukti, liberated soul
jyotir, light
jyotishi, Indian astrology
kalpa, period of time
kalyaana, happiness, welfare, benediction, prosperity
kama, love
kamandalu, wooden pot
karma, law of action and reaction
karunaa, compassion
Kashi, Benares, Varanasi

kaupeen, loincloth

kiirtana, singing praise of God

kripa, grace

Krishna, dark, name of principal character of *Mahabharata* poem

kriyamaana, work now being done

kshatriya, caste of warriors, administrators

kshema, prosperity

kusang, kusanga, the company of evil men

ladduu, Sweetmeat made of *ghii* (ghee)

lingam, phallus

maayaa, maya, delusion of

maharaja, king

maharishi, maharshi, Great sage

maharishon, sages

mahatma, mahaatma, great soul

Mahesh, name of Hindu god Shiva

maitrii, friendship

mala, maalaa, rosary, necklace, garland

mala-mutra, excrement & urine

mandir, temple

manoraajyam, the realm of the mind

mantra, word or words of spiritual power

Manu Smriti or *Manu Samhita,* law book

maryaadaa, principled code of conduct

math, monastery

mauna, maun, silent

moksha, final liberation, beatitude, redemption, absolution, salvation, freedom

muditaa, cheerfulness, delight

mukti, liberation

naastika, nastika, unbeliever

nagar, town

niraakaara, without form

nirguna, without qualities

nitya, eternal

nityaananda, always happy

paapa, sinful

pandit, learned man
parabrahma, the Supreme Soul
Paramatma, *paramaatmaa,* Supreme Spirit, Supersoul, God
parmartha, the ultimate good, salvation
pishaachinii, she-devil
praana, breath
praanon, the five vital airs
praarabdha, already commenced *karma*
prana, breath
pranaama, salutation
pranava, name of OM *mantra*
prasad, blessing
pravritti, tendency, inclination or perseverance of mind
puuja, puja, pooja, ceremony, ritual
puujana worship
punya, meritous *karma*
purnima, poornima, full-moon night
purusha, male
purushartha, human wealth or purpose, work for fulfilment of life
puurna, poorna, perfect
raaga, attachment
raaj, raja, royal, king
rajasic, energetic, passionate
rajogunii, pleasure seeking, passion of love and pleasure
Rama, Raama, Raam, name of hero of *Ramayana* poem
raurava, a hell
rish,i sage, wise man
roga, disease
Rudra, name of Hindu god Shiva
saadhaka, one engaged in spiritual discipline
saadhana, spiritual practice or discipline
sachchidananda, Truth, Consciousness, Bliss
sadguru, genuine *guru*
sadagati, salvation, good conduct
sadhu, wandering holy man
sanchita, collected *karma*
samaadhi, stillness of the mind
sampradaaya, sect

samsaara, samsara, worldly existence, mortal world,
transmigration
samsaarii, worldly
samskaara, mental impressions
sannyas, vow of renunciation
sanyaasi, renunciate
Saraswati, name of Hindu goddess of learning, name of river
Sarvashaktimaan, Omnipotent, Almighty
satogunii, purity
satsanga, to take the company of the good or pious
sattvic, satvik, pure
satya, truth
shaanti, shaanti peace
Shastras, shaastra, Hindu Scriptures
Shankar, name of Hindu god Shiva
shikshaa, instruction
shishya, pupil
Shiva, name of Hindu god of destruction, lord of the *yogis*
Shivalinga, symbol of creative forces
Shivaratri, night(s) dedicated to worship of Hindu deities Shiva
and his consort Shakti
shloka, verse
shraddha, faith, veneration, reverence
shravana, devotion
shri, blessed
shrotiyan, well-versed in *Vedas*
shruti, information heard from the *Veda*
shubha, happy, auspicious
shuudra, one of the four castes, labourer
siddha, perfected being
siddhi, one who has acquired supernatural powers
smarana, remembrance
smriti, remembered, from the *Shastra.*
sthuula shariira, gross body
stotra, hymns of praise
suukshma shariira, subtle body
svarg, svarga, swarg, heaven

swami, renunciate
swaroop, svarupa, swarupa, divine form, real self, true self
tamasik, impure
tamogunii, impure, ignorant
tapasya, tapas, austerity
tilaka, tilak, mark of sandalwood paste applied to forehead, emblem of a sect
tri, three
tyaagi, unattached renunciates
upaasanaa, sitting near, devout meditation, worship, prayer
upadesha, upadesh, lecture, advice instruction, discourse, sermon
Upanishad, texts on *yoga,* to sit near
upekshaa, equanimity, indifference
vaanaprastha, forest dweller
vaidya, physician
vairagya, freedom from worldly desires
vaishya, trader
vanaprasthas, forest dwellers
varna, caste
Veda, ancient religious texts, *Rig Veda, Sama Veda, Yajur Veda, Atharva Veda*
veshyaa, whore
vigyaana, knowledge, wisdom, science, learning, philosophy, the soul
Vishnu, Hindu god of preservation
vishvambhara, (universal support)
viyoga, separation, disunion, detachment etc
vritti, flow of mental activity
vrittiyon, mental conditions, of friendship, compassion, delight & indifference
yaatra, yatra, journey, tour, pilgrimage
yagya, yajna, ritual, religious sacrifice
yakshini, demi-gods,
karna-pishachi, demons
yogadarshanam, Patanjali's Yoga Sutras
yogamaayaa, inner power
yoga-shaastra, yogadarshanam, of Patanjali, Yoga Sutras
yuga, period of time

Sing the Song of life
and let it echo far
all to enjoy   जयगुरुदेव